BAD NEWS

Also available in the Bloomsbury Sigma series:

BAD NEWS

Why We Fall for Fake News

Rob Brotherton

BLOOMSBURY SIGMA

LONDON · OXFORD · NEW YORK · NEW DELHI · SYDNEY

BLOOMSBURY SIGMA
Bloomsbury Publishing Plc
50 Bedford Square, London, WC1B 3DP, UK

BLOOMSBURY, BLOOMSBURY SIGMA, and the Bloomsbury Sigma logo
are trademarks of Bloomsbury Publishing Plc.

First published in the United Kingdom in 2020

A catalogue record for this book is available from the British Library.

Library of Congress Cataloguing-in-Publication data has been applied for.

ISBN: HB: 978-1-4729-6285-0; TPB: 978-1-4729-6288-1;
e-book: 978-1-4729-6287-4

2 4 6 8 10 9 7 5 3 1

Typeset by Deanta Global Publishing Services, Chennai, India
Printed and bound in Great Britain by CPI Group (UK) Ltd, Croydon CR0 4YY

Bloomsbury Sigma, Book Fifty-Four

To find out more about our authors and books visit www.bloomsbury.com
and sign up for our newsletters.

For Mum and Dad

Contents

CHAPTER ONE

Fake News

Fake News

"Ladies and gentlemen, we interrupt our program of dance music to bring you a special bulletin from the Intercontinental Radio News."

The announcer spoke quickly, but there was no cause for panic. Not yet.

"At twenty minutes before eight, central time, Professor Farrell of the Mount Jennings Observatory, Chicago, Illinois, reports observing several explosions of incandescent gas, occurring at regular intervals on the planet Mars."

It was a few minutes after 8:00 p.m. on Sunday, October 30, 1938. The night before Halloween.

"The spectroscope indicates the gas to be hydrogen and moving towards the earth with enormous velocity." A Princeton University professor is quoted describing the phenomenon, ominously, as "like a jet of blue flame shot from a gun."

Then the news flash ended, and normality resumed: "We now return you to the music of Ramón Raquello, playing for you in the Meridian Room of the Park Plaza Hotel."

But this was not really a music program, and the news flash was not really news. This was Orson Welles's radio adaptation of *The War of the Worlds*, the most infamous fake news story of all time.

The musical respite is brief. An announcer again interrupts to throw to a hastily arranged interview with Professor Pierson, the Princeton astronomer quoted in the initial news flash. Ostensibly broadcasting live from Princeton's observatory, the ticking clockwork of the observatory's huge telescope is audible in the background. In fact, Welles and his *Mercury Theatre on the Air* company were broadcasting from a studio in midtown Manhattan. The ticking was just one of many special effects that would be used throughout the show to enhance the illusion of chaotic events unfolding live and unplanned.

As Pierson surveys the surface of the Red Planet through the telescope, the interviewer voices the concern that may by now have been lurking in the back of some listeners' minds: "You're quite convinced, as a scientist, that living intelligence as we know it does not exist on Mars?"

The professor sounds terse but unconcerned. Embodying scientific hubris, he delivers the famous reply: "I should say the chances against it are a thousand to one." Careful listeners would have noticed that the professor's sonorous voice was actually that of Welles himself.

It transpires that some extraterrestrial object has, in fact, crashed to Earth just twenty miles from Princeton. Events escalate quickly, and all the while the pretense is kept up of live coverage of confusing and ultimately catastrophic events unfolding on the East Coast of America at that very moment.

The interviewer rushes to the crash site, with Pierson in tow, where police and hundreds of onlookers observe a crashed alien craft of some kind. A few of the gawkers are roped into impromptu interviews. The actors, in character as bewildered bystanders, deliberately stumble over words, repeat themselves, and forget to speak into the microphone. The confusion is palpable.

Before long, a tentacled alien emerges from the spacecraft. "Good heavens, something's wriggling out of the shadow like a gray snake," the interviewer says, the professional restraint in his voice giving way to panic. Suddenly, the alien is incinerating everything around it. "Now the whole field's caught fire," the interviewer practically screams. We hear an explosion. "It's coming this way. About twenty yards to my right ..." The transmission cuts out.

After a short but excruciating silence, an announcer blithely explains, "Evidently there's some difficulty with our field transmission." The network cuts to a calm piano interlude, only adding to the horror. We soon learn that the interviewer has been incinerated, along with dozens of bystanders, by the alien, "their bodies burned and distorted beyond all possible recognition."

Moments later, the commander of the New Jersey state militia is explaining that, on the orders of the governor of New Jersey, martial law has been imposed and evacuations are beginning in the area. The broadcast facilities have been handed over to the state militia. A Captain Lansing of the signal corps informs listeners that the situation is "now under complete control" with "eight battalions of infantry ... closing in on an old metal tube."

This is more hubris.

"Ladies and gentlemen," the announcer breaks in yet again, "I have a grave announcement to make." The militia has been wiped out. The announcer gives a gruesome accounting of the carnage. "Seven thousand men armed with rifles and machine guns pitted against a single fighting machine of the invaders from Mars. One hundred and twenty known survivors. The rest strewn over the battle area from Grover's Mill to Plainsboro, crushed and trampled to death under the metal feet of the monster or burned to cinders by its heat ray."

The reality of the situation is now inescapable. "Incredible as it may seem, both the observations of science and the evidence of our eyes lead to the inescapable assumption that those strange beings who landed in the Jersey farmlands tonight are the vanguard of an invading army from the planet Mars." The Martian is on the move, trampling or incinerating everything in its path, deliberately tearing up railroad tracks and bringing down telephone lines. Even as a statement from the secretary of the interior urges calm, a second Martian craft is discovered and listeners are told of more spacecraft launching from Mars, presumably as reinforcements. Poisonous black smoke is now blanketing the countryside. New York City is being evacuated. Soon the Martians are crossing the Hudson River and all of Manhattan is being enveloped in deadly smoke.

The announcer who has been keeping us abreast of the developments from the safe confines of the news studio tells us he is now on the roof of the broadcasting building, looking down upon the chaos on New York City's streets as poisonous smoke engulfs the city. "The smoke's crossing Sixth Avenue ... Fifth Avenue ... one hundred yards away ... it's fifty feet ..."

We hear his last ragged breath, and the thud of his body collapsing.

★

As a work of fiction, Welles's masterfully staged radio play remains scintillating. But even more well-known than its story of alien invasion is the story of what happened across America as the broadcast went out: mass panic, as listeners mistook the fiction for fact.

Thousands, maybe even millions, of people, the story goes, were convinced that the country really was under extraterrestrial attack. Police and newspaper switchboards lit up. People went hunting for the downed spaceship. Families fled their homes. Highways were jammed. Churches and police stations were inundated with refugees and volunteers for the armed resistance. People died of heart attacks. Others took their own lives rather than succumb to the poisonous black smoke. Chaos, confusion, pandemonium.

At least, that's the story.

The truth is less exciting, but more interesting. The national panic is as fictional as the Martian invaders. It didn't happen. The most famous story about fake news is, well, fake news.

A. Brad Schwartz, a historian at Princeton, spent months looking for evidence of mass panic in archives of letters sent to Welles, CBS, and the Federal Communications Commission (FCC) in the days and weeks after the show aired, and in surveys and academic studies of what the American public made of Welles's prank. The evidence for nationwide panic, he discovered, is underwhelming.

As Schwartz reports in *Broadcast Hysteria*, his book-length report of his research, most of the country didn't panic because most of the country simply wasn't listening. Welles's *Mercury Theatre on the Air* had a reputation as highbrow entertainment, which made for a relatively small audience share. According to a survey conducted during the broadcast by a market research company, just 2 percent of radio-owning households had been tuned in to *The War of the Worlds*. Even a fairly generous estimate of Welles's total audience that night amounted to something like 6 million listeners, a small fraction of the audience typically commanded by rival broadcasts across the dial.

That still means there were at least a few million potential panickers. But among people who did hear the show, Schwartz found, the most common reaction wasn't fear or panic, but enjoyment and admiration. "Most people who heard the *War of the Worlds* broadcast that night loved it," he wrote.

Many listeners were aware from the outset that what they were hearing was entertainment, not news. For those who planned their evening's listening in advance, the show had appeared in all the usual radio listings, clearly labeled as one of Welles's weekly works of fiction.

And the show wasn't designed to catch listeners unaware with its pretense of breaking news flashes. At the top of the hour, the network introduced the program as "Orson Welles and *The Mercury Theatre on the Air* in *The War of the Worlds* by H. G. Wells." This was followed by two minutes or so of preamble, delivered by Welles himself, setting the show up as fiction and foreshadowing the extraterrestrial destruction to come: "Across an

immense ethereal gulf, minds that to our minds as ours
are to the beasts in the jungle, intellects vast, cool, and
unsympathetic, regarded this earth with envious eyes and
slowly and surely drew their plans against us."

At the peak of the broadcast, just as the poisonous
smoke was supposedly enveloping Manhattan, listeners
were breezily reminded, "You are listening to a CBS
presentation of Orson Welles and *The Mercury Theatre on
the Air* in an original dramatization of *The War of the
Worlds* by H. G. Wells. The performance will continue
after a brief intermission." After the commercial break
the pretense of real-time news was dropped. Welles's
Professor Pierson narrated his experience, in the past
tense, as one of the few survivors of the alien invasion.

Some listeners did tune in late or just hadn't been
paying close attention to the intro. Among those who
didn't immediately know they were listening to a work
of fiction, the mere mention of Mars and meteorites and
tentacled aliens was enough to tip some off. One listener
wrote, "Of course, when the Martians appeared, the
horror element became comedy for me in the realization
that I had been *had*." Others deduced it from the
implausible rate at which events unfolded.

Some people had believed they were hearing news
of destruction on American soil. Those who fell for
the prank were briefly, and understandably, terrified,
Schwartz writes. But even then, most didn't panic. They
listened until it became clear that the threat wasn't real.
Afterward, some wrote to Welles to tell him off for giving
them a fright, or to commend him on a job well done.
Most turned the radio off and thought little more about
it. "The infernal machines passed within a few blocks of

my house," one listener glibly wrote, "and I didn't think
to step outside and see them. After New York was
destroyed we all went to bed."

The panic wasn't entirely fictional—it just didn't
amount to anything like *mass* panic. Schwartz combed
through almost two thousand letters to Welles or the
FCC. He found just twelve from people who said they
had fled their homes. Another thirteen claimed they had
been ready to flee, though, as Schwartz points out, it is
impossible to know how much of that is exaggeration;
ten letters mentioned people suffering heart attacks
during the show, though no lawsuits were ever filed.
(One listener sued CBS for $50,000, claiming "nervous
shock." The claim was dismissed.)

True, Welles's fake-news prank did result in a lot of
telephone calls and telegrams seeking clarification and
reassurance. But if that can be considered "mass panic,"
we'd have to treat every trending Twitter topic as an
imagined national emergency.

"Panicked scenes of flight and near flight, which
turned *War of the Worlds* into the stuff of American
legend, did happen," Schwartz sums up, "but they were
very, very rare."

★

Fake news is a hot topic. Web searches for the term
spiked in November 2016, as hoax articles such as "Pope
Francis Shocks World, Endorses Donald Trump For
President" flourished during that year's presidential
election campaign. The term was declared Word of the
Year for 2017 by the people behind the Collins dictionary.

It has been used by politicians around the world, in countless news stories and think pieces, podcasts and blogs, on T-shirts and mugs, in song titles and lyrics.

What, exactly, fake news *is*, is a matter of some debate. It's not a new term, though until a few years ago it was most often used to refer to satirical news, such as *The Daily Show* or *The Onion*, which plays with news tropes but isn't trying to fool anyone.

These days, *fake news* usually means something darker. Collins defined it as "false, often sensational, information disseminated under the guise of news reporting." The term rapidly acquired broader connotations, however. It became an insult aimed not just at lies pretending to be news, but at legitimate news institutions accused of getting the facts wrong, either intentionally or innocently. Most notably, President Donald Trump co-opted the label to describe news that isn't obviously fake, but merely unfavorable to him. According to the *Washington Post*, Trump used the term more than one hundred and fifty times in 2017. Trump happily claimed credit for popularizing the term. In relation to the mainstream news media, he said in an interview, "One of the greatest of all terms I've come up with is *fake*." ("I guess other people have used it, perhaps, over the years," Trump reflected, "but I've never noticed it.")

By the autumn of 2018, the British government had decided that *fake news* was "a poorly-defined and misleading term that conflates a variety of false information, from genuine error through to foreign interference in democratic processes." At least some journalists agree. *Washington Post* media columnist Margaret Sullivan called the term "tainted" and urged fellow journalists to avoid it altogether. Nevertheless, the term still gets tossed around, and its definition is still just as unclear. One writer, in a bestselling book, declared religion the original fake news.

This book is, in part, about fake news. Thankfully, however, we don't need to get bogged down attempting to find a precise definition. Fake news, in every sense of the term, is plenty interesting. The chapters ahead will muster research in an effort to understand why people entertain or reject it, believe or doubt it, share or ignore it.

But that's just part of the aim of this book. Rather than focusing on the *fake*, we're going to focus on the *news*—because fake news, however you define it, is just one small niche within the much broader news ecosystem. To understand *fake news*, we need to understand the appeal of *all news*.

To be clear, I'm not saying that there's no difference between fake news and real news, or that journalists occasionally getting the facts wrong, despite their best efforts, is on par with intentionally deceptive fake news. What I'm saying is that fake news mimics the form and function of standard news, leveraging our collective notions of what news is or should be to its advantage. Because of this parasitic relationship, we can better understand the problem of fake news by exploring our complicated relationship with news in general.

It's hardly surprising that people are worried about fake news given how little people seem to trust regular news. A 2018 article in the *Columbia Journalism Review* summed up the findings of a recent public opinion poll as "Most Americans say they have lost trust in the media."

Outright lies and fake news were among the most common reasons people gave for lack of faith in the media. But people also had more general concerns about inaccurate, misleading, incomplete, or unbalanced reporting. They worried about reporting that is biased, slanted, unfair, or overly opinion-based or emotional, and about sensationalism, hype, and clickbait.

Likewise, in a Pew Research poll, nine out of ten people said that "breaking information that is not checked" and "factual information that is one-sided" cause confusion about current issues—the same proportion that pointed to outright "made-up" news and information as a problem. Only one in ten people said they thought things would get better within the next five years. Half expected things to get worse.

It's not just the media that is viewed with skepticism. American, British, and Canadian surveys have found that journalists are on par in trustworthiness with real estate agents, lawyers, and car mechanics. Only politicians are reliably less trusted. The communications firm Edelman monitors trust in the institutions of government, business, non-governmental organizations (NGOs), as well as the media, distilling the trends into an annual "trust barometer" reading. Lately the findings have been described in fairly dramatic terms. In 2017, the barometer declared "trust in crisis." Then 2018 was the year of "the battle for truth." The data for the United States showed that in 2018 overall trust "suffered the largest-ever-recorded drop in the survey's history," falling from 52 percent to 43 percent—meaning that people were more *dis*trusting than trusting, on the whole. Yet this wasn't even the most striking finding. Among the "informed public," trust "imploded," plunging from 68 percent to 45 percent. The informed American public was apparently less trusting of institutions even than people in Russia—a country not known for high levels of institutional trust. This American level was the lowest in any of the twenty-eight markets surveyed. (A year later, it had rebounded to 60 percent. Rather than declaring victory in the battle for truth, Edelman described 2019 more prosaically as the year of "trust at work.")

"By many accounts," media scholar John Pavlik wrote in an essay on the credibility problem facing the news media, "journalism is in crisis."

★

This is happening *now*. So why begin with a story from the best part of a hundred years ago, rather than any of the countless contemporary stories of fake news?

The seemingly timeless temptation is to assume that things are different now, that things are worse than ever. Ironically, this tendency to focus on the present and the exceptional is a habit of the news itself—you can't spell *news* without *new*. We'll talk more about that in a later chapter. But to assume that our current struggles are new and unprecedented is to assume also that new causes are responsible and that new cures are required. This perpetual scramble for new solutions to ostensibly new problems blinds us to historical insights into current predicaments.

After all, why did people think—why do people *still* think—that Welles's fake-news prank caused nationwide pandemonium? Part of the answer is because that's what the *real* news told them.

The story began to take shape even before the show was off the air. Aware of the unusually large number of calls from confused listeners, the Associated Press put out a bulletin at 8:48 p.m.: "Note to Editors: Queries to newspapers from radio listeners throughout the United States tonight, regarding a reported meteor fall which killed a number of New Jerseyites, are the result of a studio dramatization."

Reporters buttonholed Welles and his colleagues as they left the studio. John Houseman, Welles's producer, later recalled being accosted with questions like "You've heard about the family of five that was killed on the New Jersey highway. Have you heard any more around the country?" Initially, Houseman says, even he and Welles fell for the hype: "We believed for the next two or three hours that we were mass murderers."

Half an hour later, Walter Winchell, one of America's most popular radio newsmen, began his nightly newscast by assuring "Mr. and Mrs. America, there is no cause for alarm! America has not fallen! I repeat, America has not fallen!" As Brad Schwartz points out, given the small audience that Welles's show attracted, *this* was the first thing most Americans heard about the show. Already the idea that something unusual had happened was being encouraged by the nation's media.

The next morning, front pages of newspapers across the country, from the *Abilene (TX) Reporter-News* to the *Zanesville (OH) Signal*, declared that the nation had briefly, collectively, lost its mind.

The front page of the *Chicago Herald and Examiner* carried a bold headline splashed across the entire width

of the paper, blaring, "Radio Fake Scares Nation." The
Los Angeles Times went with the slightly more restrained
"Radio Story of Invasion by Mars Upsets Nation."
The *Detroit News, Boston Daily Globe, New York Daily
News*, and *San Francisco Chronicle* each carried variations
on the theme of a nation terrorized by men from
Mars. The *Austin Statesman* and the *Raleigh News &
Observer* ran with "Mass Hysteria." Perhaps the most
satisfyingly descriptive headline was from the *Amarillo
Globe-Times*: "Thousands Flee Homes, Pray, or Faint as
Fictitious Radio Program Relates Invasion by Martian
Hordes."

Not only sensation-hungry tabloids ran with the story.
The front page of the *New York Times* confidently
declared, "Radio Listeners in Panic, Taking War Drama
as Fact." A subheading continued, "Scare is Nationwide."

The *Times'* report was one of the most extensive. "A
wave of mass hysteria seized thousands of radio listeners
throughout the nation," it began. The show "disrupted
households, interrupted religious services, created traffic
jams and clogged communications systems," as many
listeners believed "that an interplanetary conflict had
started with invading Martians spreading wide death and
destruction." The story continued inside the paper,
filling most of a page with colorful tales of individuals in
distress.

As the news made its way around the world, foreign
papers got in on the action. In Canada, the *Winnipeg
Tribune* reported, "U.S. Panic-Stricken by Radio
'Invasion.'" The *Illustrated London News* reproduced
illustrations of the Martian machines from H. G. Wells's

original novel, claiming, "Many people who tuned in during the broadcast were convinced that they were listening to the description of an actual 'invasion' of America by Martians." Under the headline "The End of the World," the *Dundee Evening Telegraph* of Scotland reported "millions of Americans are today still suffering from nervous prostration after the panic that swept across the country last night." The *Falkirk (Scotland) Herald* subheaded a story "Pandemonium Reigns." A Northern Irish paper reported, "Amazing Scenes of Hysteria." As far away as Australia, the *Age* rhapsodized that "never in the history of the United States had such a wave of terror and panic swept the continent."

In Nazi Germany, the story made for convenient propaganda. An article in Joseph Goebbels's *Der Angriff*, under the headline "Death Ray Panic in New York— Half of America Flees to Bombproof Cellars," argued, "If Americans fall so easily for a fantastic radio broadcast of an 'invasion from Mars,' that explains why they so readily believe Nazi 'atrocity' tales."

A couple of days later, a writer for the *Boston Globe* commended the blanket media coverage: "The newspapers are correct in playing up this story over every other news event in the world. It is the story of the century." Yet within a few days, the news cycle had moved on. Since then, whenever Welles's "The War of the Worlds" has been mentioned, it has generally been to repeat the myth of the mass panic. In 1971, for example, the *Boston Globe* simply reprinted its original story from Halloween 1938. There were few follow-up pieces scrutinizing the reality of alleged panic, no corrections to the hyperbolic coverage.

The myth still gets retold as fact today. The reaction to "The War of the Worlds" was a "textbook example of mass hysteria," according to *Time* magazine in 2008. In August 2018, the *New York Times* wrote, "H. G. Wells's *The War of the Worlds* prompted a panic in 1938 when many listeners mistook a radio version of the novel as a real report of an attack by aliens armed with ray guns."

★

Okay, *sometimes the news gets things wrong* is hardly breaking news. But the disproportion between the reality of a handful of isolated incidents and the hyperventilating media coverage makes for such a nice example. Perhaps we could call it a day there, content to blame the media for corrupting society by occasionally playing fast and loose with the truth.

If we did, we'd be in good company. The crisis of confidence in the news isn't new. People have been criticizing the news industry for spreading fake news for basically as long as there has been a news industry. Newspapers—meaning printed news published on a regular schedule—were established in England in the early seventeenth century.* Within a few months of the first paper going on sale, one critic wrote that the new

---

* These early printed newspapers had precursors, with thousands of years of news in other written and oral forms, but I'm focusing on the English papers since they had the strongest influence on our contemporary news scene, and because the public reaction to the new form of news sweeping England is so well documented.

medium had brought both "things true and false to the presse."

Anticipating the satirical fake news of later years, a 1625 poem about falsehoods appearing in the newspapers of the day read, in part:

These shamefull lies, would make a man, in spight
Of Nature, turne Satyrist and write,
Revenging lines, against these shameless men,
Who thus torment both Paper, Presse, and Pen.

Later in the century, the poet John Cleveland took up the challenge, heaping seventeenth-century burns on the newspapermen. "I saw one once that could write with his toes," Cleveland quipped; "by the same token I could have wished he had worne his copies for socks." More pointedly, Cleveland accused the press of telling "lies by the grosse." The newsman, he wrote, "pries into each mans Breast and would faine know all mens crimes but his owne." Cleveland rounded out the criticism by comparing newsmen to astrologers, telling readers what they wanted to hear in order to sell more papers.

As weekly and daily newspapers swept the globe, so, too, did concern about their commitment to accuracy. In America, Thomas Jefferson was so disillusioned with overtly partisan newspapers' treatment of his administration that he wrote to a friend, "Nothing can now be believed which is seen in a newspaper. Truth itself becomes suspicious by being put into that polluted vehicle." He lamented that his fellow citizens believed they gained some true understanding of the world from the newspapers they read. "The man who never looks into a newspaper is better informed than he who reads them," he concluded, "inasmuch as he who knows nothing is nearer to truth than he whose mind is filled with falsehoods & errors."

Perhaps none have been more conscious of the press's credibility problem than the producers of news themselves. A 1614 newsbook began by acknowledging the predicament of the newswriter: "The just rewarde of him that is accustomed to lie, is, not to be believed when he speaketh the truth. So just an occasion may sometime bee imposed upon the pamphleting pressers. And therefore, if we receive the same rewarde, we cannot much blame our accusers." (The author went on to tell the tale of a "Strange and Monstrous Serpent, or Dragon" troubling the English countryside.)

Less chivalrous news producers have used allegations of fake news as a cudgel against competitors. In the late nineteenth century, Charles Dana, editor of the *New York Sun*, proclaimed, "I have never published a falsehood." Joseph Pulitzer, publisher of the *New York World*, responded, "That's another lie."

Accusations of sensationalism and triviality are likewise not new. Henry David Thoreau, the American writer and noted kvetch, described news as "the froth and scum of the eternal sea." Charles Dickens, the British newspaperman-turned-novelist, had harsh words for what he saw as the "ribald slander" of the American press. His novel *Martin Chuzzlewit* features New York City newsboys shouting, "Here's this morning's New York *Sewer*! … Here's this morning's New York *Stabber*! … Here's the New York *Rowdy Journal*!"

Mark Twain, in his days as a newspaperman, wryly lampooned the media's broad definition of news: "Our duty is to keep the universe thoroughly posted concerning murders and street fights, and balls, and theaters, and pack-trains, and churches, and lectures, and school-houses, and city military affairs, and highway robberies, and Bible societies, and hay-wagons, and a thousand other things which it is in the province of local reporters to keep track of and magnify into undue importance for the instruction of readers of this great daily newspaper."

It's harder to gauge how the general public felt about the press in centuries past, but the public opinion surveys of at least the past few decades suggest that the masses have similar reservations about the relationship of the news to truth. Edelman's "trust barometer" goes back as far as 2001. That year, only 20 percent of people said they trusted the media to "do the right thing." The British survey that found journalism to be among the least trusted professions has been running since 1983. Journalists have ranked near the bottom every year. Likewise, a 1985 American survey placed newspaper editors and reporters seventh and eighth on a list of ten professions in terms of honesty and ethical standards, ahead only of advertising executives and used-car salesmen.

Surely there was a better time? In the 1970s, after all, the CBS television news anchor Walter Cronkite was known as the "most trusted man in America." Another survey of American public opinion, with data from 1973 to the present, does suggest that people used to hold the press in higher esteem—but not by much. Back in the seventies, only a fifth of people said they had "hardly any" confidence in the press. That has steadily risen to almost half, as of 2019. But even at its height, the proportion of people with "a great deal" of confidence in the press has never risen above three out of ten people.

As for "the most trusted man in America," that's kind of fake news, too. The moniker was based on a 1972 poll that gauged the public's trust in a handful of politicians including senators, governors, President Richard Nixon, and his vice president Spiro Agnew. "For reasons not entirely clear," the political commentator Martin Plissner wrote later, the pollster had "added Cronkite's name to the list." Cronkite led the pack by a few percentage points, scoring 73 percent on the trust index compared to 67 percent for the average senator.* So "most trusted man in America" feels like a stretch, given that Cronkite was basically found more trustworthy than some politicians.

Anyway, fear of fake news—in the broadest sense—seems to be as old as news. John Pavlik, the scholar who noted the current crisis in confidence apparently facing journalism, quickly followed up by pointing out that this isn't unprecedented. Rather, journalism has faced "one screaming mess after another."

Contemplating the varied attacks on journalism, one magazine writer, in 1902, concluded, "No other profession is so wept over." Expressing a sentiment as true today as it was a century ago, he wrote, "Certain topics seem to recur in obedience to a rhythmic law, and to be discussed in about the same language. Society is a

---

* Nixon scored a respectable 57 percent on the trust index, though the survey came out a couple weeks before the Watergate break-in, which would eventually tarnish his reputation somewhat.

good-natured giant with no memory, and it is always safe to print a petulant article on the degeneracy of the press."

★

I'm not trying to add to the genre of media bashing. Sure, the news sometimes gets things wrong, such as the imagined panic over Welles's "The War of the Worlds." But that's not the end of the story, it's just the beginning. Deeper lessons are to be learned, though it requires a change of focus. Rather than heaping blame on the news for getting it wrong, we need to consider our own role as news consumers.

In this light, revisiting the imagined "War of the Worlds" panic is revealing. The myth endures not just because the media started it, but because people believed it. Many of the letters that Brad Schwartz found in the archives suggest that a lot of people were only too ready to believe the story that everyone else was a sucker for fake news.

"As a staunch and loyal young American," wrote one listener to Welles, "I resent the fact that the rest of the world has been made conscious of the many morons we harbor in our country." The letter illustrates a common theme among people who bought into the mass panic story: self-congratulation at not being taken in, combined with harsh criticism of the inferior mental faculties of people who apparently were.

"Of course, with an elementary knowledge of science I knew the story couldn't be true," bragged another listener, "but you must realize that the overwhelming majority of the American people do not have even an elementary knowledge of science."

"I suppose that by this time you have received many letters from numerous cranks and crack-pots who quickly became jitterbugs during the program," another writer began. "I was one of the thousands who heard this program and did not jump out of the window, did not attempt suicide, did not break my arm while beating a hasty retreat from my apartment, did not anticipate a horrible death, did not hear the Martians 'rapping on my chamber door.'"

Other letter writers questioned the fortitude as well as the intelligence of freaked-out listeners. One referred to the victims of mass panic as "molli coddled jitterbugs," and "a bunch of *cry babies*."

It wasn't just self-satisfied listeners who lamented the stupidity of their peers. Some in the media were enthusiastic supporters of the "everyone else is dumb" theory. An article in the *Chicago Tribune* argued, "Any normally intelligent man, even if he tuned in late, could not have failed to recognize it for what it was within a minute or two."

The respected journalist Dorothy Thompson was even more ardent:"Nothing whatever about the dramatization of the 'War of the Worlds' was in the least credible, no matter at what point the hearer might have tuned in." The "nationwide panic" it caused had "shown up the incredible stupidity, lack of nerve and ignorance of thousands."

Some of the criticism focused its misanthropy through the lens of elitism. One Welles fan referred to the "frothy craperoo" available on the other stations. He likely had in mind the massively popular *The Chase & Sanborn Hour*, which ran at the same time as Welles's show farther along the dial, on NBC. Many Welles fans, Schwartz writes, found *Chase & Sanborn* "moronic and inane." It became widely believed that, while Welles's "The War of the Worlds" was airing, *Chase & Sanborn* had bored its fans with an uncommonly dull show, causing an exodus of listeners. Many presumably stumbled across Welles's finely crafted fake-news drama and lacked the sophistication and discernment to comprehend what they were hearing. One listener wrote to Welles, "Perhaps this will be a lesson for those asinine individuals who blithely spin their dials haphazardly from one program to another. Hereafter they will probably refrain from jumping to conclusions before they know all the details."

A slightly different strain of elitism was perhaps evident in that, with the exception of New York and New Jersey papers, most reports were about people panicking somewhere else. The *Milwaukee Journal* explained that few people in Milwaukee fell for the fake news because "Milwaukeeans are a canny lot, given to sharp appraisal of anything." The *Austin Statesman* reported that Texas state police "did not record a single telephone query during the time easterners were panic stricken." In a humorous aside it noted, "If Texans were alarmed by the 'Invasion From Mars' broadcast Sunday night, they were too excited to call state police headquarters. 'Or maybe,' laughed Capt. Homer Garrison, director of the state police, 'they'd run too far from a telephone.'"

Added to the elitism and tribalism, some of the reporting seems tinged with racism or sexism. To be fair, nobody comes out of the media coverage looking particularly dignified or reasonable—the stories of panicking listeners are all written in a way that seems designed to elicit a smirk or a chuckle, regardless of the race, nationality, or gender of the hapless dupe. But some of the anecdotes mention details that give off a whiff of bigotry.

"Panic swept one apartment house in Greenwich Village, largely occupied by Italian families, after tenants caught scraps of the broadcast," reported the *New York Daily News*. Several newspapers, including the *Washington Post* and the *Boston Globe*, specified that the panic "gripped impressionable Harlemites," referring to the predominantly African American neighborhood of New York. "One man ran into the street," the report continued, "declaring it was the President's voice they heard, advising: 'Pack up and go north, the machines are coming from Mars.'" The *New York Times* offered a colorful anecdote about "the parlor churches in the Negro district," where congregations "took the 'news' in stride as less faithful parishioners rushed in with it, seeking spiritual consolation. Evening services became 'end of the world' prayer meetings in some."

Likewise, while both men and women are described panicking, it is almost always women who are described as hysterical and in tears. The *Boston Globe* reported, "Weeping and hysterical women swamped the switchboard of the Providence Journal." The *Baltimore Sun* related, "Freshmen in a Mary Washington College dormitory at Fredericksburg began calling for Mrs. C. L. Bushnell, dean of women, who stopped a wave of mass hysteria." Perhaps that incident was the basis of the *Washington Post*'s inflated assertion that "in girls' schools throughout the East mass hysteria was prevented by prompt and vigorous action of teachers."*

★

Some of the language and more overt prejudice aside, there are hints of the same kind of thinking about fake news today. Stories about the problem are usually about how *someone else* is falling for it.

An article on Lifehacker.com titled "How to stop your parents from sharing fake news" confidently urges readers to point out flaws, provide missing context, and share stories that the reader has personally verified— taking the reader's own powers of discernment for granted. A writer for *New York* magazine gathered stories of people "transformed" by watching Fox News, the

---

* Incidentally, I work at a "girls' school" in the East. Its student newspaper, the *Barnard Bulletin*—now sadly defunct—covered the reaction among Barnard students, in an article titled "Rocket From Mars Misses Barnard." I may be biased, but I'd say it is a masterpiece of media satire. "Here was News such as every editor dreams of," the author, Jean Ackerman, glibly admitted, "striking and sensational enough to warm the heart of even the most sophisticated and experienced reporter." Assigned the story, Ackerman gamely went looking for stories of hysteria among Barnard students, but she came up short. "Did our students so much as flick an eyelash when the end of the world approached? No, a thousand and thirty-eight times no." Only one freshman had even been listening. "Prosaically enough, two upperclassmen admitted to taking baths at the fatal hour, and another was too engrossed in an after-dinner cordial to notice that the world was coming to an end." The piece concludes with a wink: "Nevertheless, everyone questioned agreed on one point; she would never have been deceived or misled for a minute by the presentation. 'Even a college student could see though it.'"

conservative cable news channel, as if they were helpless victims of a brainwashing cult. "I asked a bunch of people how it felt watching their family members be stolen from them by Fox News," the author tweeted. "It doesn't feel great it turns out."

Again, this isn't just about the media getting things wrong. These kinds of stories just tell us what we already know: fake news is less a problem because it might mislead *us*; it's more a problem because of how it doubtlessly influences *somebody else*.

This isn't just a feature of fake news. We tend to assume that basically any persuasive communication will have more of an effect on other people than on ourselves: commercials, political ads and debates, news stories, works of fiction, even conspiracy theories. It's not that we think ourselves completely immune to influence; we just tend to think we are less gullible than everyone else. The exception is for messages we agree with. There, the effect works in reverse: we think we're *more* open to having our minds changed in the right direction, while other people will stubbornly remain in the wrong.

W. Phillips Davison, a Columbia University professor of journalism and sociology, coined a term for this: the *third-person effect*. When we think about the effects of a communication, he wrote, "its greatest impact will not be on 'me' or 'you,' but on 'them'—the third persons."

Davison gave one of the sources of inspiration for his interest in the effect as interviews with journalists he had conducted for another research project. Davison asked them how much influence they thought newspaper editorials had on the thinking of their readers. "One of the replies given frequently," Davison related, was along the lines of "the editorials have little effect on people like you and me, but the ordinary reader is likely to be influenced quite a lot."

Davison put the effect down to a kind of innocent egocentrism: "In a sense, we are all experts on those subjects that matter to us, in that we have information not available to other people." Maybe we have some genuine knowledge of the topic. At the least, we have our own likes, dislikes, and experiences. "Other people, we reason, do not know what we know," Davison went on. "Therefore, they are more likely to be influenced by the media."

More recent research suggests that we underestimate not just other people's knowledge, but their basic ability to come to their own reasoned conclusions. We tend to think of other people as less rational and more conformist than ourselves. Our own beliefs, we think, are based on objective knowledge or experiences. Other people's beliefs are more likely the result of mindlessly following the group. This is often tinged with tribalism. The more different people are from us, the more we tend to think of them as vulnerable to influence. We think our own political beliefs are informed by reason and experience, for example, whereas other people—especially those on the other side of the aisle—just believe what they're told by party officials.

Recent research has taken the third-person effect into the territory of fake news, and the pattern holds true. We think other people are more likely to fall for it than us. More generally, we think other people are more vulnerable to the risks of social media then we are, such as falling for extremist propaganda. The problem is perhaps exacerbated because fake news so often latches on to hot-button issues. The angrier we are about an issue, and the more personally invested we feel, the more we assume the best of ourselves and the worst of others.

We don't just worry about bad information corrupting people; we also worry that a lack of good information affects other people more than ourselves. After the New Orleans local newspaper the *Times-Picayune* stopped publishing a daily print edition, researchers asked people in the area if they thought the change would make it difficult to stay informed about current events. People foresaw more of a problem for everyone else than for themselves.

Public opinion surveys back up the psychological studies. More than half of the people in one survey said they find it easy to recognize misleading information in the news, including "made-up information," bias, satire, unconfirmed breaking news, and altered images or videos. But we have much less faith in other people's abilities to spot misinformation. The same proportion of people said that "it is too much to ask of the average American" to recognize fake news. Eight out of ten people said that the public's lack of effort to spot misinformation and low awareness of current events are very or moderately big challenges in addressing the issue.

In a later reflection on the body of research he had inspired, Davison offered an everyday example of how we often become less charitable depending on whom we're thinking about: "*I* enjoy good food; *you* have a tendency to overeat; *he* is a glutton." About fake news, perhaps we could say, with only slight exaggeration,

"*I* know it when I see it; *you* better be careful; *they* are getting brainwashed."

★

Fake news probably doesn't seem like a problem for *us* because *we* know it when we see it. Or, rather, we know what to do when we think we see it. The same public opinion survey asked respondents what actions they take in response to fake news. The most common response was to check the facts for themselves—eight out of ten people said they had done so.

To suppose that other people are more gullible implies that perhaps they aren't as willing to check the facts, or as able to interpret them correctly—which certainly sounds like the assumption underlying much of the condescending response to the fake national panic that Orson Welles supposedly created.

"A twist of the dial would have established for anybody that the national catastrophe was not being noted on any other station," one writer advised. "A reference to the radio [guide] would have established that the 'War of the Worlds' was announced in advance." In fact, confused listeners commonly used precisely these strategies to try to figure out what they were hearing.

Even the aspect of the "national panic" that has the strongest claim to truth—the unusually large numbers of people calling newspapers and police stations to get information about the alleged attack on American soil— was a product of people simply trying to figure out what was going on. Many momentarily confused listeners searched for information wherever they could find it, including phoning their local police station or newspaper, just as many people today would reach for their phones to check the news or Twitter.

That said, sometimes verifying evidence is easier said than done. Though there was no mass panic nationally, some people were genuinely frightened by what they were hearing. To assume that these people dumbly accepted what they thought was news of little green men also misses the lessons that can be learned by scrutinizing why some people *were* taken in by Welles's fake news. Many were doing their best to verify the news, but they came to the wrong conclusion.

Some of the people smugly criticizing others for falling for the prank seem to assume that everyone listened to the radio as attentively as a media critic. But many listeners would have had the radio on for background noise, the way we might today pay half attention to a podcast while washing the dishes. When they half heard something about an attack against America, they might have started paying more attention. But by then, families crowded around the only radio in the house were probably talking or shushing one another, theorizing about what was happening, and missing the clues that it was all a fiction.

Some only picked up on a few worryingly realistic details. The real fear among listeners was understandably most concentrated in the vicinity of New York and New Jersey. Listeners in the region might have recognized the name of the alleged landing site of the alien ship, Grover's Mill, a real town in New Jersey. (The show's writer, Howard Koch, had picked it out on a map at random and liked its quaint sound.) The script also included other plausible-sounding details, such as actions taken by

New Jersey's governor, the state militia, and a statement read by the "secretary of the interior." Moreover, the actor who played the secretary of the interior did a spot-on impression of President FDR's distinctive voice, familiar to radio listeners from his fireside chats, which explains why some listeners thought they had heard the president announcing an attack against America.

For many of the listeners who picked out a few details that convinced them that something genuinely worrying was going on, it wasn't little green men they thought were attacking the country. By October of 1938, news flashes about the ongoing tensions in Europe had become common. Just a few months earlier, as Germany made advances on Czechoslovakia, war had seemed imminent. The summer of 1938 was "the most dramatic and hysterical period of American broadcasting," one observer recalled. "Crisis followed crisis: emergency orders, mobilizations, fervent prayers, soaring hopes and bitter despondency." The idea of a surprise military attack on American soil was all too imaginable.

So, when some listeners half heard something on their radio about an unfolding crisis close to home, many didn't think they were about to be killed by aliens; they thought it was an attack by the Germans. People calling newspaper switchboards asked not about spaceships or aliens, but about bombs, gas raids, and enemy planes.

Some of the newspaper coverage considered this explanation. A *Boston Globe* article of November 1 quoted a Boston University psychology professor, Wayland F. Vaughan, speculating about the real cause of the mass panic. "For a long time people have been growing 'jittery' over the idea of war. They were in the mood to expect the worst," Vaughan said. The article went on, "Prof. Vaughan said emphatically that the Sunday night panic was not an indication of lack of intelligence on the part of the terror-stricken listeners."

Even Vaughan, though, didn't doubt that the mass panic had happened. "After all," he said, "we are really a credulous generation."

This is the irony of "The War of the Worlds" panic. The people so enthusiastically chastising everyone else for being credulous were themselves entirely credulous about other people's credulity. The most important lesson to take away from the hoopla over Orson Welles's "War of the Worlds" is, perhaps, to beware of stories that appear to confirm our worst assumptions about the people around us. When it comes to the news—fake or otherwise—things are often more complicated than they appear.

★

Other lessons are to be learned, too—lessons that hint at the psychological and historical themes that will occupy the chapters ahead.

Concern about new technologies is as strong in response to today's social media platforms as it was about the relatively new medium of radio in 1938. The *Washington Post*'s headline, "Monsters of Mars on a Meteor Stampede Radiotic America," coined a cute portmanteau suggesting that the radio was capable of turning America into a nation of idiots. Some critics accused radio of weakening people's attention spans. The *New York Post* coined the term *dialitis*, "a disease of the hand which makes it impossible for some folks to stay with any one program." Other critics reversed the causality: rather than radio making people dumb, maybe dumb people just liked radio. A writer in the *Chicago Tribune* mused, "By and large the radio audience isn't very bright."

Tied to fears of technology are questions about its potential to deceive. Welles's critics wondered how people could trust what they were hearing when special effects, impersonators, and other tricks of the trade muddied the waters—how could regular listeners be expected to tell reality from fiction? Some people took the alleged panic over "The War of the Worlds" as an indication that radio needed to be regulated so that people would never again fall for fake news.

It sounds quaint to hear people fretting about radio, a technology that is now on its way to obsolescence without having destroyed society. Yet contemporary concerns over social media, echo chambers, and deepfakes have the same ring of knee-jerk distrust of new technology and lack of faith in the intellect of other news consumers.

New technologies can present new challenges, but it's usually old human foibles that get us into trouble. Among the few people who genuinely panicked during "The War of the Worlds," many had heard about the apparent invasion from friends, rather than hearing Welles's show firsthand. The tendency to share news before substantiating it, and to believe trusted sources, still gets us into trouble today. Fake news is at its most dangerous when it becomes socially contagious.

Even deeper questions exist about how we come to our conception of reality, and the role of the news in shaping public consciousness. Part of the reason the

"War of the Worlds" myth took hold so readily, perhaps, was that it just made for such a good story. The dozens of anecdotes about panicky listeners that filled the pages of the *New York Times* and other papers had the quality of good yarns. "'My God,' roared one inquirer into a telephone, 'where can I volunteer my services. We've got to stop this awful thing.'" Another: "A man in Pittsburgh said he returned home in the midst of the broadcast and found his wife in the bathroom, a bottle of poison in her hand, and screaming: 'I'd rather die this way than like that.'" These anecdotes are nothing if not entertaining. And when we're presented with a string of anecdotes, we can't help extrapolating, turning a handful of extreme and exceptional stories into an assumed reality.

Adding to the problem, we're particularly receptive to certain kinds of story. In his search through the archives, Brad Schwartz found a letter written to Welles in the days after the show telling of a young college student who, when he learned that the invasion wasn't real, looked not relieved, but disappointed. "Too bad really," he said. "I'm almost sorry that it isn't true." It seems as though, Schwartz points out, "he had enjoyed the thrill of imminent annihilation."

It's not that we *want* the world to be ending. But it *would* be exciting, wouldn't it? And if you watch the news regularly, you could be forgiven for thinking the world is ending. It can seem like one endless stream of disaster followed by tragedy followed by atrocity.

This is the theme we'll take up in the next chapter: Why does *bad* news seem to make for good ratings?

CHAPTER TWO

Bad News

The quick fade-in from black is accompanied by a dramatic musical sting—swelling cymbals and a bass hit like something from a movie trailer.

We see the anchor. His brow is slightly furrowed, his jawline reassuringly strong, his hair stoically coiffed. No time for pleasantries. He has a lot of news to get through in the next thirty minutes—twenty, allowing for ad breaks. "Tonight, several developing stories as we come on the air," he intones with an air of hurried gravity. "Breaking news coming in *right now*."

Swishy white lines sweep across the screen, and the image pans briefly across a world map in stark blue and white. These are the top stories from around the globe, it would seem. Tonight, as most nights, though, the news is all from close to home.

The swishy lines swish the map away, and we're looking at video of police tape and bewildered bystanders. BREAKING NEWS, a bold, all-caps chyron reminds us. "The images coming in *right now*," the anchor emphasizes, before even explaining what's happened. Whatever it is, this is fresh trauma. A school shooting was "narrowly averted," we're soon told, "the alleged gunman *tackled*."

More swishy lines: F-16, MISSILES ON BOARD. In pixelated cell phone video, slowed down to jerky stop-motion, a distant fighter jet careens gracefully toward the ground and crashes into a warehouse. "The workers *stunned*. And tonight we have *now* learned the fighter jet had *missiles* and hundreds of rounds of *ammunition* on board."

Swish: SEVERE WEATHER OUTBREAK. In more shaky cell phone video, rain and wind buffet a parking lot. "The severe weather threat as we come on the air tonight. Watches and warnings *right now*. Tornadoes and severe thunderstorms. *Seventeen states*."

Swish: ABORTION DEBATE GROWS. "What the vice president is saying about it all." What's he saying? We'll have to keep watching to find out.

Swish: CHILLING NEW DETAILS about a young pregnant woman tricked with a Facebook message about free baby clothes. We're shown a selfie of the woman looking serene while we're told, "Police say she was then targeted, killed, her unborn baby *stolen*." No time to dwell on the horror. Swish.

A college doctor accused of abusing more than 170 students. "He reportedly had *nicknames*." Swish: DEADLY EXPLOSION INVESTIGATION. "A mother and father *killed*. Their son, in the home, *survives*." Swish: OUTRAGE. Uber and Lyft drivers "were *deliberately* shutting off their *apps* to increase demand, so surge pricing would kick in, so they could *charge* you more."

Swish. Now we hear the full version of the musical theme. It's not a coincidence that it sounded so cinematic. It was composed by Hans Zimmer and co-composer Steve Mazzaro, who scored the Batman film *The Dark Knight Rises*.

Graphics fly around the screen, resolving into a spinning globe with words spoken by an unseen, deep-voiced announcer: *"This* is *ABC World News Tonight."*

We return to the anchor in the studio. After the previous ninety seconds' litany of horrors, it's almost a relief to see him, safe behind his desk, looking serious but staid.

"It's great to have you with us here," he offers, as if to make up for his earlier brusqueness, "on a very busy Friday night."

★

So much bad news in just ninety seconds. These were the top stories according to one American network evening news show, on one night picked out at random. In case I had tuned in on a day unusually full of near disaster and tragedy, I collected a year's worth of headline stories from the same show: every all-caps chyron, and each short, staccato outline delivered by the anchor in those first ninety seconds or so of the broadcast.

In the aggregate, the chyrons form an abstract poetry of unease:

DEVELOPING NOW
CHILLING INVESTIGATION
DANGER AT THE DOOR

After the words BREAKING NEWS, the next most common single word was DEADLY. Over the year, there were deadly heat waves and deadly winter blasts, deadly fires and deadly floods. There were deadly plane, helicopter, train, bus, and car accidents. There was a deadly lion attack and a deadly bear attack. And there were a few more enigmatic captions: a DEADLY TRAGEDY, a DEADLY CONFRONTATION, two DEADLY MISTAKES, and a DEADLY MIX-UP.

There were plenty of scares, too. People were scared on Valentine's Day, St. Patrick's Day, and Easter. (There was horror on Mardi Gras and chaos on Christmas Eve.) Sources of scares included earthquakes, aneurysms, avalanches, and salmonella. People were scared at day care, in the hospital, on the school bus, in midair, in a tower, in the Eiffel Tower, on a cruise ship, a ski lift, at the White House, at the ballpark, and in their neighborhood. One scare chyron was followed by a tantalizing question mark— SCARED AT SEA?—suggesting that whether you should be scared at sea is an open question. But regular viewers would already be scared of stingrays, sharks, and the possibility of drowning, which all produced scare stories of their own (not to mention one SEA LION ATTACK WARNING).

In addition to the CHRISTMAS EVE CHAOS, there was chaos in the Capitol, in the cockpit, and in a cabin (chyron writers are fond of alliteration), in malls, at airports, on the highway, at the US Open, and in Venezuela.

All told, the year or so of top stories contained 131 deadly events, 42 scares, 38 dangers, 28 horrors, 14 terrors, 14 disasters, 13 outrages, 11 chilling developments, 7 tragedies, 5 crises, 3 each of fears, alarms, and monsters, 2 shocks, and a PANIC AT TRADER JOE'S.

That's a lot of bad news. Where's the good news? The closest we get is stories of disaster averted. There were 33 rescues, most of which were described as *dramatic, daring, amazing,* or a *miracle.* There were seven stories of surviving something, and six close calls. Five heroes were mentioned, though the news about three of them was that they had just died, and another was missing.

The word *happy* appeared once—a jovial HAPPY NEW YEAR! There were no words such as *calm* or *safe* or *nice,* no *positive*, no *success*, no *triumph*, no *better*, no *improvement*. *Good* appeared in chyrons just three times, but it wasn't good news. One was in a question posed that day by President Trump: WHAT GOOD IS NATO? The other two were about the actor Cuba Gooding Jr. (CUBA GOODING JR. IN HANDCUFFS read one).

It seems fair to say that, over the year, there was more bad news than good.

★

I'm far from the first person to point this out. Decrying the tropes and excesses of the news, particularly its proclivity for doom and gloom, is by now a well-worn genre. The appropriately gruesome phrase chastising the media for this bad habit is *if it bleeds, it leads*.

The phrase, now ubiquitous, seems to have first been used in print in relation to one person in particular: Boston news director Peter Leone.

A 1981 series of articles in the *Boston Globe* offered an in-depth look at the city's four major news channels. Leone was then director at Channel 7. "The news policy at Channel 7 has not been a complicated one," the article begins. "According to reporters who work there, it goes like this: If it bleeds, it leads." It's also known as the "blood on the sidewalks" approach, the article goes on. "This means a story about the municipal budget, however important, will take second billing to a story, however trivial, that is accompanied by film showing a rip-roaring fire, for example, or … well, blood on the sidewalk."

Pinning the concept on Leone, the author relates a story attributed to reporters who worked for the director.

One night, apparently, Leone was in his office watching multiple televisions tuned to the city's news broadcasts. His own nightly news show played on one of the monitors, showing some graphic video accompanying whatever sensational story Leone had chosen to lead that night's broadcast. He watched in satisfaction. On another television was a competitor, Channel 5, leading with a less sensational story. "From outside his office, reporters say, Leone could be seen pointing to the television set and the Channel 5 newscast, yelling, 'Boring! Boring! Boring!'"

Less than a year later, the network changed ownership and Leone was out of a job. A reporter for the industry magazine *Broadcasting* asked Leone's successor if the revamped news show would "continue its predecessor's policy, described as 'if it bleeds, it leads.'" The new director replied that "such tactics are those of desperation."

Despite the newcomer's disavowal, the taste for blood was not unique to Leone. "The 'if it bleeds, it leads' ethic at the old WNAC-TV was only the logical extension of the philosophy at local stations in most markets around the country," wrote another *Boston Globe* reporter in 1983. "There is an almost sadistic preoccupation with disaster. One almost has the sense that news directors think their audience is made up of people who would be cheering for the guy to jump off the 18th story."

Leone wasn't a single bad apple. It was a rotten barrel.

A *Washington Post* opinion columnist sardonically broke down the "if it bleeds, it leads" formula in 1986, in the style of an anthropologist outlining some kind of bizarre ritual: "A typical local news show begins with either a murder or a fire. If it is a murder, we see film of what is known as 'the scene.' This consists of a building, a street and maybe a close-up shot of where the body was found." Such shots, the author argued, are devoid of news, shown only for the sensation they evoke. "What we are seeing, in essence, is nothing—not the murder, not the suspect, not anything that could not be told in a sentence. It is film for the sake of film, and so accustomed are we to this that we hardly notice we are seeing nothing."

The phrase was already taking on a life of its own. It was always associated with local news, and usually an insult lobbed from one news producer at another. "'If it bleeds, it leads' is Channel 5's unwritten policy, according to a disgruntled competitor," wrote Gary Cartwright, in a comprehensive overview of Texas's dozens of local news shows. Cartwright's article ran as a cover story for a 1984 issue of *Texas Monthly*. The cover photo was of a newsreader done up in garish clown makeup, grinning maniacally into the camera, complete with bald dome and two orange triangles of hair the texture of cotton candy on either side of his head. The headline, in a huge bold font, declared, "Bozos at Six and Ten." Local TV news was becoming a punching bag.

Credit for popularizing the phrase, though, is usually given to Eric Pooley, who used it in another cover story—this one for *New York* magazine. Like Cartwright, Pooley focused his criticism on local television news, this time in the New York region. But Pooley's story was more biting than whimsical. It was titled "Grins, Gore and Videotape." The cover photo showed two telegenic newsreaders holding scripts and smiling inanely in front of a green-screen backdrop of emergency workers

carrying a body-bagged corpse. Pooley called New
York's local news industry "a machine that packages pain
as entertainment." *Some* good journalism is on television,
Pooley acknowledges. The trouble is that it's drowned
out by the blood and guts. "The thoughtful report is
buried because sensational stories must launch the
broadcast: If it bleeds, it leads." He quotes a producer:
"Context? Digging? perspective? We don't have the
time. ... What does it all mean? We can't tell you—we're
too busy putting it on the air."

From there, the phrase made it onto a 1990 *Newsweek*
list of "buzzwords," offering a behind-the-scenes glimpse
into "how the producers—both for entertainment and
news—talk off set." *Newsweek's* pithy description, for the
uninitiated, explained that the phrase is "used at local
stations that thrive on gore."

A couple of weeks later, the phrase showed up in the
pages of the *New York Times*, used by no less a writer
than the former executive editor of the *Times* itself,
Abe Rosenthal. Respectable journalists, he wrote, "are
revolted by the standards of some nightly news programs:
if it bleeds, it leads."

These were all newspaper or magazine writers, it's
worth pointing out, bemoaning the state of local
television news. Some offered scorn for their tabloid-
paper colleagues as well, but presumably these writers
felt their own publications were above such ambulance-
chasing sensationalism.

Members of the public were quicker, however, to spot
the bloodthirsty tendencies of the news media more
generally. A letter to the editor of the *Boston Globe*,
published in 1986, not only assumed that the appetite

for destruction was a long-held open secret rather than a recent innovation, but also assumed that it was a trait of *all* media, not just local news. "Perhaps we should examine the image problem that plagues the media," the writer urged, "and start with the old standard 'If it bleeds it leads.'"

Eventually the accusations broke the levees of local news and spread over television news in general, and from there, the entire news industry. The phrase is now widely used to talk about the media in general, as in a *Washington Post* article, to take one recent example, that called the phrase "the old news adage."

★

Now, I know what you're thinking. I'm thinking it, too. *Things must be worse now than ever.* If local television news ushered in the lust for blood in the eighties with its reliance on shocking visual images and lack of time for substance, things can only have ramped up since then. News shows and networks are more plentiful, broadcasting around the clock while the endless scroll of headlines on smartphone screens competes for people's limited attention. News cameras are more ubiquitous, not to mention that almost everyone now has a camera in his or her pocket capable of recording tragedy as it happens, to be posted instantaneously to social media for the world to enjoy, and for news networks to regurgitate.

With the benefit of hindsight, we can probably look back on even the blood-splattered local news of the 1980s as a quaint golden age.

Except, we've been here once before already. Even in criticizing the sensationalism of the news, we tend to paint it as a DISTURBING NEW TREND. But as we saw in the last chapter, the assumption that things must be different now makes us forget history and dooms us to repeat it. A glance at some news from before television and the internet—in old newspapers, or in newsbooks and ballads before that, or in the daily notices posted in the Roman forum before that, or what we can tell about the tropes of oral news—suggests that "if it bleeds, it leads" is not a new phenomenon. The news has always been bad.

"I hear new news every day," a British scholar wrote in 1621, the year the first regular weekly newspapers began publishing in England. He gave an overview of his sense of the news, which reads as a bewildering cacophony of calamity: "Rumours of war, plagues, fires, inundations, thefts, murders, massacres, meteors, comets, spectrums, prodigies, apparitions." There was news "of towns taken, cities besieged in France, Germany, Turkey, Persia, Poland, etc., daily musters and preparations, and such-like, which these tempestuous times afford, battles fought, so many men slain." And then there were the sundry "shipwrecks, piracies, and sea-fights, peace leagues, stratagems, and fresh alarums."

Not all the news was bad; the news of the day was a bewildering stew of "now comical, then tragical matters." It had all "the gallantry and misery of the world; jollity, pride, perplexities and cares, simplicity and villainy; subtlety, knavery, candour and integrity, mutually mixed and offering themselves."

Even before the advent of the newspaper, news of crime and calamity was commonplace. Historian Matthias Shaaber trawled through archives of sixteenth and early seventeenth century newsbooks and ballads—the forerunners of the newspaper. "The sixteenth century loved a murder as dearly as we do today," he concluded. "It hardly seems possible that a really first-rate murder, especially if it was complicated by an illicit love affair, or the hanging of any notable criminal, went unrecorded."

The earliest surviving news report of a murder Shaaber found was from 1557. A broadside reported the execution of an English peer, Baron Charles Sturton. After getting into a quarrel with a surly neighbor, Sturton had the neighbor and his son kidnapped and their throats cut. The broadside didn't just report the dry details, it claimed to present a "copy of the self same wordes, that mi lorde Sturton spake presently at his Death." This was a common feature of the murder reporting of the day, Shaaber notes. Many reports of executions claimed, implausibly, to carry "the last-minute confession and repentance of the criminal," usually "written in the first person and purported to be his own inspired work."

If anything, some of the bad news of the past was even more gratuitously gruesome than we're accustomed to today. Whenever a body turned up dismembered, the news writers often went into fine detail about the fate of each individual body part. In 1654 and 1655, what historian Joseph Frank called perhaps "the goriest single-crime story on record" did the rounds, reporting that a woman in Kent had cut out, cooked, and served to her philandering husband his mistress's vulva.

In those early days, the news writers were content to simply report the crime of the day when it crossed their desks. Beginning in the 1820s and 1830s, however, many newspapers began actively seeking out news of crime, assigning a journalist to the local police beat. The reporter would go to the police court in the early hours of the morning and report back the most sordid or amusing crimes and mishaps of the day. One publisher promised readers in 1834 that his paper would "abound in Police Intelligence, in Murders, Rapes, Suicides, Burnings, Maimings, Theatricals, Races, Pugilism, and all manner of moving 'accidents by floor and field.' In short, it will be stuffed with every sort of devilment that will make it sell."

★

Why so much bad news? As usual, it's tempting to blame the media and call it quits. Perhaps, as a lot of the "if it bleeds, it leads" punditry implied, the focus on bad news is a personal failing on the part of news producers.

A 1995 *Columbia Journalism Review* article, evocatively titled "A Generation of Vipers," noted an ostensibly new tendency among some journalists to indulge in "casual disdain" for the people they wrote about, rooted in "a deep and abiding cynicism, a reflexive suspicion of face-value explanations, an inclination to ascribe ignoble motives."

Moreover, the article suggests, the professional culture of newsrooms and the press corps actively encouraged cynicism. "Many journalists describe a kind of chemical reaction that takes place when they cluster in groups—a catalytic conversion that gets reporters thinking cynically, or more cynically, about their subjects." A journalist quoted in the piece explains, "Nothing could make you look more stupid than saying, 'I think, gee, they're doing this because they're right.' There's almost a bidding war of cynicism. It's good to be more cynical."

A related explanation casts journalistic skepticism in a more noble light. It is the media's job, this line of reasoning goes, to act as a watchdog, guarding the public interest. That necessarily entails seeking out wrongdoing, misconduct, failure, corruption, greed, cruelty, injustice, villains, and victims. In this light, being the bearer of bad news isn't a vice, but a virtue. It means you're doing your job right. "It is nothing strange that men who think themselves unaccountable, should act unaccountably," read a letter published in James (brother of Benjamin) Franklin's *New England Courant* in 1721. "The exposing therefore of public Wickedness," it asserted, "is a Duty which every Man owes to his country."

If you want to be cynical about it, we could, perhaps, say that at least there's a convenient alignment between the personal inclination to seek out the worst and the professional obligation to reveal wrongdoing. Unfettered cynicism doesn't necessarily lead to good journalism, though. "The sanctimony is frequently hard to tell from the cynicism," as Adam Gopnik put it in a 1995 *New Yorker* article on the aggressively cynical political journalism of the Clinton era: they "turn out to be a little like electricity and magnetism—two aspects of a single field, perpetuating themselves in a thought-free vacuum."

This gray area, where valiant crusading and thinly veiled cynicism are hard to tell apart, has been pointed out before. President Theodore Roosevelt coined the term *muckraker* in a 1906 speech to refer to this murky strain of journalism. The word was a reference to *The Pilgrim's Progress*, a religious allegory published in 1678 that would have been familiar to his audience at the time. "You may recall the description of the Man with the Muck Rake," Roosevelt said, "the man who could look no way but downward, with the muck rake in his hand." The man was offered spiritual reward, the allegory continues, if only he would look up from the dirt and exchange his muckrake for the "celestial crown" being offered to him. But, obliviously or obstinately, the man "continued to rake to himself the filth of the floor." It does no good—can, in fact, do great harm—Roosevelt was saying, when journalists are blinded to the good in the world by focusing purely on "things bad and debasing."

It feels as if we've wandered away from where we started, though. The noble effort to expose systematic injustice and abuses of power seems pretty far removed from the bloodthirsty focus on random murders, fires, explosions, and the like. "The highest and primary obligation of ethical journalism is to serve the public," reads one professional code of ethics. "Avoid pandering to lurid curiosity, even if others do." How the public is served, and how lurid curiosity avoided, by story after story of personal tragedy and scandal is hard to say.

Anyway, if you could ask the collective media why so much of the news is bad, it might, in a candid moment, tell you that it's just giving us what we want.

Joseph Mitchell, a New York newspaper reporter, wrote that his "editors believed that nothing brightened up a front page so much as a story about human

suffering." It was what readers wanted, the editors
thought. "The man on the street is so gloomy nowadays
that a story about somebody else's bad luck cheers him
up." To be fair, this was in 1933, in the midst of the
Great Depression. The man on the street had a lot to be
gloomy about.*

More recently, in his *New York* cover story on local
news, Eric Pooley suggested that crime and tragedy
dominate the news primarily because "they're thought to
boost ratings among the mainstay blue-collar audience."
Some station executives, Pooley said, like to personify
that audience as "Joe Beercan." The key question news
directors ask themselves when putting together the
evening news, Pooley suggests, is "What does Joe Beercan
want to watch tonight?" The answer: "Joe Beercan
wants blood."

Of course, if you could ask Joe Beercan, he'd probably
deny the unflattering allegation. A few public opinion
surveys over the years suggest that people generally
blame the abundance of bad news on the media. In a
1985 survey, around two-thirds of people agreed that
"the news media put too much emphasis on what is
wrong with America and not enough on what is right,"
and that "reporters frequently overdramatize the news."
Likewise, two-thirds of people dismissed the idea that
"the news media try not to emphasize bad news too
much." Years later, a Times Mirror poll in March 1993
found the same roughly two-thirds of the public felt that

---

* Expanding the remit only slightly, another Depression-era reporter
said he was told by his boss, "The public is interested in just three
things: blood, money, and the female organ of sexual intercourse."

the news media "put too much emphasis on negative news."

But you hardly need a psychologist to tell you that what people say doesn't always match what they do. In his article, Pooley quoted a producer explaining his take on audience demand: "People always say they want to hear what the president said, but in focus groups, when the president is on one TV and a flashing police light is on the other, which one do the heads turn to?"

It may not be flattering, but decades of psychological studies back up the producer's assessment of his audience—that is, *us*. It's not that we are force-fed a diet of bad news against our will. Rather, we're drawn toward bad news like moths to a flame. Bad things grab our attention, they're memorable, we react more strongly to them, and we want to tell other people about them.

As the title of one scholarly review of the research put it, "bad is stronger than good."

★

Allow me to demonstrate.

How would you feel if I gave you the opportunity to wear a sweater that once belonged to beloved children's television entertainer Mr. Rogers?

How about putting on a sweater that belonged to serial killer Ted Bundy?

I'm guessing your feeling about the opportunity to wear an item of Mr. Rogers's clothing was positive, but pretty mild. Something in the ballpark of "Sure, why not." Everybody likes Mr. Rogers. Maybe the idea of wearing an item of his clothing gives you a little warm feeling, but probably not too much of anything.

Imagining wearing something that belonged to a serial killer such as Ted Bundy, on the other hand, probably gives you a much stronger reaction: substantial aversion, if not outright revulsion. The bad is stronger than the good.

The idea for this kind of thought experiment came from psychologist Paul Rozin. Rozin made a career out of studying the psychology not of serial killers' sweaters, but of food. Thinking about why people like and dislike certain foods led Rozin to the psychology of disgust— what causes aversion to the taste of something that once made you sick, or outright revulsion to the mere thought of eating certain things? This led to his experiment with fruit juice and a cockroach.

The experiment, while described in the usual detached, scientific tone of a research paper, makes for excruciating reading. Had you been unfortunate enough to answer the ad in a newspaper requesting volunteers for a study of "food preferences," the experiment would have started out innocuously enough, with a sip of apple juice.

"I'm going to offer you some juices," the experimenter told volunteers. "I'd like you to taste them and rate how much you'd like to have another sip of the same juice." So far, so boring.

Then things start to get uncomfortable. "The experi-menter placed a tray covered with paper towels in front of her," the paper explains. The experimenter lifts the towels, revealing a small pair of forceps sitting next to a small clear-plastic cup. Inside the cup is a cockroach.

For anyone wishing to play along at home, the researchers helpfully provide its scientific name— *Periplaneta americana*. That means the big fuckers you dread seeing skittering around your kitchen at night, with the hairy-looking legs and twitching long antennae. Thankfully, the one in the cup was neither twitching or skittering. It was dead: dried and, participants were assured, completely sterile.

While she carefully lifts the roach with a pair of forceps, the experimenter says, "Now I'm going to take this sterilized, dead cockroach—it's perfectly safe—and drop it in this juice glass." Great. "The roach was dropped into the glass, and stirred with the forceps for 5s." It probably felt like a long five seconds to the person on the other side of the table. "The subject was then asked to count the roach's legs (to assure his attention)." Does the mere thought of being asked to count the legs of a cockroach floating belly up in a glass of apple juice make you squirm? Me, too. "The roach was then removed with a new plastic spoon that came from a new spoon container, and placed back in its original cup."

"The spoon," we are assured, "was discarded."

Finally the experimenter asked the participant how much he or she would like to have another sip of the freshly roached juice. As you might expect, people's enthusiasm for the formerly appealing juice plummeted to close to the bottom of the scale. The researchers had labeled it "extreme dislike." I'd imagine that didn't come close to capturing some people's feelings.

Now, if you're thinking that such an elaborate experiment was hardly necessary just to find out that people don't want to drink roach juice—well, yeah. But it's more interesting than that. The researchers made a show of avoiding any actual contamination of the juice. All the juices and cups were new and unwrapped in front of the participant. Even the cockroach was presented and handled with utmost scientific care. This was clearly not some roach the experimenter found crawling in a dumpster five minutes ago. To be disgusted by the juice, even while believing that the roach was completely sterile, implies some kind of magical transference of its disgusting cockroach essence to the otherwise unaffected juice, Rozin argued. He called this apparent disgust "negative contagion."

It's interesting to think about why we so readily give in to this kind of magical thinking, but that's not the point here. The point, as Rozin argued in a later review paper, written with Edward Royzman, is that contamination is largely a one-way street. While it's easy to put people off something they like by dipping something gross in it, it's hard to imagine anything you could do to make the gross thing more appealing. Being covered in apple juice doesn't make *the roach* any more appetizing, no matter how much you like apple juice.

In short, you can easily take something good and make it bad, but it's hard to take something bad and make it good. This brings us back to the idea of the borrowed sweater. Rozin specialized in beliefs around food, but he wanted to see if negative contagion applies in other contexts. Moreover, he needed to pit good against bad in a fair fight, to see if he could elicit any "positive contagion" to match the negative.

So in another study, Rozin asked people three questions about wearing a previously owned item of clothing. How would you feel about wearing a cleaned blouse or shirt of a style you like that comes from the racks of a used-clothing store? How about one that belonged to someone you dislike? And how about one that belonged to someone you like? (Rozin didn't ask about Mr. Rogers or Ted Bundy, for the obvious reason that maybe Bundy is badder than Rogers is good. It wouldn't be a fair comparison—I just used it for dramatic effect. Hey, sensationalism works!)

Rozin did find some positive contagion from the liked person's shirt, but not much. People felt only slightly more enthusiastic about wearing the liked person's shirt than the generic used-clothing-store version. But people felt much more strongly about the disliked person's shirt. The store-bought shirt was much more appealing than the enemy's shirt. The negative contagion, Rozin calculated, was three times stronger than the positive contagion.

In their review paper, Rozin and Royzman point to many other experiments that found the same trends, as well as broader cultural observations that seem to back the idea up. They found the idea illustrated, for example, in an old Russian adage: "A spoonful of tar can spoil a barrel of honey, but a spoonful of honey does nothing for a barrel of tar." In the Hindu caste system, they point out, people of higher castes can easily find their social status reduced by, for example, eating food prepared by someone of a lower caste, but people of a lower caste who consume foods prepared by higher castes will not find their status suddenly raised. Likewise, in Christianity, sinning takes a moment; redemption takes a lifetime.

"Pollution always overcomes purity," Rozin and Royzman wrote. Bad is stronger than good.

★

Negative contagion affects how we view the people around us, too. One personality flaw or ignoble deed can taint our entire impression of a person. A bad reputation is easy to acquire and hard to shake, whereas a good reputation is hard-won and easily lost. Telling the truth once does not make you honest, but telling one lie makes you a liar.

Our sensitivity to badness can influence first impressions, too. Suppose I tell you I know a guy who is industrious, critical, warm, practical, and determined. You probably picture a pretty decent guy. Maybe a Bill Gates type. Someone who works hard, possesses keen insight into problems, and uses the fruits of his labor to help his family, friends, and the broader community.

Now suppose I tell you about another acquaintance of mine. This fellow is industrious, critical, cold, practical, and determined. You will probably imagine a very different type of person. Probably more of an Ebenezer Scrooge type. Someone who uses his intellect and efforts only to his own advantage and cares not a jot for the people around him.

The two descriptions differed only in a single word in the middle of the list. Both people were equally industrious, critical, practical, and determined. But whether you saw them as *warm* or *cold* colored the entire picture. Warmth, or lack of it, is one of the first things we evaluate when we encounter someone new, and one of the most influential factors in our judgment of the entire person.

While we generally see *ourselves* in a positive light, the bad events that befall us—both small slights and major setbacks—tend to stand out in our minds more than good events. When researchers simply ask people what they're thinking about, the answer is often something bad. One study had French college students bring to mind a recent, important emotional life event. Only around a quarter of the events people brought to mind were positive; three-quarters were bad. And American college students seem to be just as dour. Threats to relationships, unexpected difficulties, and challenges are among the things that occupy American students' thoughts the most. Studies in which people are asked to keep a diary of the good and the bad things that happen to them over time suggest that people generally report more good things overall, but the bad things have an oversize influence on their mood.

You'd think, since we have such a strong reaction to anything bad, that we'd do our best to avoid the unpleasant and upsetting and surround ourselves with peace and tranquility. It seems odd, then, that when people are given the choice between looking either at pictures of death and violence or neutral scenes of people walking on the street, they're more likely than not to pick the bad ones. Even in a straight contest between negative images and equally interesting positive pictures, such as "partying people are carrying a crowd surfer," about half of people choose something bad instead, such as "a wounded boy is carried away from disaster."

In a fundamental sense, bad things grab our attention more than good things. We will look at pictures of bad stuff for longer than pictures of good stuff. Angry and threatening faces "pop out" in a crowd of neutral faces more than do happy faces (suggesting that *Where's Waldo?* would be made easier if Waldo was furious). We're quicker to respond to bad words, such as *sadistic, mean,* and *hostile,* than good words, such as *kind, sincere,* and *talented,* even when the words are just flashing up on a screen and we're not trying to read them. We remember bad experiences more than good, and we learn better when punished for wrong responses than when rewarded for correct responses.

All of which seems to help explain why we can't help slowing down to look at an accident at the side of the road. The sight is unnerving, unpleasant, upsetting. But for most of us, it's hard to look away.

*

Our negativity bias affects the stories we seek out and tell one another. One type of story that seems to thrive off negativity is the urban legend. In a study with the delightful title "Corpses, Maggots, Poodles and Rats," researchers Kimmo Eriksson and Julie Coultas wanted to see what made four urban legends involving—you guessed it—corpses, maggots, poodles, and rats, so sharable.

Here's the rat story:

Many years ago Jasmine visited Stockholm for the first time. She decided to go to a new pizza restaurant near her hotel. After eating her pizza Jasmine found that something was stuck in her teeth. She succeeded in removing the object. She examined the object: it was a tooth from a rat! She realized that the restaurant probably had used rat meat in her pizza. As far as Jasmine could remember she had never felt that sick before.

Yikes. Many urban legends are of this variety: some nasty surprise befalls an unwitting victim. But maybe we're just attuned to surprises in general. Is there something especially sharable about these kind of gross-out urban legends? To try to find out, the researchers created a second version of each legend—a sort of PG-rated version, which still contained a surprise but was stripped of the gross-out elements. Here's the pizza story again, now without the side of rat:

> Many years ago Jasmine visited Stockholm for the first time. She decided to go to a new pizza restaurant near her hotel. After eating her pizza Jasmine found that something was stuck in her teeth. She succeeded in removing the object. She examined the object: it was a stone from an olive! She realized that the restaurant probably had used green olives in her pizza. As far as Jasmine could remember they had not been listed on the menu.

Same general narrative, still with an element of surprise, but much less disgusting (unless you *really* dislike olives). The researchers had people read one or the other of these stories, and you can probably guess what happened. People who read the sensational, gross-out stories were more likely to say they'd tell the story to someone else, and they better remembered the details of the story.

So the more unpleasant the urban legend, the more likely it is to spread. But it's hard to know whether this is from the allure of the *bad* or something broader. Maybe the disgusting stories are more emotionally arousing, or maybe they are darkly humorous in a way that the tamed versions aren't.

To figure out if being bad is important in and of itself, Keely Bebbington and her colleagues at the University of Western Australia came up with a story that had no disgusting surprises. They wrote a story that wasn't emotionally engaging at all. It was a snooze-fest by design. The gist is that an eighteen-year-old named Sarah has just finished high school. She's due to get her exam results in a week, but she's decided to take a year off before going to university, and so right now she's heading off on a trip to the United Kingdom.

I told you: it's an intentionally bland story. But adding a little salt and pepper to the basic narrative were details that were either good or bad. Sarah's parents were disappointed that she wanted to go traveling instead of straight to university—that's bad. But they had always been supportive of her—that's good. She got an upgrade to business class on her flight—very good! But ended up sitting next to a guy with a cold who sneezed all over her—pretty bad!

In addition to these clearly positive or negative details, some ambiguous details were thrown in. For example, Sarah was said to be sure she knew how she had done on her exams—but the reader isn't told whether she's sure she aced them or sure she flunked them. Likewise, at the airport she sees a young man take a woman's bag—whether he is a Good Samaritan lending a helping hand or a no-good thief is left open to interpretation.

To see how the story fared in the retelling, Bebbington set the study up as an elaborate game of telephone. Arriving at the lab to take part in the study, you find yourself in a group with three other people. The four of you are randomly assigned a place in the chain. Let's say you're lucky number one. You get to read the original story. Then your job is to tell the story, from memory, to the person in position number two. Then person number two has to retell it to number three, and lastly person number three passes it along to person number four, at the end of the chain. Each person has to write his or her version down, so that the researchers have a record of how the story got warped along the way.

Around a hundred foursomes played this game. Then the researchers trawled through each unique retelling of the story, each filtered through the memory and interpretation of the various group members. (Pity the poor research assistants who had to read this same inane story retold four hundred times.) What the researchers wanted to know was how well positive and negative plot points survived in retelling, and whether the ambiguous details would take on a more overtly positive or negative spin along the way.

As you'd expect, all details, positive, negative, and ambiguous, tended to be lost in transmission. It wasn't a particularly long story, but at around five hundred words it wasn't exactly short when your job is to pass it on as completely and accurately as you can from memory. It contained more than fifty separate details, eight of them positive, eight negative, eight ambiguous, and the rest just neutral plot points.

By the time the fourth person had written his or her version of the story, typically more than half of all the details had been lost. But there was a fairly big difference between the good and the bad details. On average, around five out of the eight bad details made it into the last person's retelling, but only two or three of the good details. Around half of the ambiguous details got lost along the way, but those that survived rarely stayed ambiguous. As the story made its way along the chain, those details were increasingly likely to become negative. By the end of the chain, Sarah probably flunked her exams, and the person taking the bag was more likely a thief than a Samaritan.

This helps explain why, as one literary critic pointed out, we have no novels about happy marriages, but many about marital strife and conflict. We choose to consume stories about bad things. We're more likely to want to share them with other people. We remember the bad stuff better than the good stuff, and even innocent details can become bad over time.

*

This tour through the darker recesses of our psyches brings us back to bad news. Despite our frequent protestations that there's too much of it, it's often the bad news that we want to read and share.

In the lab, researchers can simply give people a choice between good and bad news and see which they pick. Bad often wins out over good. We don't reject good news entirely, but bad news is about 20 or 30 percent more likely to get read in these kinds of studies. We spend longer reading news stories that are accompanied by threatening graphics, and we remember the details of television news stories better when they begin with a negative image. People who say they're more interested in politics are particularly likely to prefer negative political news, and people who complain about too much negativity and cynicism in the news choose to read just as much bad news as everyone else.

As far as it's possible to make the same kind of fair comparison outside the lab, the trend seems to hold. Three German economists, led by Maria Arango-Kure, analyzed more than a decade of sales figures for three German newsmagazines, to see if sales varied with how positive or negative the cover of each issue was. They found that issues with explicitly negative covers sold between 5 percent and 12 percent more copies, on average, compared to issues with neutral covers.

Again, it seems we can't help being drawn toward the bad. To see how watching bad news affects us physiologically, University of Michigan communications researchers hooked participants up to a bunch of sensors while they watched the news. (In case you're picturing someone straitjacketed like Alex in *A Clockwork Orange*, being forced to watch hours of cable news as a researcher diligently moistens the person's eyeballs, I should point out that participants watched a news program on their own, on a large computer monitor in a quiet room, wearing noise-canceling headphones.) People's bodies reacted more strongly to bad news than to good. As they watched a bad news report, they began to sweat a little bit more than when they watched good news, as measured by the conductivity of their skin, indicating that they were getting excited. At the same time, their heart rate decreased more, indicating that they were paying closer attention. (Being excited tends to increase how fast our heart beats, but the slowdown caused by attentiveness overwhelms the increase due to excitement.)

And then, there's the sheer amount of bad news out there. When researchers have attempted to examine the obsession of the news with doom and gloom, they have tended to agree with the pundits: if it bleeds, it leads.

Despite critics' focus on television news, the majority of the research has focused on newspapers. As far back as 1900, Delos Wilcox attempted a social psychological study of the American newspaper. Wilcox would later become editor of the *Detroit Civic News* and after that went on to a career in municipal government. But in 1898, fresh from a PhD in political science at Columbia University, he was interested in how newspapers influenced the public consciousness. "The newspaper is to society much what sight and hearing are to the individual," Wilcox wrote. "It is a momentous day when the community, overwhelmed with newspaper sensations, begins to doubt and to discriminate."

Reading his research report, you can tell Wilcox suspected that day had already come. Studying in New York City in the late 1890s, he was in the epicenter of the so-called "yellow journalism" boom. Fierce competition for readers between William Randolph Hearst's *Journal* and Joseph Pulitzer's *World* spiraled into a frenzy of sensationalism. Many other papers of the day followed suit, seeking to boost sales with bold headlines screaming stories of crime and scandal. "There is a widespread prejudice against the newspapers, based on the belief that they cannot be trusted to report truly the current events in the world's life on account of incompetence or venality," Wilcox noted.

Wilcox wanted to quantify the extent to which the newspapers of the day were guilty of pandering to what he called "superficial and sometimes unhealthy interests." His measurement tool of choice was the tape measure; he literally measured the number of column inches devoted to a handful of news topics and worked out the proportions of each. Perhaps surprisingly, news of "crime and vice" made up only about 5 percent of the total news coverage. War news, however, made up close to a third. (Wilcox collected most of the news coverage in the middle of the Spanish-American War.) It's not possible to say exactly how much of the news was good or bad, based on Wilcox's categorization, but he was not impressed by what he found. He ended his report with the hope that publishers would "devote their money, their brains, and their energy to the promotion of public intelligence instead of the stimulation of public passion."

Yellow journalism appeared to have burned itself out shortly after Wilcox completed his study, giving way, it seemed, to a more restrained, ethical, objective form of journalism. Yet when Morris Gilmore Caldwell, a professor of sociology and economics at Ashland College in Ohio, followed up Wilcox's study with one of his own in 1930, he found the situation hadn't much changed. The tone of news coverage may have become more restrained, but the focus on bad news had, if anything, increased. Caldwell collected every issue of six metropolitan daily newspapers over two months. He found that the proportion of space devoted to crime and other sensation news had increased by about half since Wilcox's day. War news was no longer so prevalent, but economic news— much of it presumably bad, in the midst of the Great Depression—more than made up for it.

Caldwell concedes that the increasing coverage of crime might have been due to increased prevalence. Since the turn of the century, he writes, "crime and racketeering have become organized on a national scale. Accidents, suicides, divorces, and catastrophes have likewise increased." However, you get the sense that Caldwell doesn't much approve of the newspapers making lemonade out of those lemons. "A large percent of American newspapers have taken advantage of the fore-going situation and have deliberately engaged upon a policy of sensationalism in order to increase their sales," he wrote. Crime and other sensational news was disproportionately likely to make the front page, he found. He notes that the more crime news an individual paper carried on its front pages, the more advertising it tended to carry. "The modern metropolitan newspaper, with over one-half of its space devoted to advertising, would be a rather dull and drab affair, and hardly saleable, with-out the flashy and ostentatious display of crime news on the front page."

On television, too, there's a lot of bad news. In 1987, three journalism professors enlisted their grad students to watch and code a week's worth of local news from Syracuse, Memphis, and San Diego—the cities where each of the researchers lived. They found that bad news made up 43 percent of the stories across all the broadcasts. Around a third of the stories reported good news, with the balance made up by neutral stories. As with the newspapers and their front pages, the shows were disproportionately likely to lead with bad news.

That figure of around 40 percent bad news seems to be surprisingly stable. Paul Klite, a media critic and Executive Director of Denver-based Rocky Mountain Media Watch, analyzed a hundred stations' nightly news broadcasts from a single night in 1995. He computed what he called a "mayhem index," which included any stories with a focus on violence—stories about crime, natural and human-made disasters, and war. On average across all one hundred stations, the news was 42 percent mayhem.

Bringing things more up-to-date, computer scientist Julio Reis and colleagues collected close to seventy thousand headlines published by four major global media corporations during 2014. The outlets were the United Kingdom's BBC News and *Daily Mail*, the *New York Times*, and Reuters. They found that negativity pervaded the headlines. The *Daily Mail* led the way, with a full 65 percent of its headlines categorized as negative. Yet even at the relatively restrained BBC, close to half of its headlines were negative. Reuters and the *New York Times* were in between. Just 10 percent of all the headlines were categorized as positive. The rest were neutral.

★

What are we to make of our apparent negativity bias? Should we feel bad for watching bad news?

"A word rarely mentioned in this debate," wrote one critic of the supposed surplus of bad news, "is sadism." Wallowing in other people's pain and misfortune, he asked, indulging our morbid curiosity, "is that not what we are doing when we relish watching violent news, entertainment and sports?" Our negativity doesn't exactly reflect well on us, when you put it like that.

Yet, an ironic thing about a lot of the criticism of bad news is just how *bad* it makes it seem. Some criticism seems almost as simplistic and sensational as the news it is criticizing. "The very idea of news has been perverted into a steady diet of titillating, terrifying, and manipulative entertainment," that same critic wrote; "every child in America has witnessed a private holocaust in the media by the time he or she reaches puberty."

Some of the media reporting of bad news makes it seem as if some new epidemic is about to tear society apart. A 1984 *Washington Journalism Review* cover story about bad news bore the tagline "Scaring Us to Death on the Late-Night News." The photo accompanying the article shows an elderly woman sitting in an armchair, transfixed by the glow of the television, which looms, out of focus, in the foreground. Behind her, as if conjured by the mayhem unfolding on the screen, two men have seemingly broken in through an open window. One sports a small switchblade and a menacing grin. The other is fully kitted out in commando-style beret and aviator shades, with a rifle slung over his shoulder and a belt of large-caliber ammunition draped across his chest, Rambo-style. The impression is that the men mean to do this vulnerable woman harm, though they, too, appear to be entranced by the horror unfolding on the nightly newscast.

It's worth noting that precisely quantifying the amount of bad news is complicated. When researchers make a simple categorical distinction between good and bad news, they find no shortage of bad. But that's a necessary simplification. Any given news item isn't usually all good or all bad. Stories about a murderer being convicted, for example, or mass shootings being prevented, are both good and bad. The murder was bad; that the murderer is now behind bars is presumably good. Likewise, that somebody was planning a shooting spree is bad; that it was foiled is good.

Even more confoundingly, good or bad is often a matter of degree and interpretation. Do murderers caught and shootings foiled show that the country is on the verge of chaos, or that the safety and criminal justice procedures in place are generally working? There's no right answer. (We'll revisit the question of how we interpret the news in later chapters.) It's also impossible to say how much bad news there *should* be. After all, bad things happen. At least some of them are presumably newsworthy. The correct balance of bad and good is subjective, especially given the futility of categorizing things as unquestionably good or bad.

Besides, who's to say we shouldn't focus on the bad? As Paul Rozin and other psychologists who study the power of bad over good have pointed out, we are drawn to bad news for at least a few good reasons, some obvious, some more subtle.

Most obvious, spreading news of a clear and present danger can be an immensely valuable service. In our more parochial past, news of death, war, famine, or pestilence would usually have been of great personal importance to the recipients. Since serious illness, injury, or death can decrease your chances of passing along your genes to the next generation, it would make sense for our minds to evolve to be particularly attentive to bad news.

In *A History of News*, journalism professor Mitchell Stephens gives an example of important news spreading in oral cultures. "A group of Zulus was in hostile territory for a wedding in 1918 when suddenly they were attacked," Stephens details. The party was outnumbered. Spreading news of their predicament was an immediate priority. "The women in the group handled that task by dashing up to the hills and shouting," Stephens goes on. "Soon the alarm spread, and their tribesmen swarmed in to defend them."

From this point of view, it is *usefulness* that makes news compelling, not mere badness. In a more mundane sense, apparently most people watch the news not for the news, but for the weather. It's easy to see why: knowing if it's going to rain tomorrow tells you whether you need to take an umbrella to work. It has some direct utility. The bad news that pervades the other 28 or so minutes of the nightly news exploits our evolutionary instinct that bad means urgent and important—something you can, and probably should, act on quickly.

But stories about death and destruction don't seem to lose their news value even when the bad event is far away and poses no threat, or after the threat has passed. As Stephens notes, "Word of the ambush of that Zulu wedding party continued to spread even after the practical matter of coming to their aid had been addressed." Our zeal for bad news requires explanation beyond its occasional usefulness.

A more subtle reason for focusing on the bad is that there are just more kinds of bad things to talk about. "All happy families resemble one another; every unhappy family is miserable in its own way," wrote Tolstoy in the famous opening line from *Anna Karenina*. In a scientific paper titled "Why Good Is More Alike Than Bad," Hans Alves and colleagues at the University of Cologne explain the psychological principle behind why Tolstoy was right. To use a somewhat less sophisticated literary reference, Goldilocks discovered the problem in her dealings with the three bears. Only one bowl of porridge suited her, two didn't; one bed was just right, but two were just wrong. This is an inherent feature of human life, Alves and colleagues argue. The category of "bad things" is inherently more diverse than the category of "good things" because there are simply more ways to be bad than to be good. *Good* usually means a comfortable middle ground; neither too hot nor too cold, not too soft but not too hard. Just right.

The greater diversity of bad is even reflected in our language. You know how the Inuit people have more than a hundred different words for snow? Well, turns out that's fake news. The myth originated with early twentieth-century anthropologists, based on a misunderstanding of the complexity of the Inuit language and the ways its rules of word and sentence structure differ from those of English. The misconception has been popularized, in part, by weather forecasters trying to fill airtime with lighthearted banter. That urban legend notwithstanding, however, the English language does seem to have more words for bad things than for good.

Consider all the words we have to describe different degrees and varieties of pain compared to the relative few describing pleasure. One study came up with thirty-one adjectives describing pain (to give a few examples, *deep, intense, dull, sharp, aching, burning, cutting, pinching, piercing, tearing, twitching, shooting, gnawing, itching, stabbing, throbbing, radiating*). They came up with fewer than half as many—fourteen—to describe pleasure, "partly based," they note, enigmatically, "on a review of erotic literature" (*intense, thrilling, delicious, exquisite, deep, sumptuous, breathtaking, electrifying, delicate, sweet*). Another study found twice as many words for negative emotions as for positive emotions.

So maybe there's a lot of bad news simply because there's a lot of ways to be bad, and a lot of ways to talk about it. For news organizations trying to keep up with the seemingly insatiable audience demand for news, bad news may simply be the low-hanging fruit.

Another similarly pragmatic reason for the prevalence of bad news is that bad things often happen quickly, whereas very good things tend to unfold over time. "News time is deliberately shortsighted," wrote the political scientist Thomas Patterson: because of their circadian rhythm, daily newspapers and nightly newscasts favor events that have "taken a clear and definable shape within the past twenty-four hours." The shift online has only increased the pressure on news organizations to push new news around the clock. Assaults, murders, shootings, fires, battles, terror attacks, natural disasters—these things all usually wreak their havoc within minutes or hours. Improvements in public health, economic prosperity, crime rates—these things take time.

Again, this suggests that it's not just being *bad* that helps something make the news. When good news gets reported, it often has the same quality of having happened recently and quickly. Scientific breakthroughs, medical innovations, sporting victories, philanthropic acts—these all occur at the pace of news and so are more likely to make the news than more gradual improvements in our standard of living. This also helps explain why some bad things are more likely to make the news than others. Disasters that unfold over years, decades, or centuries are difficult to report when you're on a deadline.

In the year's worth of news intros that I collected, playing up the urgency of the news was as consistent a theme as the unrelenting negativity. BREAKING NEWS was the single most common chyron, appearing on around three out of four nights. The anchor's script frequently proclaimed that the events being reported were "coming in right now," or unfolding "as we come on the air." We will turn to this aspect of news—its breakneck speed—in the next chapter.

For now, one last feature of our psychology might be good for bad news. Paradoxically, it's that we are inveterate optimists. We *expect* things to go well, so when they don't, it's surprising. And *surprising* things—not just *bad* things—are usually relatively informative and therefore worth paying attention to.

That a plane crashed, to take one common example of bad news, tells you definitely that something went wrong; perhaps with some questioning and investigation we can get to the bottom of it. That a plane didn't crash doesn't convey the same kind of definitive information—it doesn't mean that the plane isn't going to crash on its next journey. One successful flight doesn't mean that no problems are lurking in the system, just that they weren't catastrophic this time. More generally, for the most part we expect people not to lie to us, rob or murder us, for example, so it's only noteworthy when they do. As the news historian John Sommerville points out, "Half of marriages end in divorce" makes for a better headline than "half of marriages don't end in divorce" because marriages are supposed to endure. Marital harmony is the default assumption, so it feels we have less to learn from happy marriages than from the ones that end in divorce. Both of those hypothetical headlines convey precisely the same information, but focusing on the bad highlights the lessons that might be learned.

The news value of surprise is captured in the old news cliché "man bites dog." The quote has been attributed to various newspapermen of the nineteenth century, but it was first used in print in an 1899 novel, in which a reporter explains what makes something newsworthy: "'A dog bites a man'—that's a story; 'A man bites a dog'—that's a good story." *Dog bites man* is hardly a surprise. *Man bites dog*—well, there has to be a good story behind that.

This, too, helps explain why some bad things are more likely to make the news than others. A plane crash can dominate front-page headlines for days, while the dozens of fatal car crashes that happen every day don't make it past the obituaries page, because the plane crash is so much more surprising, and therefore attention-grabbing. And again, being bad isn't necessarily newsworthy in and of itself. Rather, we are drawn to bad news because it so often feels more informative than news about good things. The good news that makes it onto the nightly news often has this same quality of unexpectedness. It's not about the many good things that happen to regular people every day. It's about people departing from expected behavior in seemingly surprising and informative ways.

Partly to counteract all the negativity on the news, it became standard practice to end on a happy note, with what's often called a human-interest story. But these aren't merely stories of regular people living regular lives—where would be the news value in that? Rather, the stories tend to be about ordinary people doing something extraordinary. As Mitchell Stephens points out, whether the news is good or bad, "whether the subject is love, birth, weather or crime, journalists' tastes inevitably run toward the unnatural, the extraordinary."

*

We began this exploration of bad news with the breathless first ninety seconds of one night's news. But, thirty minutes later, the show followed the convention of ending with some good news. It was the broadcast's regular feature, "our persons of the week," the host said by way of introduction; "a dream come true."

As the report begins, we are introduced to some patients at a children's hospital in Atlanta. One, we are told, lost the ability to walk at just eight years old. Now seventeen, she had to have both legs amputated earlier in the year. But, in addition to recovering, our host says, "She is also doing her nails. Because at that hospital one night every year they transform the hospital into the prom."

We see the teenage patients getting dressed up. "The hair, the flowers," our host gushes, "and of course the dresses." But a bigger surprise is coming. "It's what she's about to do at that prom that would move so many," the host reports. "Something she hasn't done in ten years."

Using a walker, presumably after months of grueling physical therapy, the girl is able to dance at the prom.

"This is the first time my mom saw me standing up," she says.

It's genuinely heartwarming news.

"And so we choose those brave patients at the prom," as the persons of the week, the anchor says. He smiles, warmly, for the first and only time in the broadcast.

"Good night."

CHAPTER THREE

Breaking News

On the morning of April 27, 1863, William Burgess expected to see a light on the horizon: the lantern of the Cape Race Lighthouse. Instead, he saw only fog.

Burgess was captain of the SS *Anglo Saxon*, a passenger ship carrying 360 passengers, 86 crew, vast stores of food and fuel, and a cargo of iron and other consumer goods across the Atlantic Ocean. Burgess was young for a ship's captain, just thirty-one years old, but he was experienced in the transatlantic service and respected among his peers. He had apprenticed in the shipping industry at the age of fourteen, crossing the Atlantic dozens of times as he worked his way up the ranks from bosun at twenty-three, to second mate, first mate, and captain at age thirty. This was his second crossing on the *Anglo Saxon*.

The lighthouse at Cape Race should have been the first sign of civilization beyond the ship's railings anyone on board had seen in ten days. Under Burgess's command, the *Anglo Saxon* had left Liverpool on April 16, calling at Moville at the northern tip of Ireland before starting the Atlantic crossing on the seventeenth. On the twenty-seventh, Quebec, the ship's final destination, was still another three or four days away.

For some passengers on board, the lighthouse would have been a beacon of hope. Whole families on board were emigrating from England, Scotland, and Ireland, seeking new lives in Canada's Golden West—a more enticing prospect at the time than America, which had erupted into civil war.

Burgess was anxious to see the lighthouse for a different reason. Cape Race wasn't a port of call, exactly, but it was a critical waypoint. Burgess knew the cape and its light should be getting close. Time was of the essence because the ship's cargo included another perishable commodity of great value, to be delivered to Cape Race: news.

★

Cape Race was, and is, a rocky outcropping of New-foundland's Avalon Peninsula, graced by little more than the lighthouse and a wooden hut. An 1861 issue of the *Illustrated London News* featured a beautiful full-page wood-cut dramatically illustrating the imposing cliffs, alongside an article describing the desolate beauty of the cape: "The coast at Cape Race is bold and rocky, the cliffs rising precipitately out of the water, cracked and split asunder in many places by some great convulsion of nature."

You get a sense of how treacherous the waters around the cape were. "A huge black rock lifts its head up out of the deep water immediately in front of the Cape; the eternal wash of the Atlantic has worn deep hollows, and in some cases masses of rock stand out isolated from the great granite wall that breaks the ever-restless ocean that thunders against it." Many ships had wrecked against those rocks, which, depending on the tides, often lurked just below the surface of the water.

The lighthouse had been built only a few years earlier, in 1856—by coincidence, the same year the *Anglo Saxon* was constructed. The lighthouse, a stout seventy-foot iron cylinder, was painted white with vertical red stripes. The red lantern sat atop the tower like a huge birdcage. There was no foghorn or alarm whistle. When installation of an audible warning system had been proposed in 1861, the idea was apparently dismissed by the imperial government as a "Yankee suggestion." The light was the only guide. The only warning.

Cape Race had long held significance for seafarers. Located on the "great circle" between Europe and North America, it had been used for navigation since at least the sixteenth century. But for a brief time in the middle of the nineteenth century, Cape Race held even greater significance. Residing inside the small wooden hut next to the lighthouse was a telegraph, the end point of wires that stretched west to inland Canada and south to New York City. The latest news from Europe could be received from westbound ships and conveyed in an instant to

New York, reaching the metropolis four days before the ship itself; news bound for Europe could be four days more up-to-date if it was collected while rounding Cape Race rather than at port.

The rocky coastline offered nowhere for the huge passenger ships to safely dock, however, so getting the news from ship to shore was no small feat. The service was run by the Associated Press. A small newsboat would head out from the cape to meet ships as they passed. In fine weather, the newsboat crew would board the transatlantic steamer and receive the news personally. In choppy waters, things were more difficult. The steamer crew would throw overboard a special canister about the size of a large coffee can, fitted with a special buoy and signal flag and stuffed with newspapers and mail. This would, it was hoped, be retrieved by the newsboat crew and taken to shore.

Within a few years, the Cape Race newsboats would be made obsolete by the transatlantic cable, which allowed telegraph messages to cross the ocean almost instantaneously. The first cable had successfully been operated in 1858, but it broke within a month. So in 1863, getting the news to Cape Race was a vitally important function of any transatlantic crossing. Countless news articles from the period, important and insignificant alike, carried the heading "Via Cape Race" as a mark of timeliness. "Since the introduction of the electric telegraph this lonely mass of storm-washed rock, whose existence was scarcely known to any one except the mariner, who sought it only that he might know his whereabout and carefully avoid it, has become well known," the *Illustrated London News* wrote, "its name as familiar as is that of New York or Boston."

When a typical transatlantic crossing took close to two weeks, the time saved by delivering news to Cape Race offered a massive competitive advantage, particularly for consumers of the time-sensitive business information newspapers carried. Passenger lines competed fiercely for the lucrative mail-carrying contracts. Getting the news across the ocean fast—getting it there *first*—was "an almost demonic commercial interest" that caused the operators of the passenger lines to "throw caution to the wind," wrote Arthur Johnson, a Newfoundland native, in a short but definitive analysis of the ill-fated *Anglo Saxon*. Bonuses were frequently awarded for early mail delivery. One operator, the Collins Line, went as far as to impose a penalty on their ships' masters for any trip slower than "express-rate."

"To the great peril of both crews and passengers," Johnson wrote, "caution was regularly sacrificed in favour of swift delivery."

★

Burgess knew well the imperative for speed. Though the *Anglo Saxon* carried passengers and cargo, it was a designated Royal Mail steamer. Even its schedule was dictated by the news it carried. Passengers were required to check in at the Allan Line's company offices the night before the sailing so as not to be late for the early-morning departure (lodging for the night was not included in the ticket price). This precaution was necessary, posters advised, because "the steamers being under MAIL Contract sail punctually on their appointed dates."

Burgess also knew the dangers of "rounding the cape," as did his crew, as did his employer, the Allan Line. Another Allan Line ship, the *Indian*, had run onto the rocks at Cape Race a few years earlier. Twenty-seven lives had been lost in that wreck.

The *Anglo Saxon* had both engines and sails, under which she made good speed until the twenty-fifth, more than a week into the voyage. That night, ice and fog forced Burgess to order the engines slowed, then eventually stopped. He was losing time. The ship didn't reach clear water again until after noon on the twenty-sixth. As soon as it did, Burgess ordered the engines returned to full speed and the sails raised. They steamed full speed ahead through the night.

As dawn broke on the twenty-seventh, Burgess again found his ship shrouded in fog. By 8:00 a.m., the chief officer noted that they "supposed the ship to be forty miles off Cape Race" and set a course that should have taken them around the cape seventeen miles to its south. The cape rounded, they would turn north to meet the newsboat. Either at dawn or when they changed course at 8:00 a.m., the engines were slowed to half speed on account of the fog.

But the sightings on which the crew had assumed their location turned out to be tragically mistaken. The *Anglo Saxon* was far closer to the Newfoundland coast than its crew believed. Possibly the ship's single chronometer was off. The crew of the *Anglo Saxon* could have double-checked their position to shore by taking depth soundings, but that would have required slowing the ship almost to a standstill. Even to slow to a more prudent speed, given the fog and the dangers in rounding the cape, would have cost more time.

At ten minutes past eleven, the ship's lookout cried, "Breakers!" Moments later the crew would have seen the cliffs looming out of the dense fog.

Burgess ordered the engines thrown into full reverse, but it was too late. Even at half speed, the ship was going too fast to steer clear of the rocks lurking just below the surf. Moments after the rocks had been sighted, the ship ran aground. The swell drove the ship's stern on to the rocks. Its rudder and propeller were destroyed in the impact. Water rushed into the engine room, putting out the engine fires. Nothing could be done to save the ship.

Incredibly, the clifftops were almost level with the deck of the ship and close enough that three crewmen were able to climb along the jibboom and jump ashore. They ran a rope across and shuttled close to a hundred crew and passengers—mostly women and children—to safety in a makeshift basket. But after just fifteen minutes, this means of escape was cut off as the ship shifted and began to break apart in the rough sea.

Fewer than a hundred people escaped on the lifeboats. Regulations required lifeboats only for the crew and first-class passengers; the *Anglo Saxon*'s six lifeboats had fewer than two hundred seats among them. Even that capacity couldn't be used to the full. Three of the six boats were hemmed in by the cliffs, unable to launch.

More than two hundred people remained, huddled on the deck in the fog and rain, with no hope of rescue. Within an hour of the ship's hitting the rocks, battering waves had broken it apart. Around noon, it suddenly shifted off the rocks, tipped sickeningly onto one side, and slipped beneath the waves. As it sank, those still on board were swept into the freezing sea by waves or carried away with shifting cargo and falling rigging.

In the hour or so that his ship was stranded on the rocks, Captain Burgess by all accounts performed his duties admirably. He gave the order to abandon ship as soon as it was clear that it could not be extricated from the rocks. He oversaw the loading of the lifeboats that could be launched, giving priority—against regulations—to women and children.

Burgess remained with the ship until the end—though he had no intention of going down with it. As the ship lurched and sank, Burgess was thrown into the water along with his third officer. The third officer climbed into the rigging and eventually made his way to a raft and was rescued. Burgess was not so fortunate. "I looked to see where the Captain was," the third officer wrote. "I saw him in the water, surrounded by small pieces of floating wreck, and so hemmed in that he could make no exertions to save himself. When I looked again he was gone."

Those who had been able to clamber to shore in the first few frantic minutes after the crash had no way of knowing where exactly they were. Two groups of crewmen set out looking for help, one heading north and another south. The party venturing south were the first to find civilization: the lighthouse and telegraph hut at Cape Race. There they found Captain John Murphy, captain of the Associated Press newsboat, and his small crew. The newsboat was launched in the hope of recovering survivors. By the time it reached Clam Cove, where the *Anglo Saxon* had run aground, about four miles along the coast, nothing remained of the ship but wreckage. No lives were left to save.

On both sides of the Atlantic, news of the fate of the mail accompanied that of the dead. "Two hundred and thirty-seven lives were lost by the wreck of the *Anglo Saxon*," reported the *New York Times.* "All the mails were also lost."

★

Speed has been an imperative of the news business since newspapers began publishing on a regular schedule. The first item in the oldest-surviving English-language newspaper—printed in Amsterdam on December 2, 1620—was not news, but an apology for the lack of it: "The new tydings out of Italie are not yet com."

There had been regular news before newspapers. The *Acta Diurna* were daily government notices posted in the Roman Forum. For hundreds of years, regular written newsletters circulated among select subscribers and correspondents. But most news intended for public consumption didn't come on a fixed schedule. The writers of newsbooks, news ballads, and newsletters simply reported the news whenever they got it. Occasionally they might score a scoop that could be rushed into print, but just as often their news was months old by the time it reached readers and listeners. Those writers never had to apologize for "tydings not yet com," Mitchell Stephens points out in *A History of News.* They simply waited for the tydings to com.

Even so, news makers felt the pressure to provide audiences with fresh news. A 1631 satire of the "Ballad-Monger" joked that "stale ballad-newes, like stale fish … are not for queasie stomacks." Leaning on a similar metaphor, a 1680 newspaper, admitting to having been scooped on a story by a competitor, vowed not to "nauseate the Reader this good time with cold Pye."

Publishing on a set schedule, rather than simply when some newsworthy event warranted it, represented a radical change in both how news was produced and how it was consumed. Those early papers were called corantos. The word may have referred to the running of messengers, but its relation to the English word *current*— as in, happening right now—also implies an inherent timeliness. The other meaning, the tug of flowing water, conjures the image of an endlessly flowing stream of news. As publishers realized the power of that current, the stream quickly became a torrent.

Weekly, and soon daily, newspapers flourished beginning in the 1620s. Audiences, it seems, had a formidable appetite for news. Even by 1624, "both the Reader and the Printer of these pamphlets agree in their expectation of Weekly News," one publisher noted. "If the Printer have not the wherewithall to afford satisfaction," he warned, or bragged, "yet will the Reader come and aske every day for the Newes."

Yet until the nineteenth century, even the newspaper business was relatively sedate. Those early papers were often one- or two-man businesses. The already overworked editors hardly had time to go out looking for the latest news. Instead, they would use items from other newspapers as the basis of their own reporting, often simply reprinting material from other sources in full. "I will directly proceed in my accustomed manner of searching and opening the Letters that came from beyond the seas," the publisher of England's first newspaper promised readers, "and so acquaint you with their secrets."

This dependence on the arrival of the mail led news-writers to qualify their guarantees of more news to come with caveats such as "if the Post faile us not." The post often did fail them, to the frustration of both readers and publishers. "The failure of all the mails must plead our excuse for the barrenness of our columns to-day," the *Mobile Advertiser* explained in 1833. "No mail yesterday," another paper complained. "We hardly know what we shall fill our paper with that will have the appearance of news."

Beginning around the 1830s, several trends converged to force the speed of news into higher gear. Beginning in New York City in particular, penny papers flourished, with newsboys hawking them on the street for a fraction of the cost of the old-fashioned six-penny commercial papers. By enticing working-class readers to buy a copy on a whim, rather than chasing wealthy annual subscribers, newspapers massively expanded their potential audience. This led to fierce competition among publishers. Promises of timeliness became part of newspapers' marketing efforts. For example, James Gordon Bennett, publisher of the *New York Herald*, promised readers, "In every species of news the Herald will be one of the earliest of the early."

Editors began to employ reporters and correspondents to go out and fetch the news, rather than waiting for it to arrive with the mail. Even where the mail had still to be relied upon, speed and reliability took on new significance. Some publishers sent boats far out into New York Harbor to meet ships arriving from Europe, fetching the foreign news back to the newspaper's offices before the arriving ships had even docked. Bennett's *Herald* bragged about its newsboat "skimming o'er the bright blue waters." It passed another paper's boat "almost without an effort," the article boasted, "and with a sort of gentle smile on the figurehead which adorns her prow."

Meanwhile, steamships, railroads, and the pony express helped drastically cut the time it took to convey news across oceans and continents. Producers reveled in the unprecedented speed with which they could get news into print. "In one case," a journalist of the period gushed, "an editor nearly lost his life by excitement in riding on the locomotive from Worcester to Boston, about forty miles, in as many minutes." The editor carried news of a presidential address. "In a state of syncope, he was hurried in a carriage to Congress Street, where with the greatest difficulty the President's message was taken from his clutched fingers."

Then, in 1844, the electric telegraph brought an entirely new dimension to news speed. News no longer had to be physically conveyed from one place to another. Now it could be sent over massive distances in an instant.

The first telegraphic news dispatch reported the nomination of Henry Clay at the national Whig convention held at Baltimore on May 1, 1844. As Frank Mott notes in his history *American Journalism*, the day's newspapers got the news of the nomination by train, as usual. The telegraph report had been a publicity stunt by Samuel Morse, simply to convince skeptics that his revolutionary device actually worked. But it didn't take long for news makers to realize the game-changing potential of the telegraph. The first newspaper article reporting news received by telegraph appeared in the *Baltimore Patriot* at the end of May 1844. "One o'clock," it reported—"There has just been made a motion in the

House to go into committee of the whole on the Oregon question. Rejected,—ayes, 79; nays, 86."

From that inauspicious beginning, the telegraph quickly became an essential element of news reporting. A decade later, twenty thousand miles of telegraph wire had been strung from the East Coast to the Midwest. Getting access to the telegraph wires was expensive, though. Operators charged by the word. And its limited capacity led to frustration as journalists converged on telegraph offices after some newsworthy event and were forced to wait their turn as operators tapped out the Morse-code messages. Soon, several of New York's dailies banded together to form a cooperative news-gathering service that would become the Associated Press. By 1856, North America's vast telegraphic tendrils extended to the small wooden hut next to the Cape Race lighthouse, where the crew of the Associated Press newsboat waited to race out and meet passing ships.

Again, publishers were enamored of the new technology. "The creation of the science of Electro-Magnetism and its embodiment in the Telegraph, undoubtedly ranks foremost among that series of mighty discoveries that have gone to subjugate matter under the domain of mind," a *New York Times* article declared. "Whatever may be accomplished hereafter will be a matter-of-course."

By midcentury, timeliness had been cemented as a news value. In 1851, Horace Greeley, editor of the *New-York Tribune*, confidently told a British parliamentary committee that, in America, "the paper which brings the quickest news is the one looked to."

★

Most news insiders cheered the accelerating speed of news. Judging by the unprecedented circulation figures of the nineteenth-century penny papers, readers, too, were engrossed by the daily developments that filled news pages. Along the way, however, critics have questioned whether faster is necessarily better for news.

One of the earliest skeptics was a seventeenth-century playwright, Ben Jonson. To Jonson, the very notion of news printed on a regular schedule, designed to fill a set number of pages, was nonsensical. In his satirical play *The Staple of News*, Jonson implied that periodical news ceased to be a public good and became a mere commodity, "a weekly cheat to draw money."

The eighteenth-century journalist and novelist Henry Fielding compared newspapers to a stagecoach, "which performs constantly the same course, empty as well as full." After all, publishing a paper once a week meant that it had to be filled. So what would fill the pages if nothing particularly noteworthy had happened that week? Having a set quota of news to print could change the very definition of news, the increase in quantity diluting the substance. A newspaper "consists of just the same number of words whether there be any news in it or not," Fielding wrote.

This only became more of a concern as the number of newspapers and their page counts expanded throughout the nineteenth century. New York's penny papers seemed determined, according to one observer, to fill their pages with "the name and age of every dog that dies within a hundred miles of the city, with the color of his hair and the quality of his bark." One nineteenth-century journalist complained, "Everyone now hurried to print what nobody thought it worthwhile to say."

More recently, Carl Bernstein, the reporter of Watergate fame, voiced similar reservations. "The greatest felony in the news business today," Bernstein wrote in a 1992 article for the *New Republic*, "is to be behind, or to miss, a major story." Merely to *seem* behind is a liability in the news business, he said. "So speed and quantity substitute for thoroughness and quality, for accuracy and context. The pressure to compete, the fear that somebody else will make the splash first, creates a frenzied environment in which a blizzard of information is presented and serious questions may not be raised."

To Bernstein's point about accuracy, it is undoubtedly true that breaking news often gets things wrong. To take one notable example, during the live coverage of the 9/11 attacks on the World Trade Center in New York City, BBC News mistakenly reported that a third building had collapsed, when it was still visibly standing over the reporter's shoulder. That the building did collapse twenty minutes later fueled conspiracy theories that it had been a preordained, controlled explosion. Likewise the all-too-frequent mass shootings in America are often accompanied by mistaken initial reports of a second gunman or misidentification of the culprit, again giving grist to conspiracists who take later corrections as evidence of cover-up.

Reputable news outlets acknowledge the implicit tension between breaking news and accuracy. The BBC's twenty-four-hour news channel, for example, claimed in publicity material, "We aim to be first with breaking news but our overriding commitment is to accuracy."

Many online outlets that report breaking news have taken to including some kind of disclaimer. "This is a developing story," reads NPR's. "Some things that get reported by the media will later turn out to be wrong. We will focus on reports from police officials and other authorities, credible news outlets and reporters who are at the scene. We will update as the situation develops."

Mistakes are inevitable, even when events aren't unfolding live. Reporting breaking events as they occur can have value, even knowing that some details are unconfirmed and likely to be wrong. As yet, no quantitative analysis has been made of how mistake prone reports of breaking news are, or the effects of such inaccuracy on viewers. We'll come back to the issue of accuracy and corrections in the news more broadly in Chapter 8.

In any case, the people criticizing the rush to be first weren't just questioning the accuracy of breaking news. They were questioning whether increasing the pace of news warps the very definition of news, lowering the bar of what is considered newsworthy. When it comes to contemporary breaking news, it's rarely as dramatic as the horror of 9/11 and other shocking events. "When journalists or academics talk about breaking news, they invariably focus on untypical examples of great drama or import," the authors of one study of breaking news point out, such as assassination attempts, terrorist attacks, shootings, and other tragedies. "The problem is that, *most* of the time, it is none of these things."

The researchers were Justin Lewis and Stephen Cushion, two professors of communication at Cardiff University's School of Journalism. They focused on the

United Kingdom's two twenty-four-hour news channels, BBC News 24 and Sky News, spanning from 2004 to 2007. They analyzed just over one hundred and sixty hours of news coverage, amounting to more than three thousand individual news items.

Breaking news, they found, had gradually become an increasingly common part of twenty-four-hour news culture. In 2004, stories presented as breaking news were comparatively rare. On the BBC, which is commercial-free and funded by a mandatory license fee, breaking news stories made up just 3 percent of all stories. On the commercial Sky News channel, it made up slightly more, at 4.5 percent of all news stories. But by 2007, the proportions had grown to more than 10 percent on both networks.

Just as critics from the seventeenth century onward had speculated, Lewis and Cushion found that over the three years they followed the news, the threshold for what warrants breaking news alerts had lowered, becoming more "tabloid oriented" than news overall. By that, they meant that crime, human-interest stories, and pieces about celebrities and sports had become increasingly likely to be reported as breaking news. By 2007 close to four out of ten breaking news stories covered those topics—double the proportion of regular news items on those topics.

Crime, in particular, made up a quarter of all breaking news stories in 2007. Yet, curiously, the breaking news often wasn't all that new. Looking at a subset of breaking news stories that both the BBC and Sky News had covered, Lewis and Cushion found only a single breaking story that reported a *new* crime. Indeed, most of the stories reported as breaking news were not unexpected events, but actually "anticipated developments of ongoing stories"—trials, verdicts, and the like.

More disconcertingly, much of the breaking news contained little in the way of original reporting or substantive insight. Most breaking stories basically repeated wire alerts, sent to every newsroom by services such as the Associated Press. Compared to regular news, breaking news stories tended to feature fewer outside sources such as members of the public, politicians, or experts.

This might all be defensible if the stories covered as breaking news had real news value. Yet Lewis and Cushion also observed a decreasing tendency for the breaking news items to be followed up. Around half of breaking news stories were revisited in later reporting, suggesting that the other half weren't important enough to follow up on. Moreover, only about a quarter of the stories that the researchers sampled in 2007 were covered as "breaking news" on both channels. About one out of five stories that were reported as breaking news on one of the channels didn't warrant a mention on the other channel at all, suggesting surprisingly little consensus about which specific events are worth covering as breaking news.

Lewis and Cushion's conclusions were cutting: "The emphasis on being first appears to have created an assembly line of breaking news production that has little to do with being informative or communicating news well." The most time-consuming aspect of reporting news well is the application of professional judgment that goes into checking facts, providing context, and communicating the story effectively—not to mention deciding whether a story is worth reporting as breaking news in the first place. Rushing news to audiences means churning out information with little regard for these processes. "To boast of being first," Lewis and Cushion wrote, "is, effectively, to boast of abandoning such judgments."

We could, once again, blame prioritizing speed over substance on news producers and smugly absolve ourselves of responsibility. One historian of the news accused journalists of "fetishism of the present." It is a "ritual of the media tribe," he wrote. "Getting the story first is a matter of journalistic pride, but one that has little to do with journalistic quality or public service."

But by blaming the problem on a personal failing of news producers, we'd be ignoring our own role as news consumers. After their dispiriting analysis of breaking news, Lewis and Cushion concluded that, like the nineteenth-century publisher bragging about speed of his newsboat, the contemporary push toward breaking news is largely about marketing. In the arms race of news speed that has been escalating since the nineteenth century, labeling some recent or ongoing event "breaking news" is the current pinnacle of expected timeliness. The rush to break news doesn't improve the news; indeed, it probably makes it worse. But fail to regularly provide breaking news and your audience's attention might wander elsewhere. "Breaking news is there because it has a certain *feel*," Lewis and Cushion write, "rather than because of the significance of its content."

★

Research exploring how we think about time—past, present, and future—offers some clues about why this feeling of immediacy can make for effective marketing. There's psychological truth, it seems, to the famous opening line "The past is a foreign country; they do things differently there."

Think: What were you doing this day a year ago? What did you do yesterday? Or, for that matter, what will you do tomorrow? What do you think you'll be doing a year from now? It's amazing that these are even meaningful questions. As philosophers have long argued, we are prisoners of *now*—the eternal, ever-fleeting present. Our direct experience is only ever of *this precise moment*. When we find ourselves reminiscing about the past, or trying to imagine the future, it is always from the vantage point of the present. Psychologically speaking, it seems this kind of mental time-traveling is not unlike physical travel. The farther you go, the more foreign the landscape becomes.

Yaacov Trope and Nira Liberman, psychologists at New York University and Tel Aviv University, respectively, have each spent decades researching *psychological distance*. "Psychological distance is a subjective experience that something is close or far away from the self, here, and now," Trope and Liberman wrote in a review of research on the topic. In other words, whether something is distant in space or in time, the psychological effects are the same.

Specifically, the greater the psychological distance we must traverse, the more abstract our mental representations of things become. Up close, we focus on the nitty-gritty, idiosyncratic details. From a distance, we take a broader, more holistic view. By way of analogy, Trope and Liberman point to the old saying about "missing the forest for the trees." In simple, literal terms, they write, it seems "intuitive that from a distance we see the forest, and as we get closer, we see the trees." Literally getting closer to something can change how we construe it. They argue that this is also true, in a more metaphorical sense, of psychological distance. "We do not literally see either tomorrow or next year. Yet we may think about tomorrow in terms of trees and about next year in terms of the forest."

In one study, Liberman had people rate how well they expected to cope with everyday minutiae—such things as keeping their apartment clean, getting along with the people in their life, making the right decisions, avoiding arguments, reading books for pleasure, remembering people's birthdays, getting enough sleep, finding time to relax. Some participants rated how well they would cope over the following week, others rated their probable coping for the week beginning a year from today. People didn't imagine the week next year as being any better or worse, on average, than the coming week. But their ratings for the coming week were reliably more variable. Some challenges, they thought, would be a cinch, others a slog. Their ratings for the week a year away were more uniform—all the challenges, they imagined, would be about average.

We may be more aware of all the specific circumstances that could make next week better in some ways, worse in others—the project that's due at work, the day off you've scheduled, the gently simmering argument between you and a friend, the dull ache in your knee

that seems to be getting worse. But we're aware, too, that
next year probably won't be so different. The specific
grievances and blessings may change, but life will be as
richly unpredictable as always. When they were filling
out the survey, Liberman's test subjects could just have
extrapolated from the week ahead to the year ahead,
rating them about the same. But something about the
psychological distance in time flattened their mental
image of what would come. Next week, the challenges
each appeared unique, as different from one another as
an oak tree is from a spruce. From a distance, every
challenge looked about the same, a forest of indistinct
daily hassles.

That's not to say that one way of looking at things is
necessarily better or worse than another. Sometimes we
need to scrutinize the trees, sometimes we need to survey
the forest. If you've ever been struggling with some
seemingly intractable problem, perhaps someone advised
you to "take a step back and look at the big picture"—
another turn of phrase, Trope and Liberman point out,
that reflects our intuitive association of distance and
abstraction. "We do not literally take a step back to
forget the daily hassles and consider our life in general.
Yet, when thinking of the general aspects of our life
rather than about daily details, we may find ourselves
looking farther into space."

Though most of the research has had people imagine
the future, Liberman and her colleagues argue that the
same general pattern holds for thinking about the past.
The further into the past we attempt to peer, the more
abstract our mental image becomes. In one study,
researchers found that people use more abstract language

when talking about the distant, as compared to the recent, past. Recalling an argument from just a week or two ago, for example, you might say, "We yelled at each other." Recalling an argument from a year or two ago, however, you'd be more likely to use increasingly abstract terms, such as "we fought," or "we were angry."

The researchers also found that the relationship worked in reverse: they could make people remember things from the more distant past by asking more abstract questions. For example, if I asked you to bring to mind an occasion when you helped somebody, you would probably remember something more recent than if I asked you to remember an occasion on which you were helpful. It seems a subtle distinction, but *helping* is concrete behavior, while being *helpful* is an abstract characteristic. People who were asked the relatively abstract questions brought to mind events that were around twice as distant as people who had been asked concrete questions.

Fascinatingly, different types of psychological distance seem to be inseparably associated in our minds. For example, Trope and Liberman suggest it's no coincidence that the events portrayed in the film *Star Wars* were said to have taken place both "a long time ago," and "in a galaxy far, far away." Linking distance in both space and time "reflects not only a literary convention," the researchers suggest, "but also an automatic tendency of the mind." It would simply seem incongruous if the saga took place *a long time ago in a galaxy nearby*.

This all suggests one reason why emphasizing timeliness could be an effective marketing strategy for news organizations. Whereas an epic movie franchise such as *Star Wars* might benefit from leveraging psychological

distance to create a fantastical sense of scale and timeless-
ness, the news depends on constant story churn. To keep
people coming back day after day, hour after hour, each
story has to appear unique. Emphasizing how recent
events are, through frequent reminders of *breaking news*, or
this just in, or *latest developments*, likely helps create the
impression of an endlessly diverse parade of idiosyncratic
events. Up close, every fire, murder, scandal appears
unique; from a distance, the particular details are less salient
than the overall pattern. And because psychological
distances are linked in our minds, being closer in time also
creates the impression of being closer to our own direct
experience in every way. Events that are in the more
distant past might simply make for less engaging news.

Trope and Liberman point out, however, that psychological distance is subjective. It isn't only the absolute
number of minutes, hours, days, or months that have
passed that determine how psychologically distant some
past event feels. It depends, too, on what that amount of
time means to us. Sometimes news can overcome the
bonds of psychological distance, whether of space or
time.

Mitchell Stephens, in *A History of News*, gives the
example of the death of King William III. The king of
England, Scotland, and Ireland—and by extension, the
colonies of what would become the United States—
died on March 8, 1702. Yet rumors of the king's death
didn't reach New England until May 17. Official news,
in the form of a copy of the *London Gazette*, took even
longer, arriving in Boston on May 28.

Nowadays, it's unimaginable that it might take close
to three months to learn of the death of one of the

world's most powerful leaders. Yet, Stephens points out, American colonists in 1702 were "accustomed to a delay of months while news from their homelands made its way across that seemingly irreducible impediment— the Atlantic Ocean." News of the death of their king may not have been timely in an absolute sense, but it was as close to breaking news as technology permitted at the time. So, even though the news had taken more than two months to reach the colonies, it was no less shocking. "Indeed," Stephens writes, "on June 4, 1702, the colony of Massachusetts officially and un-self-consciously grieved for a king who had been dead for nearly three months."

To take a more recent, and much more frivolous, example, in late 2019 headlines reported that scientists had potentially uncovered evidence about the reality of the Loch Ness monster. As the *Washington Post* noted, legends of the mythical monster date back to AD 565, though Nessie became a fixture of offbeat news in the 1930s. Despite the age of the myth, headlines about it appear to remain attention-grabbing. The scientist behind the discovery had deliberately linked his work to the monster, knowing that it would catch the media's attention. "Loch Ness attracts people in a way that few other things ever could," the canny scientist admitted. "I am unashamedly using the monster as a way to attract interest so I can talk about the science I want to talk about."

So timeliness isn't everything. Technological advances, coupled with competition among news publishers, may have pushed our expectations for breaking news closer and closer to *right now*. But, as the Loch Ness monster story goes to show, another aspect of the fast-flowing news current is psychologically satisfying: our desire simply to hear something that we haven't heard before.

★

As with most things, we seem to appreciate novelty best in moderation.

Karl Halvor Teigen, a Norwegian psychologist, seems to have an unusually high tolerance for novelty. Over his long and prolific career he has studied countless quirks of human thinking, from our grasp of probabilities, to beliefs about climate change, to the psychology of luck, to give just a few examples. He even received an Ig Nobel Prize—awarded, so the Ig Nobel committee says, for research that first makes you laugh, then makes you think. Teigen earned the award for a study trying to understand why people sigh. The study found that we assume that other people sigh because they are sad, whereas our own sighs are more often believed to express a state of "giving up" on something. Teigen defined sighing, with his tongue in his cheek, as "the sound of hope leaving the body." He is a professor emeritus now, though he still actively researches and publishes.

Back in the eighties, though, Teigen was interested in the news. What is it, he wondered, that makes news appealing? Part of the answer, his research suggested, is its *new*ness. But how much new information we can stomach is limited. Over a series of studies, he found we prefer new information about familiar things.

In one study, Teigen asked a group of Norwegian students how familiar they were with a list of various countries. Some emerged as more familiar; Denmark and

England were close to the top of the scale. Some countries were unanimously unfamiliar; Macao and Malawi scored close to zero. Some countries, such as Thailand and Bulgaria, averaged out in the middle. Meanwhile, Teigen had a second group of students imagine themselves reading a newspaper containing a section of "news from abroad." They had to indicate how interested they were in reading news from each of the same countries the other group had rated for familiarity.

When he looked at the data, Teigen found an almost perfect correlation between the two sets of ratings. News from familiar England and Denmark was among the most appealing; news from the completely unfamiliar Macao and Malawi was the least. The countries of middling familiarity, among the Norwegian students, were of middling interest.

Perhaps, though, his students merely saw the unfamiliar countries as relatively unimportant, and therefore less newsworthy. To rule out this possibility, Teigen ran a second study. This time, he combed through reference books to come up with a list of all twenty-six of the world's capital cities that had a population between 1 million and 2 million at the time. That way, the cities should presumably be of roughly equivalent news value. Again, he had one group of students rate the cities for familiarity. A second group of students indicated how much they'd be interested in reading newspaper articles by correspondents in each of the twenty-six cities. Once again, the correlation was almost perfect: the more familiar the city, the more interesting its news.

To try to make sure this was something particular about the news, Teigen had another group of students

answer yet another question: Imagine you have a friend
who has won a round-the-world tour. How much would
you like to receive a postcard from each of the countries
the friend visited? Now pattern was the opposite. For
postcards, the unfamiliar countries were generally
preferred over the familiar.

This is evidence, Teigen argues, of the psychological
tension between familiarity and novelty. Postcards, Teigen
says, are not generally expected to contain much in the
way of new information. The message tends to be a
fairly formulaic variation on "Wish you were here!"
Given that we're familiar with the person sending the
postcard and the kind of message the person is likely to
write on it, we'd prefer it to come from somewhere we
don't know well—a familiar message from an unfamiliar
place. That way, at least some novelty will be in the
exotic city pictured on the front of the postcard and the
unusual stamp used to mail it. *News*, however, inherently
contains new information. So to achieve a pleasing
balance of familiar and unfamiliar, we prefer to read
news about somewhere we know.

"Ideally," Teigen concluded, what we want out of news
is "'food for thought,' digestible but not pre-digested."
This helps explain the "constant demand for news about
the most well-known subjects, however insignificant,"
Teigen says, while unfamiliar topics go unmentioned. As
cases in point, he noted the endless coverage of "minor
events in the fields of sports, pop music, the lives and
activities of movie stars, famous politicians, etc." Perhaps
we could add the Loch Ness monster to the list.

A similar line of thinking concerns not familiarity,
exactly, but surprisingness. It seems our interest is piqued

most by ideas that are simultaneously intuitive and surprising. Specifically, the most appealing ideas are "minimally counterintuitive." The term is a mouthful, but it basically means that we respond best to ideas that are neither too surprising, nor entirely unsurprising.

The idea was pioneered by Pascal Boyer, an anthropologist who specializes in the study of religion. The most successful religious ideas, Boyer argued, have, in part, endured because they are minimally counterintuitive. They defy intuition enough to get remembered and passed around, but not so much as to be confusing or impossible to explain.

More specifically, minimally counterintuitive claims remix the properties of the natural world. Boyer argues that, evolutionarily speaking, people have spent most of their time thinking about five basic categories of stuff: people, animals, plants, natural objects (such as rocks), and human artifacts (such as tools). The recipe for minimal counterintuitiveness is to take something that has most of the attributes of one kind of entity and add just one or two additional attributes from a different category.

Take a weeping statue. Every now and then, religious statues—most often, of the Virgin Mary—are claimed to have spontaneously started secreting tears. Sometimes the tears are rose-scented water, sometimes oil, sometimes blood. They still crop up now and again—a painting of the Virgin Mary in a Chicago Greek Orthodox church apparently started crying in September 2019.

What makes the idea of a weeping statue so compelling, according to the idea of minimal counterintuitiveness, is that it blends attributes of different categories in just the right way. A weeping statue has all the properties of a typical human artifact. It is immobile, mute, liable to break if hit by a hammer, and so on. But crucially, it possesses an attribute that statues usually don't: it weeps, like a human.

That one category-crossing feature is enough to grab an audience's attention. Adding more counterintuitive features would just make it confusing. We could imagine a statue that not only weeps, but grows thick fur and barks like a dog while floating two feet above the floor and glowing bright, radioactive green. That would be inexplicable, all right, but the story probably wouldn't do as well as that of the more modest weeping statue. It'd be *maximally* counterintuitive, too hard to remember and explain to get any traction.

News might seem like a far cry from religion. Religious claims are some of the oldest, most enduring ideas that humanity has retained, for millennia. For individuals, religious beliefs can be among a person's most deeply held beliefs. News, on the other hand, is disposable by design. Yesterday's headlines are forgotten today, just as today's news will be replaced by tomorrow's. Yet minimal counterintuitiveness might give news items just enough of a competitive advantage in the vast market of ideas vying for our attention. (Note that weeping statues, like mythical lake monsters, invariably generate news coverage.)

To see how counterintuitive content affects how people read news, psychologist Aiyana Willard and colleagues had people read three real science-news stories, each with some minimally counterintuitive component.

One reported the story of Jim the Wonder Dog, a dog that had apparently predicted the results of the 1936 World Series. "Jim was just a plain black and white setter, but in all the annals of dogdom there has never been anything his equal," gushed the first sentence of the article, which had originally been published in *Ruralite* magazine. "Psychology professors from Washington University in St. Louis and the University of Missouri in Columbia observed the uncanny things he could do." Apparently Jim wasn't just a baseball fan; he also picked the Kentucky Derby winners seven years straight. He could also predict the gender of unborn babies, and the winners of presidential elections. The psychologists "shook their heads in wonder and had absolutely no explanation for his behavior," the article said.

The other two articles were more contemporary. One bore the headline "Teleporting Larger Objects Becomes a Real Possibility." The story explained that physicists had proposed a method that could, in theory, be used to "entangle" absolutely any kind of particle, permitting atoms, molecules, and even larger objects to be teleported from one place to another. Another article reported on a self-organizing electronic circuit that was baffling engineers.

Willard pitted those minimally counterintuitive stories against three run-of-the-mill, intuitive science stories. She chose the stories to be just as interesting and unusual, but without the intuition-defying element. One reported on a new type of window capable of producing electricity through solar power. Another reported on a twenty-two-year-old physics wiz earning a professorship. The third reported a new email plug-in designed to check messages for hostility.

A week after the participants read all these news stories, Willard had them come back into the lab and tested their memory. She found that the counterintuitive stories had stuck in people's minds. The odds of someone remembering the gist of a story were boosted by 80 percent—a substantial increase—by the minimally counterintuitive content. Interestingly, while the counterintuitive stories were better remembered, it wasn't because people *believed* the stories. Willard found that stories with counterintuitive content were rated far less believable than intuitive stories. When she threw some made-up stories into the mix, Willard found that people even considered intuitive-but-fake stories to be more believable than counterintuitive-but-true stories.

Afzal Upal, a cognitive scientist who works for Canada's Department of National Defence, more explicitly suggested a link between the appeal of fake news and our responsiveness to counterintuitive ideas. He began a 2011 report by juxtaposing two stories. The first was the myth of the windigo, "a superhuman giant about thirty feet tall, who lived in the forest and preyed on human beings." The second was a fake news story that had done the rounds in 2005, claiming that a monstrous crocodile was prowling New Orleans in the wake of Hurricane Katrina. "21 FT long, 4500 lbs, around 80 years old minimum. Specialists said that he was looking to eat humans because he was too old to catch animals."

What the two stories have in common, Upal suggested, is minimal counterintuitiveness. Just as Pascal Boyer argued, the myth and the fake news story both violate expectations by mixing attributes of different categories, imbuing the monstrous animals with humanlike malice.

Upal also points out that counterintuitiveness depends on our expectations. The windigo might sound maximally counterintuitive to modern, secular city dwellers, with its heart of ice, lipless mouth, huge jagged teeth, blood-filled, protruding eyes, and yard-long feet with only a single toe. Yet the Algonquian Native Americans who originated the myth believed many monstrous spirits inhabited the forest. The windigo was the only cannibal, setting it apart as minimally counterintuitive. A massive crocodile with a taste for human flesh might be just the right blend of intuitive and surprising for contemporary audiences.

Fake news about killer crocs is all good fun. But Upal suggested that a frivolous story like that isn't so different from the false rumors about looting, rioting, murder, and rape in New Orleans that were widely reported in the wake of Hurricane Katrina. In the high-churn context of news, ideas that are minimally counterintuitive today might be accepted wisdom tomorrow. So, tomorrow an even more counterintuitive variant of the claim might be required to keep the audience's interest.

The escalating Hurricane Katrina rumors demonstrated this pattern clearly, Upal argued. "The first reports from New Orleans about thousands of poor people unable to evacuate from the city and being housed in poor conditions without water and food were initially shocking, but soon they became conventional wisdom." A new, surprising twist was required. "Later news reports added lawlessness to the mix to keep the interests of their viewers," Upal went on. "Once theft and looting in New Orleans became conventional wisdom and were no longer news-worthy, reports of rapes and murders began to emerge." These were initially reported as a small number of isolated incidents, but soon the number of alleged incidents began to swell, as did the shock value. "It was no longer the adult women who were getting raped, now it was underage girls, and once that lost its shock-value, babies!"

★

News can be a matter of life and death. The last battle of the War of 1812 was fought two weeks after the war ended. The peace agreement that put an official end to hostilities, the Treaty of Ghent, had been signed in the Belgian capital on December 24, 1814. It took close to two months for the news to reach America. In the meantime, British troops attacked New Orleans. In a single short battle on January 8, nearly two thousand British troops were killed or wounded, including eight colonels and three generals. Despite General Andrew Jackson's inferior forces, only eleven American soldiers were killed, and twenty-three wounded.

But the race to get the news as fast as possible brings dangers of its own.

Delivering the news was doubtless not the only consideration that drove the SS *Anglo Saxon* onto the rocks four miles north of Cape Race. One newspaper reporting the tragedy argued that the simple ambition to make "a 'quick run' is the besetting temptation and snare of the commanders of steam vessels." Since it saved fuel and pleased passengers, the paper argued, speed was not discouraged by owners. An official inquiry acknowledged that "the steamer would, of course, have landed her news had she called off the Cape," but argued that "her immediate purpose" was to receive, rather than deliver, news: "Instructions were to be telegraphed to the Cape for her as to whether the St. Lawrence was sufficiently free from ice to admit her going to Quebec, or whether it would be necessary for her to go to Portland [Maine] instead."

Arthur Johnson, the Newfoundlander who wrote about the wreck of the *Anglo Saxon*, was unpersuaded by these excuses. "There can be little doubt," he wrote, that Captain Burgess's "chief overriding motive was to make the Cape early to deliver the news canister." This was not malice or incompetence on Burgess's part, Johnson points out, but a requirement of his job. But whatever its cause, this "unholy haste" ultimately caused "the travesty of errors and omissions that led to the loss of the *Anglo Saxon*, and the death of her captain and 236 others."

Today, the repercussions of news speed are more likely to be felt in more subtle, but perhaps more wide-ranging ways—in erroneous reports, in less substantial reporting, perhaps even in the spread of fake news. So it's ironic that the endless speed arms race might not even be entirely about timeliness. Part of the rush to get the latest news seems to be simply about supplying a steady stream of information to satisfy the seemingly endless audience demand for pleasingly familiar-yet-surprising stories.

"If the celebrated 'man bites dog'-paradigm for good news is a psychologically sound one," Karl Teigen concluded, "it is perhaps less due to the sensational or unexpected message itself than because of its new twist to a recognizable, familiar theme." Stories that have the right blend of novel and familiar, intuitive and surprising, are more attention-grabbing, if not necessarily believable. But for news organizations, it's not belief that pays the bills—it's attention.

The increasing speed of news raises another set of questions, though. Are we in danger of being swept away by the torrent of news? How can we possibly keep up with the endless barrage of news? How much information is *too much information*?

CHAPTER FOUR

Too Much News

For seventeen days in the summer of 1945 there was no news in New York City. Well, there were no newspapers. Well, it was hard to get a newspaper. (Sensationalism is a difficult habit to kick.)

The newspaper deliverymen were on strike. The walkout had been called for midnight on June 30, a Saturday night. Apparently many of the disgruntled workers couldn't wait. According to the *New York Times*, something like a thousand men who were due to work that afternoon failed to report for duty. Some had called in sick. Many more just didn't show up. The *Times* sarcastically reported three hundred deliverymen "struck by the epidemic."

The deliverymen were equally droll. As they mingled on the picket line, according to the *Times*, "There was much horseplay, men asking each other: 'Well, how d'ye feel, buddy?' with the answer being, 'Oh, I guess I shouldn't have had that mayonnaise for lunch.'"

All told, fourteen major papers were left without their usual means of distribution. According to an estimate in the *New York Times*, some 13 million customers in the city and surrounding area were deprived of their daily newspaper.

Bernard Berelson, the project director of Columbia University's Bureau of Applied Social Research, saw an opportunity. Berelson wasn't just *a* behavioral scientist, he was *the* behavioral scientist; later in his varied and distinguished career, he would be instrumental in establishing the concept of the behavioral sciences, including coining the name *behavioral sciences*.

His initial passion, though, had been library sciences, in which he had earned his master's and doctorate degrees. So when the deliverymen's strike hit New York City's newspapers, Berelson's enduring fascination with reading and readers mingled with his research interest in public opinion to inspire him to study the public's reaction to being deprived of their daily reading matter.

He quickly put together a plan. As the first week of the strike came to an end, Berelson dispatched research assistants around Manhattan to conduct in-depth interviews with sixty people affected by the strike.

The interviews included some scripted questions, but their primary purpose was simply to let people talk about what the newspaper meant to them, and how they felt about going without it. The sudden absence of people's daily paper, Berelson figured, would bring its significance into sharp focus. "Such studies can most readily be done during a crisis period like that represented by the newspaper strike," he wrote. "People are not only more conscious of what the newspaper means to them during such a 'shock' period than they are under normal conditions, but they also find it easier to be articulate about such matters."

Most of the people interviewed complained about being deprived of their regular reading material. By design, Berelson wanted to interview people who usually read the paper, so these were all people who were being forced to abstain from a regular pastime. But one of the questions Berelson asked was "Are there any reasons why you were *relieved* at not having a newspaper?" The answers revealed how torn some readers were about keeping up with the news.

"Papers and their news can upset my attitude for the whole day—one gruesome tale after the other," a "middle-aged housewife" confessed. "It was rather a relief not to have my nerves upset by stories of murders, rape, divorce, and the war." She contemplated the other uses she could put her time toward without the daily newspaper demanding to be read. "I think I'd go out more," she mused, "which would be good for me."

Another interviewee had similar thoughts about better possible uses of his time. "I usually spend my spare time reading the papers and put off reading books and studying languages or something that would be better for me," he said, calling the paper "just escape trash." Whether he was successfully pursuing those loftier habits in lieu of his daily newspaper is not reported.

The interviews revealed the compelling, almost addictive, and not always pleasurable quality keeping up with the news possesses for some people. "The typical scrupulousness of the compulsive character," Berelson wrote, "is apparent in this case of a middle-aged waiter who went out of his way to read political comment with which he strongly disagreed."

"I hate the policy of the *Mirror*," the waiter complained, naming a particular columnist whom he particularly disagreed with, despite reading regularly. "It's a pleasure not to read him."

In other cases, Berelson reported, people were compelled to keep up with news of the war. By that point in the summer of 1945, Hitler was dead and Germany had surrendered, but the official armistice was still a few weeks away, as was the nuclear bombing of Japan. Some people forced themselves to follow the news out of obligation, Berelson said—as the least they could do for the war effort, or as a kind of atonement for the guilt of not doing more. It felt like her duty, a young housewife said, to follow the latest developments "for the boys—the spirit of it."

Some people seemed to feel that keeping up with the war news was bad for their well-being. "Under the stress and strain of wartime conditions my health was beginning to fail," one said. Thanks to the newspaper delivery strike, she "enjoyed being able to relax a little."

"I've been reading war news so much, I've had enough of it," said another.

For these people, conflicted for one reason or another about following the news, the newspaper strike provided "a morally acceptable justification for not reading the newspaper as they felt compelled to do," Berelson concluded. Though they wouldn't voluntarily have given up their newspaper, "once the matter was taken out of their hands, they were relieved."

★

Does this sound familiar? Feeling compelled to keep up with the news, even while suspecting that it isn't good for you. Suspecting that your time could be better spent. Perhaps even yearning for the imagined tranquility of simply tuning it out.

As I write this, the world is not at the tail end of a devastating world war, as it was during the 1945 strike—but if you follow the news closely enough, it can feel like it. A relentless procession of political corruption and disorder, war, famine, global warming, disease outbreaks—one crisis after another. Each story seems important at the time. But the next day's news brings a fresh scandal or tragedy to learn about. It never ends.

And the news seems to be *everywhere* now, in a way that it wasn't before. It's hard to avoid when the smartphone in your pocket buzzes with breaking news at any moment of the day. Back in 2002, researchers coined the term *ambient news*. Even then, news had already become something that we expect to be available just about everywhere, free of charge, and free of effort, the researchers said. "News is, in a word, ambient," they wrote, "like the air we breathe."

Ambient news may be convenient when you *want* to hear the news, but what about when you don't? Unlike the air we breathe, sometimes it's nice to take a break from constant news of chaos and discord. Yet, "escaping the news is as difficult as escaping advertisements," wrote another scholar, invoking a more conflicted comparison. Ads can be useful when you're in the market for a new laundry detergent or cell phone carrier, but sometimes it'd be nice to watch or browse without the constant interruptions.

So maybe escaping the news has a nice ring to it. According to a 2018 Pew Research public opinion poll, around seven out of ten Americans say they "are worn out by the amount of news" these days. Likewise, in

2010, researchers at the University of Texas at Austin's
School of Journalism asked people if they often felt
"overloaded with the amount of news available these
days." Around seven out of ten felt at least somewhat
overloaded; only three in ten said "not at all."

The Associated Press commissioned a different kind
of study in 2007, employing a team of anthropologists to
analyze in depth eighteen young people's news habits.
They found that "news fatigue" was a problem for almost
all of the young people they studied. "It's a nonstop
machine, just churning information out," said one of
their subjects. "It doesn't matter what it's about ... it's just
churning."

Think pieces about the dangers of "news addition,"
and the joys of kicking the habit, have proliferated. The
instructional website wikiHow.com offers a helpful
guide titled "3 Ways to Curb Your Addiction to News."
"Abstaining from seeking news will likely be challenging
due to the constant influx of news that fills online, TV
and radio channels," it warns. "Divert your eyes and ears
from news sources and focus on your work or an activity."
Seek help from family and friends, it suggests, or simply
"turn it off."

More generally, *digital detox* has become a popular
buzzword, implying that toxic technology has dulled our
intellects and diminished our attention spans. An article
in the *New York Times* bears the subtitle "How I Ditched
My Phone and Unbroke My Brain." Unwittingly
reinforcing the parallel between inescapable news and
advertising, the photo accompanying the article shows
its author sitting on the subway, contentedly reading an
advertising poster. Meanwhile, the only other passenger

on the subway car looks down at her phone. Presumably her brain remains broke.

Some companies will gladly take your money in exchange for helping you live without your smartphone for a few hours or days. Lack of Wi-Fi or phone reception has become a selling point for some vacation destinations. If you find yourself in New York City when you get bored of staring at ads on the subway you could indulge in a two-hour Digital Wellness Escape treatment at the Mandarin Oriental hotel. "Concentrating on the head, eyes, neck, shoulders, hands and feet, this restorative treatment aims to ease the stress and strain resulting from the frequent use of digital devices," the promotional material boasts. Only $345.

★

So, if you count yourself among the overwhelmed, it's easy to imagine yourself in the place of one of Berelson's interviewees relieved at the sudden absence of news in their lives.

Except, those people were in a small minority. The more common reaction, by far, was displeasure, occasionally even despondency, and in many cases an active effort to get the news.

While newspapers were missing from mailboxes and newsstands, some publishers kept printing daily issues throughout the strike, selling copies directly to customers at the publisher's offices. This proved remarkably popular.

The *Times*, for example, had initially set up a makeshift sales desk in the main lobby of their building on

Forty-Third Street. The number of takers greatly exceeded expectations. "A news-hungry public swamped the newspaper offices for copies of the Sunday papers," the front page of the *Times* declared the Monday after the strike began. "The difficulty of handing the crowds made it necessary later to set up the large counter in the truck entrances."

The article boasted of how "buyers arrived afoot, in taxis, in private cars and on crutches. A 'parade of taxis' formed on West Forty-third Street late Saturday as after-theater crowds stopped for their papers on their way home." One purchaser, a headline bragged, had driven all the way from New Haven just to pick up a copy. "All copies of the limited editions printed were snapped up during the day by the scores of thousands of persons who traveled to publication offices to purchase them."

The *Times'* truck-depot sales desk became a twenty-four-hour service for the duration of the strike, and the sales figures became a running theme of its strike coverage. The figures climbed from 42,500 on the first day of the strike to more than 100,000 on July 11. On the penultimate day of the strike, the *Times* reportedly sold 155,000 copies. "Despite the length of the strike, the public showed no weariness yesterday in trooping to publication offices to buy papers," the *Times* reported. "As on other nights before press time, thousands assembled in long lines to wait for the appearance of the papers."

The day the strike ended, the *Times* reported, "Deliverers of afternoon papers were back at their jobs by noon, and soon thereafter the news-hungry public was swamping newsstands for its favorite dailies." More pointedly, the *Herald Tribune* asserted that "probably no strike in the history of labor relations in this community has so angered the public."

Now, at the risk of sounding cynical, the papers would hardly have run headlines such as "Readers Doing Just Fine Without Us." It was in their interests to play up the sales and public unrest over the news deprivation, both for the sake of their reputations and their bargaining position with the deliverymen's union. But Berelson's interviews, along with other surveys carried out during the strike, support the picture conveyed in the newspaper coverage. The few people who were unreservedly relieved to be without the news were a small minority. Most found it genuinely hard to live without the news.

"Something is missing in my life," one of Berelson's interviewees said.

"I am suffering! Seriously! I could not sleep, I missed it so," claimed another.

The interviews indicated a fascinating array of reasons for missing the paper. For some people it was simply a matter of habit, the 1940s equivalent of reaching for your phone to check the news first thing in the morning or on the commute home. "I sat around in the subway, staring, feeling out of place," reported one commuter.

Some readers missed the specific information that helped them plan their days, such as radio listings, movie times, ads, or the weather forecast. Friends or relatives of returning soldiers worried they would miss embarkation news. "A couple of women who regularly followed the obituary notices," Berelson reports, "were afraid that acquaintances might die without their knowing it."

Others felt a broader sense of disconnection from the world. "It practically means isolation," a reader complained. "We're at a loss without our paper."

Still others articulated a more general fear of missing out on something—*anything*—important. "I don't know what I am missing—and when I don't know, I worry," one interviewee admitted.

Another admitted to feeling as if she were "just a little cog in the wheel." She "felt cut off" without the paper. "Things go on whether you know about it or not," she remarked sadly.

For some, the paper served a social function. "You have to read in order to keep up a conversation with other people," another interviewee explained. "It is embarrassing not to know if you are in company who discuss the news."

Other people had a sense of social connection with the columnists and the people discussed in the paper. "You get used to certain people; they become part of your family."

In a mirroring of the rising sales figures reported by the *Times* and other papers hawking copies from their offices, most of Berelson's interviewees said they missed their paper more, not less, as the strike dragged on. The finding was confirmed in two other larger surveys conducted during the strike.

"Different people read different parts of the newspaper for different reasons at different times," Berelson concluded. But whatever their reasons, "something that had filled a place in their lives was gone, and the adjustment to the new state of affairs was difficult to make."

★

Now, as then, we seem torn about our news habit. Sometimes it can feel as if there's too much information to keep up with. Yet most of us wouldn't want to live without it.

In October of 2009, three communication studies researchers loitered in a retail corridor connected to the MGM Grand Hotel in Las Vegas, offering to pay passersby for their thoughts on the news. The report of their research reads like a contemporary parallel to Berelson's interviews with news-deprived New Yorkers. Where Berelson had been inspired by the temporary absence of news, however, Eszter Hargittai and her colleagues were responding to an alleged overabundance of news.

Over the years, Hargittai noticed, claims about "news overload" had become commonplace. She wanted to know if typical news consumers really felt there was too much news. With her colleagues, Hargittai recruited seventy-seven people to be part of their Vegas focus groups. The sessions revolved around a single, simple question: "How do you feel about the amount of information out there?"

Like Berelson's interviewees, a few seemed to find the abundance of news hard to deal with. "There are way too many sources," one woman said. "I feel sometimes just stressed-out like Robin Williams in the movie *Moscow on the Hudson*. He has to go pick up a can of coffee at the supermarket and he hyperventilates because there are so many choices," she explained. "That's how I feel with all these sources of information."

Another focus group member felt "overwhelmed and amazed that there's that much out there, and kind of feeling, you know, underinformed." His coping strategy, he said, was "to avoid news as often as possible."

Just as Berelson had discovered, however, only a small minority of people seemed to think there was too much news. Just eleven out of the seventy-seven people mentioned some feeling of overload, even though the researchers pressed the issue repeatedly. "In one instance where we asked the group at large if they felt overwhelmed," the researchers reported, "many people nodded. But minutes later, most of the participants were enthusiastically discussing media choice."

Many people, the researchers report, felt "empowered and enthusiastic, not overloaded" by the amount of information available to them. A few expressed "nothing less than delight." Most people just didn't feel too strongly one way or the other, saying they felt neutral on the subject or that they had "mixed feelings that balanced out in the end."

These findings seem at odds with the public opinion surveys, where, for example, seven out of ten Americans are apparently worn out by the amount of news in their lives. Taken as a whole, however, the opinion polls are more equivocal than they first appear. True enough, Pew found a lot of people agreeing in 2018 that they felt "worn out" by the news. But Pew has also asked people specifically if they feel "overloaded by information" and found that the feeling is not widespread. In 2016, only

20 percent of people said they felt overloaded. On the contrary, more than three-quarters of people said they *like* having so much information at their fingertips. Two-thirds said that having more information at their disposal helps to simplify their lives. More people, 27 percent, said they felt overloaded back in 2006—a year before the first iPhone went on sale.

The findings are also revealed to be somewhat complicated by studies that allow for more nuanced responses than the simple yes/no options offered by many public opinion polls. The study by University of Texas journalism researchers that I mentioned before, for example, asked people, "Would you say you often feel overloaded with the amount of news available these days, or not?" I told you that only around three out of ten people said "not at all." That's true, but the five options to select from ranged from "not at all" to "a lot." Less than 10 percent of people selected "a lot." Most people put themselves somewhere in between, neither completely overloaded nor *not* completely overloaded. The most common response, chosen by three out of ten people, was the midpoint of the scale—the public opinion polling equivalent of a shrug.

Another study asked a few hundred Ohio residents, "Have you ever felt overwhelmed in terms of the information provided by various media?" This study offered three response options. Roughly a quarter of respondents said "not at all," and around a third said "yes, frequently." Again, the most popular option was the midpoint: just under half said "sometimes."

Yet another study asked a handful of questions rather than just one, in an effort to get a more rounded measure of news overload. The questions were along the lines of "It is sometimes hard for me to concentrate because of all the information I have to assimilate" and "I feel overwhelmed learning a new subject or topic because there is so much information." On a five-point scale, the average of everybody's answers to all the questions was below the midpoint, once again suggesting that, on the whole, people don't feel entirely *not* overloaded, but feeling overloaded is far from universal.

We seem to be confronted here with another eternal aspect of our complicated relationship with the news. We might occasionally say it's exhausting to keep up with, but, at the same time, we act as if we can't get enough.

Publishers have long been aware of this seeming contradiction. The inaugural issue of Philadelphia's *Public Ledger*, which went on sale in 1836 in the midst of an explosion of penny-paper start-ups, began by acknowledging the overabundance of news. "In offering to the public *another newspaper*, we are fully aware of the objection which may be urged, that, *the community is already overstocked with this commodity*." But the publisher didn't foresee a problem. "It is true that throughout the land, and more especially in our great cities, newspapers abound; the whole number daily issued almost amounting to millions," the editor wrote. But it is also true, he argued, that a massive, underserved audience of people remained "whose thirst for knowledge generally outruns its provision."

Now, approaching two hundred years later, more news is available to us more easily than ever before. But we seem to be just as charmed, and just as overwhelmed, as ever. Which raises a psychological question: What, precisely, *is* our capacity for news? More generally, how

much information is *too much* information? At what
point does abundance become overload?

★

The answer, happily enough, starts with a joke.

It comes from a keynote address given at the April 1955
meeting of the Eastern Psychological Association. The
talk was given by the cognitive psychologist George
Miller. As the punch line to the joke, he used the title of
his talk: "The Magical Number Seven, Plus or Minus Two:
Some Limits on Our Capacity for Processing Information."

Like all the best jokes, this one takes some explaining.

Miller had been ambivalent about giving the speech.
Fearing that the two strands of research he was working
on at the time, one on judgment, another on memory,
were each insufficiently developed for such a prestigious
address, he sent a lengthy letter declining the invitation.
"Fortunately," Miller later recalled, "I was writing to a
psychologist. He replied that anyone who needed two
pages to say no obviously wanted to say yes, so why
didn't I reconsider."

Miller reconsidered and got to work on the talk. "In
order to provide an hour's entertainment, I had to report
on both lines of work," he realized, but "the stylist in me
refused to give two 30-minute talks having nothing to
do with one another. So I asked myself whether there
was *anything* in common to the two of them." Eventually
he discovered something in common: a number.

So he took to the stage at the Benjamin Franklin
Hotel, in Philadelphia, in front of thirteen hundred or so
other psychologists, and began building up to the punch

line. "I have been persecuted by an integer. For seven years this number has followed me around, has intruded in my most private data, and has assaulted me from the pages of our most public journals." He imbued the number with cosmic, even conspiratorial, significance. "The persistence with which this number plagues me is far more than a random accident. There is, to quote a famous senator, a design behind it, some pattern governing its appearances." Then, with typically self-deprecating charm and wit, he undercut the premise, giving the whole buildup the air of an elaborate shaggy-dog story. "Either there really is something unusual about the number or else I am suffering from delusions of persecution," Miller deadpanned.

The number was seven, give or take a couple. In his studies of judgment, Miller found that people can reliably distinguish around seven different musical tones at once (with the exception of trained musicians, who perform much better). Likewise, people can accurately judge the number of shapes briefly flashed on a screen up to around seven. In his studies of short-term memory, Miller found that people can remember around seven pieces of information at a time.

Miller assumed it was just a coincidence, but the findings were consistent enough that he came up with the amusing formulation, the "magical number seven plus or minus two." That's the joke: the grandiose buildup leading up to the revelation of a "magical" number so small and inexact; the tongue-in-cheek toying with mysticism and numerology to explain a probably coincidental similarity in the findings of some fairly dry psychological experiments. As Miller himself explained later, "The idea of a magical number with a confidence interval tickles the fancy."*

What started as Miller's tongue-in-cheek way of summarizing two lines of research became one of the most influential lines of research in cognitive psychology. In the more than half century since it was published, Miller's keynote paper has been cited close to thirty thousand times.

The focus has been on the memory component of Miller's thinking. Short-term or "working" memory is the gateway to long-term memory. Everything you're aware of at this moment, you are conscious of only because it is available to you in your working memory. When you need to write down a phone number and you repeat it over and over, you are keeping it rattling around in your working memory. Everything you remember about your childhood, about state capitals, about the toppings available at your favorite pizza place, or about the pattern of freckles on your partner's neck you remember because it passed through your working memory.

So to say that the capacity of working memory is *seven* is, you can imagine, a provocative claim. Plenty of quibbling over the details has occurred over the years. If seven sounds like a horribly limited capacity for information, I regret to inform you that more recent

---

* Well, I didn't say it was a laugh-out-loud joke. Actually, I'm not sure a lot of psychologists get the joke. *I* didn't get the joke until I looked into the history of Miller's magical number. Like anyone else who studied psychology as an undergrad, I first heard about Miller's magical number seven (plus or minus two) in Intro Psych. I don't remember it getting a laugh. If the professor was in on the joke, he didn't feel like explaining it.

research suggests that Miller's magic number was overly generous. Nelson Cowan, a University of Missouri psychologist who has been studying working memory for decades, suggests an even smaller capacity of closer to four items.

Debate continues about whether our information-processing capacity has a meaningful single answer. Even to talk of "working memory" is a simplification. Numerous hypothetical interacting systems allow us to comprehend the world around us and remember bits of it for immediate or later use. But after more than half a century of research, Miller's main point appears to hold true: our capacity for information seems to be, in an absolute sense, astonishingly small.

★

This creates the impression of a hopelessly limited cognitive system. With so small an information capacity, we *must* perpetually be overloaded by the deluge of information we face. How *couldn't* we be?

So how is it that we're not all quivering wrecks, cowering in fear of one more piece of information overloading our delicate systems? Instead of being glad to be rid of the daily newspaper, why were most of Berelson's interview subjects dismayed?

Well, if we have a processing capacity of seven (or four, or whatever), the question is, Seven *what*?

Miller's research, like a lot of psychological thinking in the 1950s, was inspired by the blossoming field of computer science. It saw the brain as an information-processing machine, like a computer. A computer has a "limited channel capacity," measurable in bits or bytes. It would be convenient if our brain's channel capacity could likewise be measured so precisely. Miller quickly realized, however, the human brain handles information not nearly as orderly and predictably—as inflexibly—as a computer. Our capacity for information, Miller argued, must be measured not in bits or bytes, but in *chunks*.

Suppose, for example, that I want you to remember a sequence of twelve letters: MLBNHLNBANFL. If I showed you the letters on a screen just long enough for you to read them, then distracted you with some pictures of kittens or something, chances are you probably wouldn't remember all the letters half a minute or so later. Maybe you'd get a few from the start and two or three from the end. As long as the individual letters are the unit of measurement, you probably wouldn't be able to keep the whole set in your working memory. There are just too many.

But Miller's concept of *chunking* would prove even more influential than his magic number. What he meant is that the individual letters don't necessarily have to be the unit of measurement. If we can somehow combine individual letters into larger chunks of information, then each chunk becomes a unit of information. The trick is simply making each chunk meaningful in its own way.

So, if you're vaguely familiar with American professional sports, you might have noticed that those twelve letters could be chunked into four acronyms—MLB (Major League Baseball), NHL (National Hockey League), NBA (National Basketball Association), NFL

(National Football League). Now instead of twelve letters to remember, you've got a mere four chunks. Those four chunks should fit comfortably within your limited working memory capacity.

Here's another example of how making information meaningful can ease information overload. In a classic psychological study, researchers had people read the following paragraphs:

> The procedure is quite simple. First you arrange things into different groups. Of course, one pile may be sufficient depending on how much there is to do. If you have to go somewhere else due to lack of facilities that is the next step, otherwise you are pretty well set.
>
> It is important not to overdo things. That is, it is better to do too few things at once than too many. In the short run this may not seem important but complications can easily arise. A mistake can be expensive as well.
>
> After the procedure is completed one arranges the materials into different groups again. Then they can be put into their appropriate places. Eventually they will be used once more and the whole cycle will then have to be repeated.

If you let this rattle around in your brain for a few moments and then try to recall as many details from it as you can, chances are you will only get a few. It's difficult because the passage probably doesn't make much sense. It just sounds like a weird, arbitrary list of instructions. Each step has to be remembered individually, and there's just too much information for the limited capacity of our working memory.

However, the addition of one more piece of information changes the whole thing. That seemingly bizarre paragraph is actually instructions for doing laundry. Read it back knowing that, and it'll suddenly make sense. If I'd given you that crucial piece of information before having you read the paragraph, then instead of seeming like a strange list of unrelated steps to be remembered individually, it would have been a single, coherent, meaningful explanation of a familiar process. In the study, people who were told before reading the passage that it was about doing laundry remembered about twice as many details as people who were given no context.

If you've ever tried to read a newspaper article about something you know nothing whatsoever about, you've probably experienced information overload. Without some background knowledge—a hook on which to hang the new information we're encountering—it can be hard to make sense of, like the decontextualized laundry list. But even a fairly dense article about something you're already familiar with is much easier to process. You can slot the new information alongside what you already know, rather than having to try to remember each individual talking point as you sort through the information.

The news often helps us in this regard by framing stories in relatively familiar, generic ways. For example, Stephen Pyne, a former firefighter and expert on wildland fire, has pointed out that media coverage of wildfires generally conforms to one of two templates. One, he says, is "fire as a disaster." This kind of coverage emphasizes the fire as a fast-moving threat that towns are bracing themselves against or have just been ravaged by. (The same template, Pyne notes, is used for hurricanes and floods.) The second template for forest fires is "the fire fight as battlefield." Pyne says this flavor of report, borrowed straight from war coverage, will be accompanied by footage of firefighters in uniform, using heavy equipment and air support to do battle with the fire.

The use of familiar news frames resonates with our desire for familiar novelty, as we saw in the last chapter. But it also helps us absorb information about some new event by fitting it into our existing schemata for those types of events. Same fire, different day.

As Pyne points out, the relatively limited templates the news tends to use to report events such as wildfires doesn't necessarily enhance the public's understanding of the phenomena. "We're not at war with fire, and if we are, we're gonna take a lot of casualties, we're gonna spend a lot of money and we're going to lose," Pyne said in an interview. "If I were to frame the larger story, and I do this as a fire historian, I would say the problem is that we have too much bad fire, too little good fire, and too much combustion." Pyne has written fifteen books on wildland fire exploring these relatively nuanced ideas. For all the media's fascination with fire, he notes, none of his books have received much media attention.

Regardless of whether generic news frames actually help us understand the issues at hand, we *feel* as if we better understand what we're learning about when stories are framed in a way that resonates with our existing beliefs and expectations about the topic in question. News about stem cell research, for example, might highlight the moral and ethical questions such research raises. Or it might focus on the potential of stem cell technology to cure illnesses. If you already tend to think about stem cells as a potential medical benefit, then that framing will resonate with you, and a story dwelling on the ethical dilemmas won't. When the frame matches how we already think about the issue, we absorb more of the information, have more thoughts about it, and come away with stronger attitudes about it than when the news frame doesn't match our existing schema.

★

Another valuable strategy at our disposal helps us avoid overload: directing our attention toward information we are interested in, and away from information we aren't. Put more simply, we can ignore stuff.

"Can consumers be overloaded? Yes, they can," Jacob Jacoby reported back in 1984. As a professor in marketing at New York University, Jacoby's research focused on how consumers choose between different products. When people have too many choices, the research suggested, they make objectively worse choices. Like Eszter Hargittai's focus-group subject who pictured herself hyperventilating in a grocery store trying to pick a can of coffee, people in consumer research studies do often pick worse options when there are too many to fully consider.

But, Jacoby argued, the more important question than *can* consumers be overloaded is *will* consumers be overloaded? The answer, he concluded, is "generally speaking, no, they will not."

The discrepancy exists because, in researchers' labs, people are deliberately force-fed information until it's too much to handle. People taking part in studies expect their memory to be tested or their choices scrutinized, and they try to consider and remember as much as possible. But the researchers are actively looking for the point at which people become overloaded, so it's no surprise that they find it.

The real world, Jacoby points out, is rarely like the psychologist's lab. In the real world, we don't usually feel that we have to consume all the information that's available to us. We can be selective in how much and which information we access, and we tend to stop well short of overloading ourselves.

In the coffee aisle, for example, we latch on to one or two features—the design of the can maybe, or some emotional tug toward one brand, as from a childhood memory for the aroma of Grandma brewing up her daily pot of Folgers. We simply ignore the vast amounts of other information that could potentially be relevant to the decision. If we didn't, we'd be stuck there all day, weighing up the relative benefits of price ratios, caffeine contents, flavor profiles, countries of origin, and on and on and on.

In our consumption of news, a similar discrepancy exists between research in the lab and real-world behavior. Recent research, for example, has focused on multiscreening—trying to watch the news on one screen while also tapping on a laptop or scrolling on a phone. As you might expect, when people are given a test on the news content they saw on the main screen, they do worse when researchers had them splitting their attention between two screens. They remember fewer facts, and with less accuracy. That seems to give credence to the idea that the hyperabundance of information and devices with which to access it are eroding our ability to retain any of the information that's available to us.

But again, back in the real world, it doesn't necessarily mean that people *will* get overloaded by information. We often don't want or need to remember absolutely everything that we're idly perusing to pass the time.

Here's another of those research findings that makes you say, "You needed a study to find that out?": we spend more time reading news articles we find interesting than ones we don't. People are often criticized for skimming headlines without reading the articles below. But when something catches our interest, we give it our attention. When it doesn't, we keep on scrolling.

We can be even more fine-grained in our choices of how to consume the information available to us than by simply consuming or ignoring it. One study of people's Web browsing habits found four main ways that they engaged with news stories. The majority of news articles people clicked on warranted merely what the researchers called a *bounce*. Users took a brief look at an article, decided it wasn't for them, and moved on. The researchers labeled the other three categories *shallow*, *deep*, and *complete* engagement. *Shallow* engagement referred to reading less than half an article. *Deep* meant reading the whole thing, and *complete* meant engaging with the news story by, for instance, posting a comment on it.

Few articles earned the Holy Grail of deep or complete engagement. And why should every article get read in full? A lot of news is out there—it's not all going to be of interest to everyone. We know our time and attention are limited resources, and we act accordingly. Given that more information is out there than we can possibly consume, we avoid overload by being selective about what we watch, read, and listen to.

So, from a psychological perspective, our absolute capacity for processing information through short-term memory is less important than how we use that capacity. We can understand and remember massive amounts of information by being selective and flexible with our attention and by turning an unmanageable slew of factoids into meaningful, manageable chunks of information.

Knowing all this, most psychologists who study our information-processing capacities have never been overly worried about information overload. Sure, we have inherent limitations on taking in the plethora of information available to us at any moment. This can cause problems in certain situations, such as when pilots have to make critical decisions quickly based on the vast amount of information potentially available from cockpit instruments. But in everyday life we have a range of strategies we use to deal with the buzzing confusion of information that we encounter. These strategies aren't all for the good, as Stephen Pyne's criticism of the news's formulaic treatment of forest fires shows. But information overload generally isn't overly distressing or problematic. For the most part, we manage just fine.

*

If you're still worried about information overload, the best way to soothe your fears is to read what people have said about it in the past. The fear that we're on the verge of being swamped by the unprecedented availability of new information is very much precedented.

Even at the dawn of news going online, some people felt that the amount of information made available

would make it incomprehensible. In his memoir of
more than four decades in the journalism business, the
former editor in chief of the *Guardian* Alan Rusbridger
describes a trip to "visit the internet" in 1993. "It's a
cacophony, a jungle," he wrote to a colleague after the
trip. "There's too much information out there. We're all
overloaded." This was a time, Rusbridger notes, when
the *New York Times'* Web department, @Times, consisted
of just four full-time staff and three freelancers, with a
total of two PCs between them. Most newspapers
didn't even have a website, and only 3 percent of
households owned a modem. If the internet was
overloaded then, it's a wonder that it hasn't melted
down by now.

But we can trace fears of information overload back
further than the internet. The eighties was a decade in
which "the executive suite is awash with paper," as a
1983 *Chicago Tribune* article put it. "Office computers
undoubtedly have improved the efficiency of many a
businessman," it begins, "but amidst piles of printouts
and stacks of statistics, managers are finding at least
one unfortunate side effect to advanced technology:
information overload."

In 1987, the *New York Times* ran a cute article quoting
a business consultant who used juggling as a metaphor
for information overload: "Every executive I know has
got more balls in the air, so to speak, than he or she can
handle. Learning to remain calm and balanced in the
face of information overload is an essential managerial
skill. Juggling is a really wonderful metaphor for that."
Actually, juggling is more than just a good metaphor, the
article suggested; it can be a good way to deal with
information overload. "Juggling helps me to concentrate,"

a manager is quoted as saying. "I find it helps me to subconsciously work through my mental blocks."

Even as early as 1963, an article in *Nation's Business* offered suggestions for managers on how to "reduce the pressure of your daily information load." It's interesting to note, historian Nick Levine points out in a paper on the history of information overload, that the stress that results from dealing with too much information is almost always discussed as an affliction of high-status, white-collar workers.

The reality of the affliction was often taken for granted. A 1979 *New York Times* article began, "Although there is no objective evidence that modern America is more stressful than societies in the past, a number of researchers suspect that it is." The piece quotes the chairman of the University of Chicago's psychiatry department, who said, "I doubt if the people of other times had the information overload that we have." Hardly the strongest evidence that 1979 was the "age of anxiety," as the article's title suggested.

But the history of information overload goes back even further. Much further. Though they didn't use the term *information*, there is a long history of people complaining that simply too much information was out there to deal with, that it was proliferating out of control. Before the internet, and before fax machines and printouts, the culprit was the most advanced information technology of the day: books.

"We have reason to fear that the multitude of books which grows every day in a prodigious fashion will make the following centuries fall into a state as barbarous as that of the centuries that followed the fall of the Roman Empire," warned the French scholar Adrien Baillet in 1685.

Baillet was not alone in his concerns. Abraham Rees, the author of *The Cyclopædia; or, Universal Dictionary of Arts, Sciences, and Literature*, wrote in his entry on books, "Books, *the multitude of*, has been long complained of : the complaint is as old as Solomon, who lived three thousand years ago : they are grown too numerous, not only to procure and read, but to see, to learn the names of, or even to number."

Antiquated declarations of the information apocalypse make for fun reading. But I'm not trying to trivialize the fears here. It's easy now to look back and see that the printing press didn't bury society in books, as some of those thinkers feared, but at the time the concern was entirely reasonable. Information was growing at a staggering and unprecedented rate. Where it was going to end up was impossible to know.

Daniel Rosenberg, another historian who has written about early-modern information overload, notes that Europe experienced a kind of "information explosion" around the sixteenth through the eighteenth century, when "the production, circulation, and dissemination of scientific and scholarly texts accelerated tremendously." Another scholar notes that, around the turn of the sixteenth century, the largest personal libraries might have contained something like sixty books. A century later, that number had grown to a thousand. Another century later, perhaps three thousand.

The proliferation of information contained in books can even be seen in how artists represented scholars at work. Early medieval art typically showed a scholar hunched over a single book. The first depiction of someone studying multiple books didn't appear until the year 1200, and it wasn't common until around 1400.

Thereafter, a scholar was usually depicted nestled among a multitude of open and closed books scattered on the scholar's desk, bookshelves, and even littering the floor.

It's easy to imagine how the rapid multiplication of books created a sense that the world was on the verge of drowning in information. But what the people fretting about the possible consequences couldn't have known then is the range of creative solutions people would come up with to manage the glut of information.

One of the first bright ideas was the index, a thorough list of a book's keywords, stuck in the back of a book, organized alphabetically, with a reference to the page number where the topic could be found. If you've ever had to look up some obscure topic in a thick textbook, you'll appreciate how useful an invention it is. The index points you to exactly the information you need, so that you can overlook all the information that you don't need. Pioneered in the thirteenth century, the index proved a popular and enduring innovation (you can find one at the end of this very book). Printers boasted of a "most complete" or "augmented and corrected" index. Some enterprising readers, when they found the publisher's index unsatisfactory, would go to the trouble of creating their own.

That a solution to the problem of books containing too much information was to add even more information has a pleasing irony. Increasing the page count with the addition of the index made books more manageable. Other solutions favored the creation of entirely new books. The dictionary and the encyclopedia (both of which have long histories spanning many cultures, but owe their modern forms largely to the fifteenth and sixteenth centuries) offered bite-size pieces of information intended to be consumed piecemeal, rather than read cover to cover. Epitomes, commonplace books, and florilegia collected interesting quotations and abstracts from other books.

Other strategies for dealing with the plethora of information advised the use of specialized reading and note-taking strategies. Isaac Newton apparently favored dog-earing, turning the corner of a page to point to a passage of interest. Using a fingernail to mark an important passage was common enough in the eighteenth century to earn a satirical reference to women who cherished their "nails for the convenience of making marginal notes." Other readers, more averse to such permanent defacement, left bookmarks to easily find key pages.

For taking notes, various people offered advice on the most efficient methods of underlining or making notes in the margins using different marks—crosses, circles, half circles, numbers, letters—with various meanings assigned to them. As with the index, and books summarizing and abstracting other books, the solution to too much information was *more* information, designed to help tame and navigate the glut.

Other thinkers noted that a variety of reading styles could be employed, tailored toward specific goals. A key insight was that not every book had to be read cover to cover. Francis Bacon argued, "Some books are to be tasted, others to be swallowed and some few to be chewed and digested; that is, some books are to be read only in parts; others to be read, but not curiously; and some few to be read wholly, and with diligence and attention."

Then, as now, some people kvetched about what these "shortcuts" portended. "So many summaries, so many new methods, so many indexes, so many dictionaries have slowed the live ardor which made men learned," one scholar moaned. "All the sciences today are reduced to dictionaries and no one seeks other keys to enter them."

Other hoity scholars mocked people for owning more books than they could read, seeing it as an intellectual weakness. "Be careful," the ancient Roman philosopher Seneca warned, "lest this reading of many authors and books of every sort may tend to make you discursive and unsteady." His favored solution was simply to only read the good books. "You must linger among a limited number of master-thinkers, and digest their works, if you would derive ideas which shall win firm hold in your mind."

Abraham Rees, the author who had noted the frequent warnings about the "multitude of books," didn't put much stock in the complaints. Even his own weighty tome—his *Cyclopædia* came in 39 volumes, close to a thousand pages each—wasn't part of the problem, Rees argued. "In reality, there are few of the immense number of books which deserve seriously to be studied: for the rest, part of them, like this, are only to be occasionally consulted, and the rest read for amusement," he wrote. "Life is too short, and time is too precious, to read every new book quite over, in order to find that it is not worth reading."

★

It's remarkable how much the historical fears of information overload resemble current complaints about the internet. Even complaints about news becoming "ambient" have historical forebearers. In 1837 a New York paper noted, "The first thing you hear in the morning is the newsboy's cry, and the last thing at night is the importunity of the Chronicle carrier. They waylay you as you go down Wall-street, up Broadway, into the Theatre, on board or away from the steamboat, and even as you go into church. One lives, while in New York, in a complete rustle of newspapers."

Possibly this time is different; maybe the internet will really cause us to fall into a barbarous state. Right now, it's impossible to know. But, for all our complaining, we seem to be fairly adept at dealing with the ever-increasing amounts of information in the world.

Many of the strategies that the early-modern scholars came up with to manage the swelling supply of information mirror innovations that help us deal with the amount of news and other information available today. Keywords and search terms are the new indexes. Readers are constantly rediscovering Francis Bacon's system of tasting, chewing, and digesting as they bounce from article to article. With the tap of a screen, we can save articles for later and share them with friends and followers. News aggregators do the hard work of trawling through the world's collective news output and showing us the articles most likely to catch our interest. Commonplace books and florilegia aren't so fashionable nowadays, though a 2012 article in the *Atlantic* compared these kinds of compilations to the modern-day website Tumblr. And unlike the cries of nineteenth century newsboys, the news alerts emanating from your phone can be easily silenced. If you feel that you need to, you can install an app that will monitor how much time you spend reading the news and cut you off when you've had too much.

News overload is a matter of perception. The historian John Sommerville, in a study of news from ancient times to the modern day, wrote, "The news has the magical quality that if you have a compartment in your brain that is set aside for it, it will always be full." In general, we engage with the news to the extent that we want to. People who enjoy reading news read more news than others and don't feel overloaded by it. People who enjoy the news less feel there's too much of it, but they tend to seek out less of it to compensate. When we start feeling overloaded, we get more selective in the news we seek out, and we avoid the news that we're least interested in.

Bernard Berelson interviewed newspaper readers when they were being deprived of their newspaper. It's hardly surprising that he found, for the most part, that people missed it intensely. Presumably the people who didn't habitually read the paper didn't miss it. Rather than being a highly addictive substance, capable of hijacking our attention and overloading our fragile synapses, news is more like a mild recreational drug. We control our dosage, taking in as much or as little news as we're interested in. If you're sick of hearing about the news, it's probably not because there's too much of it out there to handle. It's just because there's more of it than you want to hear right now.

So take a break. Life's too short, and time's too precious.

Perhaps, however, all this necessary sorting and sifting, bouncing and ignoring, is leading us into a new kind of problem. Perhaps we are sealing ourselves into ideological echo chambers, where the only news worth hearing is news that tells us what we want to hear.

CHAPTER FIVE

Echo Chambers

"Every morning, instead of being printed as in antiquity, the *Earth Herald* is 'spoken.'" This was what journalism would be like in the year 2889, imagined science fiction writer Jules Verne and his son, Michel, in an 1889 short story. But more than a mere change of format, the Vernes imagined a fundamental change in consumption. News would become personal. "It is by means of a brisk conversation with a reporter, a political figure, or a scientist, that the subscribers can learn whatever happens to interest them."

Alexa, what's in the news? Siri, play news from CNN. Hey, Google, listen to news about NASA. It took a little over a hundred, rather than a thousand, years, and instead of speaking directly to news makers, we listen to recorded or digitized sound bites. But with the idea of a personally curated news feed, which anyone can summon at any moment of the day, Jules and Michel Verne hit the nail on the head. First thing in the morning, last thing at night, or at any convenient moment in between, you can seek news from your digital assistant of choice, your preferred news aggregator, or any one of countless websites and apps. Or, even though the technology is *so* last century, you can still turn on the television or radio and find dozens of news channels catering, more or less, to your personal taste in news.

Even by 1995, this brave new world of customized news was closer to science than fiction. Technologist Nicholas Negroponte, in his bestselling book, *Being Digital*, speculated then that artificial intelligence would soon be used to skim the world's headlines and keywords and construct a personalized news summary for each user, filtered according to the user's preferences. "This kind of newspaper is printed in an edition of one," Negroponte wrote. "Call it *The Daily Me*."

Both the Vernes and Negroponte envisioned this as a potentially utopian development. Negroponte likened automated information personalization to the best kind of personal assistant. It could be a supreme "digital butler," he hoped, available to everyone, not just wealthy CEOs. For the Vernes, the technology that permitted individualized news (along with other sci-fi touches such as flying cars and pneumatic transportation tubes) was "a work of genius"; the inventor was "a real benefactor of humanity, that great man!"

As with any vision of utopia, though, there are portents of trouble. In the Vernes' story, personally tailored news has boosted readership and profits immensely and, in doing so, concentrated the newspaper's influence and power. "The plenipotentiaries of every nation and our very ministers" flock to the paper's editor, the Vernes wrote, "peddling their advice, seeking his approval, imploring the support of his all-powerful organ." In the story, the seat of American government has relocated from Washington to a new city, Centropolis. "The newspaper had followed the government—if it were not that the government had followed the newspaper," the narrator notes darkly.

"Done well," Negroponte's hypothetical *Daily Me* could be "a magnificent news medium," he argued. "Done badly, it will be hell."

★

In the popular imagination, it seems, the current state of affairs is definitely leaning toward dystopia. Far from each of us carrying around a benign butler to help us parse the news of the day, some pundits argue that we are gorging ourselves on—or being force-fed—a diet of news and information that tells us only what we want to hear. We are increasingly isolated from opposing points of view, pundits argue, to the detriment of democracy and society as a whole.

Obligatory, poorly defined but catchy buzzwords describe what is apparently going on. In 2001, the prolific science writer Cass Sunstein coined the term *echo chamber* to describe how the internet urges people to connect with like-minded others. Sunstein, a lawyer and First Amendment specialist, argued that mutual awareness, if not understanding, of opposing points of view, only possible through unfettered exposure to a wide range of viewpoints, is an essential element of democracy. Online, however, "you need not come across topics and views that you have not sought out," Sunstein wrote. "Without any difficulty, you are able to see exactly what you want to see, no more and no less." The walls of our self-constructed echo chambers resound with our beliefs being fed back to us in a smug cycle of confirmation and amplification.

Eli Pariser, a tech entrepreneur and author, coined a related term in his 2011 book, *The Filter Bubble*. Whereas echo chambers are ideological enclaves of our own choosing, *filter bubbles* are the result of technology imposing sameness upon us. Pariser initially focused on how search results can be tailored to individual users, the same search producing different results depending on who is doing the searching. The term has since expanded to acknowledge the proliferation of social media platforms such as Twitter and Facebook, which customize users' news feeds and suggested connections based on their previous activity.

For Pariser, this was a dark development indeed. "More and more, your computer monitor is a kind of one-way mirror, reflecting your own interests while algorithmic observers watch what you click," he wrote. "Left to their own devices, personalization filters serve up a kind of invisible autopropaganda, indoctrinating us with our own ideas, amplifying our desire for things that are familiar and leaving us oblivious to the dangers lurking in the dark territory of the unknown."

Both echo chambers and filter bubbles received renewed attention in 2016, in the wake of two unexpected political events, the Brexit vote in the United Kingdom and Donald Trump's victory in the US presidential election. A common explanation, at least among opponents of either outcome, was that echo chambers and filter bubbles were responsible for the apparent collective failure to take either possibility seriously. Information personalization suddenly began to look a whole lot more hellish.

"Your filter bubble is destroying democracy," claimed a 2016 *Wired* headline. Like the Vernes' century-old sci-fi, the *Wired* writer painted a picture of utopia turning to dystopia: "The global village that was once the internet has been replaced by digital islands of isolation that are drifting further apart each day. From your Facebook feed to your Google Search, as your experience online grows increasingly personalized, the internet's islands keep getting more segregated and sound proofed." While Sunstein had seen echo chambers as bad for mutual awareness, the *Wired* writer suggested the bigger problem was that by preaching only to the choir, we are neglecting our duty to persuade those outside our echo chamber of the wrongness of their ideas. "Our digital social existence has turned into a huge echo chamber, where we mostly discuss similar views with like-minded peers and miserably fail to penetrate other social bubbles that are often misled by fear and xenophobia."

A 2019 *Forbes* article concluded, "In the end, social media's greatest influence has not been to bring the world together, it has been to tear it apart."

Even some of the pioneers of social media have acknowledged their technology's ostensive role in creating a problem. Twitter's Jack Dorsey said, "I think Twitter does contribute to filter bubbles and I think that's wrong of us, we need to fix it."

Chamath Palihapitiya, who had been Facebook's vice president for user growth before leaving the company in 2011, said, in 2017, "I think we have created tools that are ripping apart the social fabric of how society works." By desiring to please their audiences, Palihapitiya suggested, companies such as Facebook were precipitating disaster: "If you feed the beast, that beast will destroy you."

This all sounds pretty dire. And to me as a psychologist, it reads as only too plausible. Psychological research can sometimes seem like a ruthless accounting of all the ways our minds are flawed. Some of those flaws seem like a recipe for echo chambers and filter bubbles. For decades, psychological studies have seemingly confirmed that we like talking to people who are just like us, and consuming information that confirms what we already believe about the world.

We're going to explore that research in this chapter. But first, I'm going to give away the plot twist coming up later: echo chambers and filter bubbles don't seem to be that big of a deal. Researchers using massive data sets looking for evidence of filter bubbles and echo chambers in the real world haven't been able to find much. Echo chambers and filter bubbles are not *not* a problem, necessarily—they just don't reflect the world that most people inhabit. As it stands, the fears about technology causing society to rip itself apart at the seams appear to be greatly overstated.

So, I'm going to give you all the psychological reasons we should be suckers for filter bubbles and echo chambers. Then I'm going to tell you that the internet doesn't seem to be coalescing into impenetrable filter bubbles or fostering democracy-shattering echo chambers. Then we'll try to figure out why.

★

First up, echo chambers. It seems little more than common sense that, given the chance, we will congregate with people who share our views. A 2016 *Washington*

Post headline asserted echo chambers and their dangers as fact: "Confirmed: Echo chambers exist on social media. So what do we do about them?" The pronouncement was based on a single new study, coauthored by Cass Sunstein, no less. But the study, the *Post* columnist wrote, only "confirmed what we already knew about social media—or at least had suspected."

But the thing about common sense is sometimes it covers all the bases, leaving you none the wiser.

"There is much difference of opinion as to the nature of friendship," wrote Aristotle, more than two millennia ago. "Some define it as a matter of similarity; they say that we love those who are like ourselves: whence the proverbs 'Like finds his like,' 'Birds of a feather flock together,' and so on." (The proverb in Aristotle's day was "Jackdaw to jackdaw," but "birds of a feather" has a better ring to it.)

Other commonsense turns of phrase, Aristotle noted, suggest exactly the opposite: "'Opposition unites,' and 'The fairest harmony springs from difference,' and ''Tis strife that makes the world go on.'" More poetically, Aristotle quotes Euripides, who wrote, "'Earth yearneth for the rain' when dried up, 'and the majestic Heaven when filled with rain yearneth to fall to Earth.'"

So which is it? Opposition unites, or jackdaw to jackdaw? Psychological research overwhelmingly favors the jackdaws. When it comes to whom we spend our time with, "opposites attract" is the exception. Like Aristotle's jackdaws, we tend to associate with people who are a lot like us.

"Similarity breeds connection," wrote sociologist Miller McPherson, who has spent much of a long and productive career studying human relationships. The technical term is *homophily*, meaning, basically, "love of the same." According to McPherson, homophily "is one of our best established social facts." In a review of more than half a century of research on the subject, he concluded that homophily is so pervasive it can be considered "a basic organizing principle" of human social life.

Take intelligence, for example. In 1922, John C. Almack, a professor of education at Stanford University, gave a few hundred fourth-graders through seventh-graders in Californian public schools intelligence tests. Then he asked each kid which of their schoolmates would be the first person they would invite to a party. The correlation between each child's own intelligence score and that of their chosen friend was fairly strong. Kids who scored higher on the intelligence tests tended to choose someone who scored similarly high to party with; kids who scored lower usually wanted to party with someone who also scored low. More interestingly, Almack also asked the kids which of their schoolmates they would ask for help if they had a project to work on. Here, you might think everyone would just choose the class brainiac, but that wasn't the case. Instead, the same correlation showed up. Kids wanted a project partner who had scored similarly to themselves.

The finding was recently replicated, close to a hundred years later, by looking at pairs of best friends from across the United States. Again, kids who hang out together tended to have similar levels of intelligence, according to standardized tests.

Our attraction to people of similar intelligence seems to endure beyond childhood, and beyond mere friendship.

Assortative mating is the starkly unromantic technical term for the observation that romantic couples often share similar traits. Intelligence seems to be a particularly important driver of coupling. The correlation between spouses' intelligence is about as high as it was for the 1920s school chums. When researchers measured more nuanced types of intelligence, they found that spouses are especially closely matched on indicators of verbal intelligence, such as having an extensive vocabulary, as compared to nonverbal intelligence, such as being good at spatial reasoning—perhaps because verbal intelligence is easier to gauge in a potential mate than nonverbal intelligence, making it easier to pair up accordingly.

So when it comes to general cognitive ability, like goes with like. How about more specific attitudes and beliefs? Here, too, considerable evidence suggests that we are drawn to friends, confidants, and lovers who think the way we do.

Donn Byrne earned a PhD in clinical psychology from Stanford. But what he was really interested in was attraction, in its many forms. Later in his prolific career Byrne served as a member of the US President's Commission on Obscenity and Pornography and conceptualized "erotophobia–erotophilia" as a personality dimension (basically quantifying that some people are more into sex than others). But in 1965, then a young professor at the University of Texas, Byrne set out simply to study what makes one person attracted to another.

He used University of Texas undergrads as his guinea pigs. In his initial studies, Byrne had had dozens of students read questionnaires supposedly filled out by four other participants in the study, indicating the strangers' attitudes on a long list of topics. It was an intentionally wide range of topics, some important, some trivial. There were questions about fraternities and sororities, integration, science fiction, welfare legislation, tipping, discipline for children, community bomb shelters, and gardening, to give a few examples. After the students had skimmed each questionnaire, they rated how much they thought they would like the stranger, and how much they would probably enjoy working together.

The four strangers' responses, however, were fake. The scales had been filled out by Byrne himself, "using different colors of ink, various pencils, different styles of checkmarks, etc.," he noted, to convince the participants that they were genuine. He called the fake questionnaires "simulated strangers."

Each of the actual students had initially completed a questionnaire of his or her own. When Byrne reached for his colorful pens to fill out the counterfeit questionnaires, he made some of the simulated strangers agree with the student's own attitudes and some disagree. He also varied whether they agreed on the trivial stuff, such as gardening, or the weightier issues, such as welfare and integration.

There was a large and consistent difference. Students rated the simulated strangers more favorably when the strangers appeared to agree with the student about stuff, less favorably when they disagreed. The importance of what they agreed about didn't matter at all. Strangers who seemed to have the same beliefs about gardening and sci-fi were as attractive as strangers who agreed about welfare and integration. In another variation on the procedure, Byrne found that the absolute number of attitudes the rater and the stranger shared didn't matter either. More important was the *proportion* of attitudes they shared. Strangers were judged more alluring when they shared four out of four beliefs than eight out of sixteen.

Wary of assuming that his simulated strangers reflected real-world preferences, Byrne followed up these studies with a more ambitious project in 1970. Here, he played matchmaker for real potential couples.

He had more than four hundred Intro Psych students complete a questionnaire about fifty attitudes. Then he fed all the responses, on punch-hole cards, into the university's hulking new mainframe computer. The computer calculated the level of agreement between every potential couple. On the basis of these scores, Byrne identified the twenty or so couples who had the most in common, and the twenty or so couples who disagreed the most.

Byrne then invited each couple into his lab to see how well they would hit it off in an endearingly innocent-sounding "Coke date." Explaining the idea to the couples, Byrne played up the high-tech computer angle, making it sound as if that were the whole purpose of the study. "Earlier this semester, one of the test forms you filled out was very much like those used by some of the computer-dating organizations," Byrne explained. "The answers of several hundred students were placed on IBM cards and run through the computer to determine the number of matching answers among the fifty questions for all possible pairs of male and female students." Byrne filled the couple in, truthfully, about their computer-calculated compatibility. Then he gave the potential couple fifty cents to get themselves a Coke and get to know each other.

Apparently the study caused a stir on campus. Word about the "computer dating" study got out, and many of the students showed up dressed to impress. "The subjects were attired more attractively than is usual among undergraduates," Byrne noted with scientific detachment. "From anecdotal olfactory evidence, even the perfume and shaving lotion level was noticeably elevated."

The big question was whether attitude similarity would really affect how the dates went, the way the results from simulated strangers predicted. When he analyzed the data, Byrne found that it did. The real strangers hit it off better when they shared more attitudes. They rated one another as better date and marriage material, as more intelligent, and more attractive overall. They even stood closer together while the researcher debriefed them at the end of their "date."

When Byrne followed up with the couples at the end of the semester, a few had actually kept dating in the interim. Unfortunately he doesn't mention how many, though he does note that the only follow-up dates had been among couples who had the most in common.

★

And then there's politics. Though Byrne found that agreeing about trivial and important subjects alike predicted attraction, political disagreements often seem particularly hard to overcome.

A 2017 article in the *New York Times* reported a seemingly trivial occurrence: somebody had posted an ad on Craigslist advertising a room for rent in her house. What made the ad newsworthy was the list of exclusions it carried. "Alcohol, pets and meat products are not allowed in the house," the roommate seeker wrote. "Neither are Trump supporters."

The ad was not, apparently, a one-off. Several Craigslist posts in late 2016 and early 2017 shared the same criteria. "We're open to any age/gender identity/non-identity … so long as you didn't vote for Trump," another ad read.

"I can't live with someone who supports a 'leader' with those types of ideals," the author of another ad explained.

Some of the ad authors admitted that their posts had started off as a joke. "Please no Imperial Sympathizers, Borg, Vogons, Lannisters (some exceptions), Sith or Trump supporters," wrote another. But the joke, he said, reflected genuine underlying frustration. "As a black man, Black Lives Matter is sort of important to me, and Trump supporters aren't known for their fondness of that movement."

That people tend to hang around with politically like-minded people is not news. We last encountered the behavioral scientist Bernard Berelson surveying newspaper-deprived consumers during the 1945 delivery strike. A decade later, he had moved on to studying people's political attitudes. In 1954 he published, together with colleagues Paul Lazarsfeld and William McPhee, an influential book titled *Voting: A Study of Opinion Formation in a Presidential Campaign.* Among other findings, Berelson and his coauthors report that people who say their best friends are all Democrats are more likely to vote for the Democratic candidate in an election than people with Republican friends. As a *New York*

Times article on the topic put it, "Those who liked Ike, in other words, liked each other."

Likewise, a 1987 study found that eight out of ten people who said their friends were mostly Democrats said they were a Democrat themselves. On the other side of the aisle, about eight out of ten people whose friends were all Republicans were themselves Republican. More recently, in a study that would have no-doubt pleased Donn Byrne, researchers examined real data from an online dating website. They found that people whose profiles indicated similar opinions about politics were more likely to message one another. Even teenagers hang out with other teens who share their political views—though, according to one study from the seventies, shared affinity for smoking pot was a far stronger predictor of friendship than shared politics.

So, whether the topic in question is our preference in gardening techniques or politicians, we are more drawn to people who seem to share our beliefs. A common explanation is that it's just easier talking to someone who is like us. Having a shared set of experiences, references, and cultural touchstones means you can gossip, joke, and understand each other more easily. Talking to someone very different from you just takes more work. You have to explain yourself more, and there's more scope for misunderstanding.

And it just feels *good* when somebody agrees with you. What could be worse, for example, than telling a joke to a roomful of your friends and being met with blank faces and uncomfortable silence? Telling a joke and getting a laugh—or sharing an opinion and receiving enthusiastic agreement—is rewarding and reassuring.

Your joke was funny, the stuff you like is good, and your views are right on.

★

Which brings us to filter bubbles. It seems like common sense that we like being told that we're right—so why leave it up to chance? Surely, if technology offers to filter information according to our beliefs and preferences, we'd be only too happy to settle into its bubble. The technical term here is *selective exposure*, or the only slightly catchier *congeniality bias*, meaning we pick information based on how compatible it is with our existing beliefs.

A team of psychologists led by William Hart reviewed the research on the congeniality bias in 2009. They kicked their report off with a tidbit of information about former vice president Dick Cheney. According to a document obtained by the website the Smoking Gun in 2006, Cheney made some specific requests of the hotels he stayed at as vice president. The scoop was somewhat unusual for the Smoking Gun, which generally published those kinds of "riders" from pop musicians and rock stars—think Van Halen's infamous demand for "no brown M&Ms" backstage at their concerts. By comparison, Cheney's requirements were tame: a queen- or king-size bed, a supply of diet, caffeine-free Sprite, and the thermostat set to sixty-eight degrees. In addition, all the televisions in the room were to be tuned to Fox News, the conservative news channel.

Cheney's desire to surround himself with news that would presumably conform to how he already saw the

world is not unique. Psychological studies have been
churning out evidence of our congeniality bias for
decades. As Hart and colleagues explained in their
review of the research, a typical experiment begins by
asking people their views about a topic—abortion or
smoking or gun control or whatever. Then the researchers
offer a choice of reading material about the topic, some
of which supports the person's belief and some of which
contradicts it. The researchers simply tally up how often
each person chooses to read congenial or uncongenial
articles.

An early study approached the topic from the angle of
consumer preferences. In 1957, Danuta Ehrlich and
colleagues at the University of Minnesota tracked down
Minneapolis residents who had bought a new car within
the past month or two. Those new car owners said that,
in the weeks since the purchase, they had read more ads
for the model of car they bought than for other models.
When the interviewer offered them the chance to look
at more ads for a number of different car brands,
including their own, fifty-one out of sixty chose to look
at the ad for their own model. Ehrlich explains that
looking at ads for rival brands would be uncongenial
information for the new car owners, possibly invoking
buyer's remorse. So, it seems, they steered toward the
congenial ads to reassure themselves that they'd made
the right choice.

In the realm of opinions, rather than purchases,
Stanford psychologist J. Stacy Adams asked a hundred or
so mothers of young children back in 1961, "On the
whole, would you say that a child's behavior is mostly
learned or would you say that it is mostly inborn?"

Almost all of the mothers believed that behavior is mostly learned—perhaps reflecting the idea, so congenial to parents, that we can shape our kids in our own image. When offered the chance to attend a talk advocating one position or the other, most mothers preferred the talk that supported their belief that behavior is more about the environment than genetics.

Researchers have long been interested in whether the congeniality bias influences the kind of news that people consume. There, too, we often seek out the news we think will best conform to our existing beliefs. It seems we, like Cheney, would all like to have the TVs tuned to our preferred sources of information.

In the same study that found evidence of homophily in people's political opinions, Bernard Berelson, Paul Lazarsfeld, and William McPhee also discovered evidence of congeniality. People with a firm intention of whom they would vote for in the upcoming presidential election appeared to be consuming information that supported their preferred candidate. About two-thirds of people said they were predominantly exposed to campaign information for their preferred candidate. Less than a quarter of people said they primarily encountered information supporting the other side.

Back in 1953, Columbia University sociologist Seymour Lipset found that people tend to read newspapers whose editorial policy generally agrees with their existing beliefs. In more recent experiments, people given a choice of news that appears to confirm or contradict their existing opinions lean toward the congenial news and are more likely to say they would share the information with others.

After analyzing the collective findings of close to a hundred studies, Hart and his colleagues reported that, all else being equal, people are almost twice as likely to select information congenial rather than uncongenial to their preexisting attitudes, beliefs, and behaviors. We don't *always* choose the congenial information, but it's a substantial and consistent leaning.

Explanations for our congeniality bias have generally chalked it up to the unpleasant feeling of suspecting you're wrong about something. Again, like telling a joke and being met with crickets, holding an opinion that is challenged by something we read can be uncomfortable. Better, surely, to avoid challenges whenever possible by limiting our information environment to a warm cocoon of comforting reassurance.

★

Okay, so, based on all this psychological research, *of course* digital echo chambers and filter bubbles must be real. If we like people who are like us so much, of course the internet would devolve into ideological echo chambers. If we tend to pick and choose information that fits our existing worldview, of course we'd be happy to let algorithmic filter bubbles present us only with what we want to see.

But I already spoiled the twist: researchers have consistently failed to find compelling evidence we're losing our minds to echo chambers or filter bubbles online.

In 2018, four academics headed up by Andrew Guess, a Princeton political scientist, produced a report on echo chambers. "The evidence," they wrote, "is more equivocal than the alarmist tone of popular discussion suggests." Echo chambers and information bubbles are not entirely imaginary, they argued, but the ideas "at most capture the experience of a minority of the public." Guess and his fellow researchers were left with the ironic impression that something of an echo chamber exists around the idea of echo chambers. The title of the report was squarely aimed at people residing within that particular echo chamber: "Selective Exposure to Like-Minded Political News Is Less Prevalent Than You Think."

The lack of evidence for the corrosive effects of echo chambers and filter bubbles is not for lack of searching. Researchers have combed through massive data sets looking for echo chambers and filter bubbles. The research began at the same time that personalization was becoming more common.

Matthew Gentzkow and Jesse Shapiro, both academic economists, examined the Web-browsing histories of a few hundred thousand people between the years 2004 and 2008. Using independent data sets, they estimated the political leaning of each user, as well as of each news site that the user visited. By doing so, they gauged the degree to which people consume information that fits, and that challenges, their political views.

"The data clearly reject the view that liberals only get news from a set of liberal sites and conservatives only get news from a set of conservative sites," Gentzkow and Shapiro concluded. Liberals and conservatives did have slightly different information diets, leaning toward congeniality. But both were largely omnivorous. Only a little less than half of the news they consumed came from sources slanted toward the opposing political point of view. Conservatives got around 40 percent of their news from liberal-leaning sites, while liberals got around 47 percent of their news from conservative sites. According to this analysis, the congeniality bias was less an irresistible urge, more a gentle nudge.

In another early study, a team of social scientists led by Elanor Colleoni studied the entire network of 2009 Twitter users—all of the more than 40 million users at the time and the close to 1.5 billion follower/following relationships among them. By using machine learning to guess the political orientation of users who had posted about politics, and then looking at whom they followed and were followed by, Colleoni and colleagues worked out the degree of homophily in the network. If a typical user was following a hundred other people, for example, eighty of them would be of the same political persuasion as the user.

That sounds like a lot of homophily, but it's important to compare it to some kind of baseline. To do so, Colleoni and colleagues calculated how much homophily you'd expect if everyone had just chosen whom to follow entirely at random, with no consideration of politics whatsoever. Suppose the network was a perfectly even split between Democrats and Republicans; pick a hundred people to follow at random, and fifty would happen to share your political views. But in reality, the split was far from even. Democrats outnumbered Republicans on 2009 Twitter by about ten to one, which meant that, if you were a typical user who signed up and followed a hundred people entirely at random, in all likelihood seventy-seven of them would share your ideology. So 2009 Twitter was pretty echoey by virtue of the sheer number of Democrats using the platform, but people weren't exactly going out of their way to add to the reverberation. The network was slightly more of an echo chamber than you'd expect by chance alone, but only by about three out of a hundred followers.

More recently, Eytan Bakshy, Solomon Messing, and Lada Adamic, a trio of researchers employed by Facebook, analyzed a huge set of data collected in the second half of 2014. It contained information on more than 10 million American Facebook users who had stated their political leaning in their profile. People whose profiles stated that they were liberal did tend to have more liberal friends, and conservatives were better connected with other conservatives. But, once again, the echo chamber wasn't as echoey as you might think. Around 40 percent of liberals' friends were not self-described liberals (20 percent were conservative and 20 percent described themselves as independent). The trend was the same in reverse for conservatives.

Bakshy and colleagues also examined their massive data set for evidence of Facebook's algorithms imposing a filter bubble on users. The Facebook News Feed shows users certain stories shared by their friends in an order determined by many factors, including how often they interact with the person sharing an update, and how often they tend to click links from certain friends or to certain websites. The news feed reduced cross-cutting content by around 5 or 10 percent, the authors report. So some filtering was going on, but hardly a bubble permeable only to congenial news stories.

Moving from social media to search engines, researchers have looked at the extent to which different people searching for the same keywords on Google see different sets of results. In the run-up to the 2017 elections in Germany, researchers had fifteen hundred people install a browser plug-in that automatically searched for the names of various German politicians and political parties at regular intervals several times a day over the five weeks leading up to the election. Each time the plug-in performed one of its automatic searches, it sent the results to the researchers. This allowed them to compare different people's search results to see the extent of any algorithmic filtering.

A typical Google search returned around nine first-page results. Taking pairs of randomly chosen users and comparing their search results when searching for a particular politician, the researchers found that, on average, the two users would have seen about seven or eight of the same links. Often, the researchers note, the links were even presented in exactly the same order. In other words, the degree of personalization was about one link out of nine. On Google News, there was even less personalization. Of about twenty results, only two or three, on average, differed between different people. "If there were filter bubbles here," the authors admit, "at least some of them would be quite spacious."

These are just a few studies; there are others, and the findings are fairly consistent. "Overall," concluded Axel Bruns, author of a review of the research titled *Are Filter Bubbles Real?*, "the more carefully researchers have pursued echo chambers and filter bubbles, the more elusive these structures have become."

★

So if the siren songs of homophily and congeniality are etched into our psychology, why hasn't social media sucked us into inescapable echo chambers? Why aren't we happily ensconced in algorithmic filter bubbles of purely congenial information?

As usual, there are a few explanations.

First, the congeniality bias is more complicated than simply avoiding any potential challenge to our beliefs. Most of the early accounts of congeniality bias centered on the idea that our overriding motivation is to defend our existing beliefs from challenge at all costs. In other words, we want to feel validated. But, in their review of the research, William Hart and colleagues pointed out another important motivation. Sometimes we want, or need, our beliefs to accurately reflect reality. Congeniality bias can set these motives at odds. Sometimes *being* right is more important than merely *feeling* right. Sometimes there's value in learning that we're wrong about something.

So the strength of our congeniality bias varies along with our motivation either to feel validated about our current beliefs, or to check those beliefs against reality. When some important personal outcome is on the line, being accurate trumps being defensive. We take into account the quality of information; when we think some source of information is dubious, we're less likely to give it our attention, even when it's telling us what we want to hear. And congeniality bias is weaker the more confident we are in our beliefs. Presumably, when we're particularly sure of ourselves, challenges are less threatening and so we're more open to potentially challenging information.

Another issue complicating the congeniality bias is an interesting, and often overlooked, asymmetry. Enjoying having our beliefs reinforced isn't necessarily the same thing as avoiding having our beliefs challenged. We could be drawn toward information that confirms what we already think without being equally repulsed by information that calls our beliefs into question.

Kelly Garrett, a professor of communications at Ohio State University, has explored this distinction across several studies. In one, Garrett surveyed fifteen hundred Americans just before the 2004 presidential election. He asked them whether they'd heard a set of arguments about the two leading candidates, George W. Bush and John Kerry. For each candidate, half of the arguments were favorable ("The Bush administration's policies have helped the economy begin to recover"), and half were critical ("Some Bush administration policies are a threat to basic civil rights and civil liberties"). If seeking reinforcement and avoiding challenge were simply two sides of the same coin, you'd expect that people would generally be familiar with congenial arguments and not with uncongenial arguments. But that wasn't the case. Garrett found that people were generally more familiar with the congenial statements—but only slightly. On average, people had heard about three of the four congenial arguments, but they had also heard two or three of the uncongenial arguments.

In another study, Garrett created a custom news platform that served up four news stories about abortion—a contentious topic that should be conducive to congeniality bias. A little icon next to the headline gave viewers an indication of exactly how much pro-life and pro-choice content each article contained. An article could be high in one or the other perspective, or high or low in both. Again, Garrett found that the more people thought an article aligned with their current perspective, the more likely they were to click on it; congeniality mattered. But the same was not true of *un*congeniality; the degree to which people thought an article would support the other side of the debate had no effect on whether they clicked it.

This calls into question the idea that news organizations seeking to maximize profits ought to simply ply their audiences with news and opinions that reinforce everything they already think about the world. While we sometimes prefer news that fits our worldview, we aren't necessarily opposed to news that challenges it. Sometimes, the challenge can be appealing—especially when we're more interested in knowing what's true than simply feeling as if we already know. Even the most devoted political partisans need to keep an eye on what the other side is saying, so that they know what they are disagreeing with. More cynically, who hasn't read an article one knows one will disagree with, just for the satisfaction of picking it apart or ridiculing it on social media? Whatever the reason, much of the time we are more open to challenging information than we're given credit for.

The media had this all figured this out long before psychologists caught up. As we've seen in previous chapters, surprising news—which often means, but isn't limited to, *bad* news—is attention-grabbing. And we delight in novelty—at least, certain kinds of familiar novelty. Coupled with how we often genuinely want to learn about the true state of the world, rather than just having our existing assumptions fed back to us, this means that producing engaging news often means telling the audience something they don't know.

Which is perhaps why proclaiming that "You Won't Believe" something or other makes for such good clickbait headlines. It's an overt challenge, practically demanding to be clicked, just to see if you believe it. More generally, and only slightly more subtly, the entire business model of news (not to mention pop science) sometimes seems to depend on telling your audience that things aren't quite what they think—either that something they think is good is actually bad, or something they think is bad is actually much worse than they think. In the business of providing information, telling people what they already know doesn't have much value.

Homophily, too, is more complicated than always choosing to surround ourselves with our own doppelgängers. Our choices play a role in our relationships, but another large part of the equation must be considered. Many of our relationships are influenced by whom we happen to find ourselves in contact with.

Say you're a member of Mensa, the high IQ society. You're obviously some kind of brainiac—you have to be to become a member. And obviously all your Mensa pals are going to be similarly brainy. Yet the surplus of eggheads within your social circle doesn't necessarily mean you are picking and choosing your friends based on IQ. You just happen to spend a lot of time around a lot of boffins.

Much of society is structured in ways that push similar people together and separate people who are different. Schools group kids by age, and, in some cases, ability. Workplaces are often fairly homogenous and are further stratified by job title and seniority. Neighborhoods are increasingly segregated by education, income, even political persuasion. The relative contribution to the homogeneity of our social networks of our personal choices and these broader structural forces are difficult to tease apart. Things such as the neighborhood we live in, the career path we follow, and the groups we join are partly the result of our decisions, partly the result of our abilities, efforts, and motivations, and partly the result of sheer happenstance. Yet research suggests that these structural forces are at least as potent as choices in breeding similarity.

Ironically, given all the fretting about how the internet is driving us apart, people's online social networks tend to be, if anything, more diverse than their offline networks. Matthew Gentzkow and Jesse Shapiro, the economists who studied ideological segregation of online news consumption back in 2004 to 2008, compared online news consumption with face-to-face interactions. They found that people's in-person relationships—their family members, friends, and acquaintances—were substantially more homophilious than their online connections. The people in our neighborhood, our closest friends, and the people we discuss politics with in person are much more likely to think like we do when it comes to politics.

Digital social networks can, in some ways, push back against the ways in which society is structured around homophily. In the old days, you might have lost touch with most of your high school friends when you moved away for work or college. Now you can remain Facebook friends indefinitely. You might not interact with them much, but the links they share can still pop up in your news feed, exposing you to a point of view you might not find among your new IRL friends.

Indeed, search engines, news aggregators, and social media can, at least some of the time, help us encounter information that we wouldn't otherwise have. Gentzkow and Shapiro found that the internet appears to be a better source of uncongenial information than either your face-to-face pals or national newspapers (though good, old-fashioned, mainstream broadcast news exposes people to the most ideologically balanced diet of information). According to another study, people who used social media and search engines to find news tended to consume more partisan information favoring their own political team than people who got their news from aggregators like Google News or by going directly to a news outlet's home page—but they also tended to read a higher percentage of opposing articles, as well. They simply read more news overall, increasing the variety of what they read. Likewise, research conducted in Sweden in the early 2000s found that, as high-speed internet became increasingly available to the Swedish public, users consumed more news online, but didn't noticeably change their political attitudes.

*

One last reason that the internet hasn't devolved into inescapable echo chambers and filter bubbles is that most people just don't care that much about the news.

As one indication of how relatively unimportant the news is to most people's information diet, consider a study by political scientists Gary King, Benjamin

Schneer, and Ariel White. The study wasn't about echo chambers and filter bubbles, exactly. Rather, King and colleagues wanted simply to know whether media coverage of a particular news topic results in people talking more about that topic. They went to heroic lengths to find out. They established collaborative relationships with close to fifty news outlets, which agreed to publish stories on predetermined topics at randomized times. This wasn't some exercise in generating fake news—the individual outlets retained complete control over what to write about within the broad topic, what kind of article to produce, and how to promote it. The topics were things that the news outlets would routinely cover, but also were relatively timeless. The important thing was simply that by randomly deciding when articles on a particular topic would run, the researchers could then measure how much more people were talking about those topics on social media, over and above the week before or after, when the topic hadn't been in the news.

Social media posts about the topics spiked by 20 percent the day after the articles ran, then trailed off over the next few days. Typically, the randomized blast of news coverage for a topic amounted to around thirteen thousand additional social media posts. Not too shabby for a few articles from relatively small outlets. Putting their findings in context, however, King and colleagues note, "The effect sizes and baseline volumes for our study are small relative to huge entertainment events." For example, "they are about one-hundredth the size of the Twitter frenzy generated by a new episode of the television series *Scandal*."

To be fair, significant breaking news stories from large news organizations can result in far greater social media frenzies than King and colleagues found. They point to a story the *New York Times* broke about fracking affecting drinking water, which produced a one-day spike of about 300 percent. Topics that ignite public interest even more than fracking would undoubtedly produce even greater spikes. But, in general, viral news events are small-fry and infrequent compared to run-of-the-mill weekly entertainment.

Other studies provide similar indications of the relative unimportance of news in most people's digital lives. Another set of researchers had a dataset consisting of the browsing histories of more than a million internet users, but the researchers wanted to limit their analysis to "active news consumers." Their definition of an active news consumer was someone who had read at least ten substantive news articles and at least two opinion pieces over three months. If that sounds like a low bar to you, you are unusual. The reading requirement reduced the initial pool of more than a million people down to just over fifty thousand (or 4 percent of the total).

News just isn't the biggest thing in most people's lives. It's not the reason most people are scrolling through Facebook and Twitter. It's not what they're searching for. Studies find that only about 10 percent of people's posts on Facebook and Twitter are about politics. Eytan Bakshy and colleagues at Facebook found that people only click on 7 percent of the news links that appeared in their news feeds. Another group of researchers observed that only one in every three hundred outbound clicks from Facebook corresponded to substantive news. Video- and photo-sharing sites were, the authors report, "far-and-away the most popular destinations." According to another study, only about one in ten internet users has visited an overtly politically partisan website.

When most people *do* go looking for news, they stick to a small range of sources with which they are familiar, and those tend to be mainstream and centrist. Studying people's online news consumption in 2015 and 2016, Andrew Guess found that, even at the height of the 2016 election, roughly half of the news consumed online by Democrats and Republicans was the same. Most people just didn't go looking for partisan news. Instead, most people got most of their news by visiting "large, one-stop informational hubs," such as AOL, MSN, and Google. These kinds of huge, mainstream portals generally avoid ideological extremism, Guess notes, "sifting news about political affairs from relatively nonpartisan sources and presenting it in such a way that people from across the political spectrum may encounter it." The portals' editorial judgments are much like those of broadcast networks, which aim for mass appeal by avoiding ideological extremism.

"Despite a wealth of available information from diverse perspectives," Guess wrote, most people "are satisfied with what's in front of them."

★

So, as usual, things are complicated. If you think you live within an information bubble, maybe you're right. But, if so, you are the exception, not the rule.

"Polarized media consumption is much more common among an important segment of the public—the most politically active, knowledgeable, and engaged," Andrew Guess and his colleagues wrote in their report on the echo chamber about echo chambers. Significantly, this group includes many of the journalists and pundits who end up writing the articles about echo chambers and filter bubbles, which get everyone else worried about echo chambers and filter bubbles.

There is a danger, notes Axel Bruns, that "we are paying far too much attention to the aberrant practices of a handful of 'political junkies' rather than the experiences of ordinary, mostly politically disinterested citizens." Algorithms make small tweaks to our news feeds, but most people still end up seeing the same stuff. A few people seek out hyperpartisan news online, but most people simply don't. Even the most fervently politically partisan readers rarely expose themselves only to one side of the issues. "In the main," Bruns argues, platforms such as Facebook and Twitter "appear to make serendipitous encounters with counter-attitudinal content more common."

Indeed, recent research by Levi Boxell, in collaboration with Matthew Gentzkow and Jesse Shapiro, suggests that the people who are the most isolated from a broad and diverse range of information and viewpoints are people on the wrong side of the "digital divide." Looking at data from 1996 to 2016, they found that political polarization had grown the most among people least likely to use the internet and social media. The strongest predictor, they found, was age. For example, less than one in five of those aged seventy-five and older said they used social media in 2012, compared to four out of five young to middle-aged people. While polarization had risen dramatically over the two decades among the oldest age groups, it had barely budged among the youngest.

"Our findings are difficult to square with a straight-forward account linking the recent rise of polarization to the internet," the researchers concluded.

Which is not to say we're living in utopia. "We would not claim that all is well with American media," Guess and his coauthors conceded. "Even if echo chambers are not widespread, partisan media can still spread misinformation and increase animosity toward the other party among a highly visible and influential subset of the population."

These real dangers make it even more important not to get carried away with the oversimplified idea that the internet is destroying society. As is often the case, we seem to be blaming new technology for old problems, as if technology spontaneously presents itself to us and we—or, rather, *they*—inevitably fall under its spell. The lure of homophily and congeniality have been within us all along. But our psychological tendencies are more nuanced than to simply push us inexorably into echo chambers and filter bubbles. It's reasonable to worry that technology could amplify our darker impulses, but there's no reason why it shouldn't encourage our better behavior, as well. It would be naive to assume that a technology with such potential to influence the very news we consume would be an unmitigated good, but it could be equally misguided to write it off as a catastrophic mistake.

Usually we use technology to indulge both the best and worst of ourselves; we use it to do what we've always done. The internet is not to blame for our problems; it may even be helping—or at least holding the beast at bay. The difficult part is realistically assessing the various nuanced ways in which it could affect us without our becoming jaded and losing sight of what technological tools to connect with one another, and to manage the astounding variety of information available to us, can offer.

"The men of the twenty-ninth century live in a perpetual fairyland, though they do not seem to realise it," began Jules and Michel Verne's imagining of the year 2889. "Bored with wonders, they are cold towards everything that progress brings them every day. It all seems only natural."

CHAPTER SIX

Deepfakes

In 2019, some of the world's most powerful political leaders came together in an unprecedented show of international solidarity. It didn't involve any agreements or treaties. There were no historic summits or accords. There was only a YouTube video.

It begins with the slow, familiar piano chords and ascending motif of John Lennon's "Imagine." The first line is sung in Lennon's plaintive tone, but it's not Lennon we see singing. It's President Donald Trump.

He mouths along with Lennon's vocal, sitting in front of two flags, the Stars and Stripes and the Great Seal of the United States, as if addressing the nation with news of national importance. He looks directly into the camera, delivering the line with a serious semi-squint, and adding his signature half nod, half head-tilt as a flourish at the end. There's no mistaking this for a look-alike or an impersonator in makeup and prosthetics. This is the president of the United States of America, inexplicably lip-synching to a corny song, by an inveterate hippie, about world peace.

The next line is mouthed not by Trump, but by Vladimir Putin, the Russian president, standing in front of a backdrop of Moscow by night. After delivering the line, Putin tilts his head back and arches an eyebrow slightly, as if to say, "This is pretty surprising, no?"

The verse continues with Theresa May, British prime minister, posed in front of a Christmas tree. Then former president Barack Obama, looking somehow younger than he did when he left office. Shinzo Abe of Japan is next, followed by North Korea's Kim Jong Un, then Chinese president Xi Jinping. Canada's Justin Trudeau croons his line.

Interspersed with the mugging world leaders are shots of people watching the video. A couple gaze at their television in quiet reverence in their dimly lit, tastefully decorated living room. A young woman watches a stream on her cell phone, its blue glow illuminating the look of delight on her face. Tourists in Times Square point and smile as the video beams out over massive digital billboards. A group of friends around a small campfire have set up a projector to watch under the starry sky. Another group are watching over drinks at a bar, transfixed. The surprise and awe at the momentous event they are witnessing is obvious. One man has his hand on his chin as if in disbelief. He briefly turns to a friend, perhaps to check that he isn't imagining things.

Some of the images are particularly on the nose. A soldier in combat fatigues watches on a portable screen, set up in front of what looks like mortars ready to be fired, as Putin mouths along with Lennon suggesting that in his imaginary world there would be no cause for war; the soldier is speaking into a walkie-talkie, presumably calling off the strike. The line imagining no religion is simultaneously mouthed by Israeli prime minister Benjamin Netanyahu and Iranian president Hassan Rouhani.

The video ends with a slow pan out on a grid of nine of the featured world leaders simultaneously singing along with the hopeful final line, suggesting that if we join them in their imaginary world we will all come together as one.

Who'd have thought, amid all the political turmoil of our age, that the world's most powerful politicians would agree to come together in such a simple, heartwarming, endearingly goofy show of goodwill.

★

Of course, they didn't. The video is a fake.

I mean, it's a real video, in the sense that it exists. You can watch Trump and colleagues mugging along to Lennon's "Imagine." But the video was created entirely without the involvement of the world leaders it features.*

It was made by a software company that digitally altered file footage of each of the leaders to make it look as if they were mouthing the words of the song. It was intended, the company suggested, as an inspiring hint of what could be achieved if only the leaders of the world would set aside their differences. "*AI* brings people together," the company tweeted. "Imagine a world in sync." While the video did not, unfortunately, precipitate world peace, it did serve as a nice piece of viral marketing for what the company's software was capable of. The

---

* And, apparently, without the permission of the song's copyright holder. The official video was removed from YouTube due to a copyright claim by the Recording Industry Association of America, though you can still find it floating around online—it's easy if you try.

results are uncannily good, though the politicians'
movements have a difficult-to-pin-down unnaturalness.
In any case, the video was absolutely not created to fool
anyone. It opens with a disclaimer that "what you are
about to see is not real"—adding, to help sell the
aspirational intent, "but it can be."

But the technology used to create the video has set
some people's imaginations running wild. Surely, if
computers can now put together convincing videos of
people saying (or singing) things they never said (or sang),
the potential for malicious use is virtually unlimited.

As usual, there's a catchy buzzword for the technology
used to create the video and others like it: *deepfake*. *Deep*,
because it involves "deep learning" artificial intelligence
processes (or something). *Fake*, because, obviously, the
results are fake. *Deepfake*. Has a good ring to it, no?
Rhymes with *deep state*. Sounds spooky. Sounds exciting.

One of the first political deepfakes to get widespread
attention was of former president Obama, one made to
look as if he were saying things that are actually coming
from an impression by comedian Jordan Peele. "We're
entering an era in which our enemies can make it look
like anyone is saying anything at any point in time," fake
Obama says. "So, for instance, they could have me say
things like … 'President Trump is a total and complete
dipshit.'"

Okay, that one was all in good fun. The most
controversial fake video to date showed House Speaker
Nancy Pelosi seemingly slurring her words during a
speech as if she had had a few drinks too many. The
video wasn't even, strictly speaking, a deepfake. The
effect was achieved by simply slowing down the speed of

the video. Anyone sounds drunk if you slow down their speech while keeping it at the same pitch. ("Call it a 'cheapfake,'" a Slate.com writer quipped.)

But the way the manipulated Pelosi video quickly went viral got people worried. In June 2019, three members of Congress sent a letter to the director of national intelligence urging scrutiny of the new technological threat. "We are deeply concerned that deep fake technology could soon be deployed by malicious foreign actors," they wrote.

The media took up the idea with gusto. Not only could deepfakes be used by our overseas enemies to subvert elections, the thinking went, but perhaps they would erode our very ability to know what's real and what's not.

"It's certainly clear that deepfake technology will get better and better," an article in *Forbes* argued. "Over time, this may make it difficult to really know what's true."

A *Vanity Fair* headline proclaimed, "Fake News Is About to Get Even Scarier Than You Ever Dreamed."

Even more bluntly, the *Guardian* claimed, "Deep fakes are where truth goes to die."

★

So … really? Is the idea of truth in danger of being killed off by fake videos?

Well, at the risk of repeating myself, we've been here before. In this case, quite recently.

"Faster than you can say 'visual credibility gap,' the 1980s are becoming the last decade in which photos can be considered evidence of anything." So said a 1989

Washington Journalism Review article titled "Photographs That Lie." It was part of a spate of articles in the late eighties and early nineties pontificating on the impact that new tools to digitally alter photographs might have on truth and the credibility of what we see.

Expensive machines for digitally scanning and manipulating photos were already common in newsrooms by the end of the eighties. Then, in 1990, Photoshop, the relatively cheap and accessible image-manipulation software, launched, bringing digital trickery to the masses. The term photoshop quickly became synonymous with "fake photos."* Such tools enabled anyone to "alter the content of photographs in virtually any way," the *Washington Journalism Review* piece claimed. "It's all done electronically, with no trace of tampering."

Understandably, people speculated about the potential use of such fakery for political ends. "Consider what might happen if the Soviet KGB or a terrorist group used such technology to broadcast a bogus TV news bulletin about a natural disaster or an impending nuclear attack—delivered by a synthetic Dan Rather," the *Washington Journalism Review* piece's author urged readers.

As with the concern about deepfakes and videos today, the assumption then was that the ability to alter *any* photograph would undermine the credibility of *every*

---

* I should note that colloquial uses of the term *photoshop* are frowned upon by Photoshop's distributor, Adobe. "Trademarks are not verbs," and "Trademarks are not nouns," Adobe's website scolds. For example, it would be incorrect to say, "The image was photoshopped." The correct way of expressing the sentiment, Adobe suggests, would be to say, "The image was enhanced using Adobe® Photoshop® software."

photograph. "In the future, readers of newspapers and magazines will probably view news pictures more as illustrations than as reportage," said a *New York Times* think piece, "since they will be well aware that they can no longer distinguish between a genuine image and one that has been manipulated."

Bringing things full circle, the *Times* article presciently speculated about the fate of video in a world of digital trickery: "If photographs can no longer be perceived as unalloyed facts peeled from the surface of the real world, what will replace them?" Video was a tempting answer, it said, given how ubiquitous it had quickly become in the era of burgeoning twenty-four-hour news. "But the prospect that video will inherit photography's former truth-bearing function is limited by its even greater susceptibility to computer manipulation."

Foreshadowing deepfaked Obama calling President Trump a dipshit, the *Times* speculated about how this could have been achieved thirty years ago, no deepfakery required. "An enterprising computer wizard could, for instance, create a visual data bank of all of former President Ronald Reagan's speeches and then, using a montage of the recorded images and sounds at his disposal, make the President's video image speak entirely new sentences—literally put words in his mouth." (Maybe something like "Future president Donald Trump is a total and complete dipshit"?)

★

The fears are understandable. Images seem to hold special significance to us as a species. From ancient cave paintings, to medieval woodcuts, to modern-day selfies, we seem to have an irresistible desire to visually represent and document our environment, activities, and selves.

Moreover, we do sometimes seem to place undue faith in images as representations of reality. Photographs and videos, especially, as the pinnacle of currently available technology to document the world, feel like the closest we can get to capturing a moment in time. Sometimes it seems as if we value these representations of the world more than the world itself. Daniel Boorstin, who published an influential book, *The Image*, exploring the sometimes tenuous link between image and reality, opened his book with a joke.

> Admiring Friend: "My, that's a beautiful baby you have there!"
> Mother: "Oh, that's nothing—you should see his photo-graph."

The news has long used visual images to imbue dry reporting with immediacy and excitement. Newsbooks and news ballads often featured crude woodcuts to illustrate their sensational tales. But not until the middle of the nineteenth century did printing technology make it feasible for large and detailed images to be printed along with text on every page of a newspaper. "The dry details of the telegraph becomes a living fact beneath the pencils of our artists," boasted one early American illustrated paper. "The text of the journalist resembles the dull unlit paper firework in the frame—our illustrations light it up, and immediately the public attention is aroused into action."

Beyond adding mere sensation to "dry reporting," images were often presented as enhancing the credibility of the reporting. The *Illustrated London News*, in its first issue, published May 14, 1842, boasted, "The public will have henceforth under their glance, and within their grasp, the very form and presence of events as they transpire, in all their substantial reality, and with evidence visible as well as circumstantial." Photography was still in its infancy; the pictures it boasted about were drawings. Yet that didn't diminish their credibility as far as the editor was concerned: "If the pen be ever led into fallacious argument, the pencil must at least be oracular with the spirit of truth."

More recently, an editor at Newsweek, Mark Whitaker, expressed a similar sentiment: "What makes a news photo distinctive is the fact that it is real."

Because of the trust we often seem to place in images, the fear of manipulated photographs and videos sounds entirely resonable—especially now that the news is more reliant on visual images than ever. Photojournalism scholar David Perlmutter noted, "News pictures have a special ability to focus attention on one time, place, event and issue." The availability of compelling pictures or footage can even determine the amount of coverage an event receives, and how the audience reacts. Events pictured in the news get attention, Perlmutter noted. Events not pictured often get ignored.

Sometimes we trust what we can see more than we should. Whether it's something we've seen in person or through pictures or videos, we often act as if seeing is believing. "I saw you with my own eyes," says a character in a Marx Brothers movie, catching one of the brothers in a lie. "Well, who are you going to believe, me or your own eyes?" came the pithy reply. The joke is in the brazen absurdity of instructing someone to doubt the evidence of their own senses. Seeing is believing, after all. And the camera never lies.

As we'll see, fake and manipulated images can predictably distort our beliefs. But before we get to that, it's worth noting that images can have surprisingly subtle influences on how we think about the world. Even a picture of a pair of shoelaces can, under the right conditions, affect what we believe.

True or false?—the little plastic or metal tube things on the ends of your shoelaces are called aglets. If you don't know, just take a guess.

If you said true, congrats, you're right! The word comes from the Latin *acus*, meaning "needle," by way of the Old French *aguillette*. The aglet is one of those underappreciated innovations that you only notice when it's missing or broken. Imagine trying to thread laces through the eyelets of a new pair of shoes if the end of each lace was a limp, frayed bundle of threads. It would be difficult and annoying. The aglet is an elegant solution to the problem. It forms a sturdy end, preventing the threads from unraveling and making threading laces a breeze.

Aglets have been around for a long time. Before buttons were invented, tunics and the like were fastened with threaded ribbons, often with decorative aglets at the ends to make life easier, and, presumably, to impress other aglet aficionados. Shoelaces have been around for a long time, too, but the modern version with an aglet at the ends of each lace is generally credited to British inventor Harvey Kennedy. Kennedy patented the lace in 1790. He apparently made $2.5 million off his invention, equivalent to over $70 million in 2020 dollars. So don't feel too bad for overlooking the aglet—it made Kennedy rich.

But I digress; this isn't a history of the aglet. The reason I ask is because the question about aglets is, for most people, an obscure piece of trivia. When cognitive psychologist Eryn Newman and her colleagues posed the brainteaser, around half of the people they asked got it right, which suggests most people were just guessing. You'd do as well just flipping a coin.

The interesting thing for our purposes is that Newman provided some people with a picture of shoelaces to look at while they contemplated the question, showing the aglets in all their humble glory. It's important to note that the photo didn't provide any evidence—the aglets didn't have AGLET written on them or anything. But the people given the photo were more likely to rate the claim as true than people who hadn't been looking at a photo. Something about seeing the object they were thinking about made them lean toward accepting the claim as true.

The trivia statement about aglets was true. Showing people the photo nudged them toward being correct. But obviously this power can be used for nefarious purposes, too. In her studies, Newman also included some false items of trivia mixed in with true ones.

Did you know, for example, that macadamia nuts are in the same evolutionary family as peaches?

Well, they're not. But people were more likely to rate this piece of bogus trivia as true when it was accompanied by a photo of a bowl of macadamia nuts, even though the photo again provided zero evidence about the claim in question.

Nudging people's beliefs around like this doesn't just affect what they say in the moment, it seems to leave a lasting effect. In a later study, Newman used the same procedure, asking people items of true-or-false trivia, some accompanied by a useless picture, some not. As before, people were more likely to say the questions accompanied by photos were true. But this time the researchers got the same people back in the lab two days later and asked them the same questions again, this time without seeing any photos. The ones that had been accompanied by photos two days before were *still* judged more likely to be true.

This is not just an academic curiosity. Newman cites a real court case in which a lawyer, attempting to persuade the jury that his client had been defrauded, showed a stock photo of a cash machine to illustrate his argument that his client had been treated like an ATM. Put like that, it sounds nonsensical. Obviously the photo adds nothing to the argument. But, Newman argued, simply seeing the photo may have nudged the jurors to take the argument more seriously.

Its not entirely clear why photos, devoid of any actual evidence, nudge us toward accepting the claims they illustrate. Maybe we find evidence in the photos that isn't actually there. "I'm going to go with yes," one participant in Newman's research reasoned when contemplating the "macadamia nuts are related to peaches" question, "because they kind of look like peaches, so that would make sense."

More broadly, Newman argues, looking at a picture just makes it feel easier to process a claim. Seeing the shoelaces or macadamia nuts helps jog your memory for shoelaces or macadamia nuts. This makes it a bit easier to turn the claim over in your mind. The relative ease with which you can think it through gives you a misleading feeling of being better informed about it. It helps you imagine how the claim *might* be true. And to the extent that you can easily imagine it *might* be true, it's easier to take the next step and assume that it *is* true.

Newman's first paper was published back in the pre-post-truth golden days of 2012. In it, she related the effect to fake news—but of the quaint, satirical variety rather than our new spooky variety. Photos can inflate the *truthiness* of claims, Newman said, borrowing the sardonic term coined by Stephen Colbert on his fake news comedy show, The Colbert Report. In this sense, *truthiness* means going with our gut. If it *feels* true, it *is* true. Photos, regardless of whether they tell us anything at all, can just make things *feel* true.

★

Naturally, this line of reasoning led to *real* fake news. If pictures that provide evidence of nothing can influence what we think is true, what about pictures that do appear to provide evidence of something—something that never happened?

In one of the largest studies of its kind, a group of psychologists led by Steven Frenda collaborated with the online newsmagazine Slate to run a survey asking people about their memory of things in the news. They ran the survey in 2010. All the news events they asked about were from the previous decade or so. Do you remember, for example, in 2003, when US secretary of state Colin Powell presented evidence, later discredited, of Iraq's nuclear weapons program to the United Nations Security Council? Or in 2000, when Florida's secretary of state, Katherine Harris, declared George W. Bush the winner of the presidential election in Florida? How about the passing of the 2005 law by the House of Representatives aimed at preventing the death of Terri Schiavo, a forty-one-year-old woman in a persistent vegetative state?

The five thousand or so people who took part in the research were asked if they remembered each event, and, if so, how they had felt about it at the time. As each person read the brief description of the story, they were shown a real, unaltered photo from the news to help jog his or her memory. There was Powell giving his speech to the United Nations; Harris at a podium joined by then-governor Jeb Bush; and House majority leader DeLay at a podium, advocating passage of the Schiavo law.

Those three events were each true. However, each participant was also asked about a fourth story, innocuously mixed in with the real stories. Unlike the other stories, this one was fake news.

Different people were asked about different made-up stories. Some, for example, were asked if they recalled President Obama shaking hands with Iranian president Mahmoud Ahmadinejad at a United Nations conference in early 2009. "White House aides say the encounter was unplanned and the handshake was a formality," the description lied. Right there next to the description was a photograph seemingly documenting the handshake— Obama and Ahmadinejad in the midst of a hasty handshake outside some official-looking building. The image was a fake. "A photograph of Obama shaking hands with a man in a suit was altered to make it appear that the man was Ahmadinejad," the researchers explained in their report. "In fact, there is no public record of the two men ever meeting or shaking hands."

Other participants were asked about a fake story from 2005, concerning President George W. Bush. "As parts of New Orleans lie underwater in the wake of Hurricane Katrina, President Bush entertains Houston Astros pitcher Roger Clemens at his ranch in Crawford, Texas," the description read. An altered photograph depicted the baseball player in the passenger seat of a truck. From the driver's seat, Bush looks out the window smiling, one hand on the wheel, his other arm resting casually on the windowsill. This photograph, too, was a digital alteration. "In fact," the researchers clarify in their report, "Bush was at the White House when Hurricane Katrina hit, and Clemens never visited Bush's Crawford ranch."

A third fake story concerned an attack ad that Hillary Clinton had supposedly run against her rival Obama during the 2008 Democratic presidential primaries. "Trailing in the delegate count for the Democratic presidential nomination, Sen. Hillary Clinton airs an ad in Pennsylvania linking Sen. Barack Obama to the Rev. Jeremiah Wright. Under criticism, she pulls down the ad but wins the primary." In this case, the ad was real, but it had nothing to do with Clinton. It had actually been created by a Republican organization, not Clinton's campaign. The researchers simply edited the logo in a screenshot from the ad to make it look as if Clinton had approved it.

People claimed to remember the real news stories well, for the most part. Eight out of ten of the people who completed the survey said they remembered all three of the real events. But almost exactly half said they remembered the fake event, too.

Moreover, many of those who said they remembered the fake event claimed to have more than just a vague recollection of something like the event described taking place. Half said they remembered seeing the events happen on the news. Some even had strong and detailed memories of what they had thought about it at the time. "I was torn because I think it is fair to ask Obama why he was associating with someone like Wright," one participant recalled of the fake Clinton ad attacking

Obama. Another felt the ad had even influenced his or
her evaluation of Clinton at the time: "I thought it was a
desparate [*sic*] move and it solidified my disgust with
Mrs. Clinton as a candidate."

★

Even more disconcertingly, seeing photographs can
seemingly influence our memory for things that
happened—or, rather, *didn't happen*—to us.

As part of her PhD research into the psychology of
memory at New Zealand's Victoria University of
Wellington, Kim Wade became interested in the potential
power of Photoshop over people's memories. She published
the results of her first study in 2002, with an attention-
grabbing title: "A Picture Is Worth a Thousand Lies."

"Image-manipulation technology has recently
become widely available, inexpensive, and easy to use,"
she explained in the first sentence of the research report.
Wade knew from experience just how easy it was to use.
For the study, she had taken people's childhood photos
and manipulated them, using simple digital trickery, to
put the child in a situation the child had never actually
been in. The question was whether the false evidence of
their eyes could make people "remember" an experience
that they had never had.

Photoshopping* the photos was the easy part. Getting
the photos in the first place was more of a logistical
challenge. Wade began by recruiting twenty volunteers,

---

* Sorry, I mean enhancing the image using Adobe® Photoshop®
Software.

but they weren't the ones who would be the actual guinea pigs for the study. Instead, these volunteers were tasked with recruiting a family member who would become the *actual* participant. The volunteers also had to surreptitiously gather up some childhood photos of their relative from childhood birthday parties, vacations, and things like that.

Finally, the volunteers had to confirm that their relative had never taken a ride in a hot-air balloon. This was the imaginary experience that Wade and colleagues would try to get their subjects to remember. She chose the balloon ride because it was plausible that the New Zealanders taking part in the study could have had such an experience—hot-air ballooning is fairly popular in New Zealand. But a hot-air balloon ride also seemed like a suitably significant false memory to try to implant in people's minds. It's the kind of thing you'd think you would remember if it had happened to you. And something, you'd think, that you would be unlikely to remember if it hadn't happened to you.

So Wade and her fellow researchers scanned the childhood photos of the unwitting participants, digitally cut out their smiling visages, and pasted them convincingly into a hot-air balloon, making it look as if they were soaring through the air, smiling down at the photographer.

Finally, one by one, Wade met with each of the twenty people into whose minds she would try to implant the false memory. She began by asking about some real childhood events they had experienced, accompanied by real photos. Then she produced the fake hot-air balloon photo. "Tell me everything you can remember," she said benignly.

Initially, as you might expect, nobody remembered the balloon ride. Wade told them not to worry: "Many people can't recall certain childhood events at first because they haven't thought about them for such a long time." She had them close their eyes and think about what it might have been like, who was with them, what the weather was like, what they saw when they looked over the side of the basket. By the end of that first interview, after Wade's coaxing, seven of the twenty subjects said they had some recollection of the balloon ride, though most couldn't recall it clearly. Wade gave each person a copy of the photo to take home. Spend a few minutes each night looking at it, she suggested, and focus on recalling the event.

A week or so later, Wade met with each person again to repeat the procedure. A week after that, she met with them a third and final time. By the end of that third interview, ten of the twenty people said they remembered the balloon ride to some extent. Of those, four said they remembered it clearly. One, for example, was able to recall the day of the week it had happened, how much it had cost, and who had been on the ground taking the photo.

The other six people were less sure of themselves, but still seemed to think the balloon ride had happened. "I'm sort of like my mind's playing tricks on me," one confessed. "I sort of think I remember being up in it. But I don't know whether that's just me thinking that I have been." The photograph seemed to be evidence that the person couldn't discount. "I actually, until I had seen this picture, I didn't even believe I had been up in a hot-air balloon," the same person said.

*

So this all kind of makes it sound as if the editorials from the eighties had it right when they said we wouldn't even be able to trust our family snapshots, let alone photos in the news.

Except, it's thirty years later, and Photoshop hasn't led to a world in which nobody trusts anything they see. Selfies and snapshots are more popular than ever now that most of us carry a high-quality camera with us at all times. Photos still fill the pages of newspapers, television screens, and social media feeds. We seem to trust them about as much as we always have. If their credibility was in trouble thirty years ago, it's taking a long time to erode completely. It's too early to say whether deepfakes will usher in the post-truth apocalypse. But if the premature predictions of catastrophe that Photoshop provoked in the eighties are any guide, it seems unlikely.

One cause for hope that deepfakes won't destroy society is that we've been dealing with the power of images to inform or mislead for quite a while, and we've been doing okay. The trouble predates even Photoshop and its digital predecessors. Manipulated photos have been blurring the line between fact and fiction since the dawn of photojournalism.

The August 22, 1863, issue of *Harper's Magazine* included an uplifting story about "old man JOHN BURNS, the only citizen of Gettysburg who shouldered his rifle and went out to do battle in the Union ranks against the enemies of his country." Burns was a sixty-nine-year-old veteran of the War of 1812. When the Civil War came to his doorstep, *Harper's* reported, "The old man made his appearance in a uniform which he had worn in the last war, but he fought as stoutly as any young man in the army. Honor to his name!"

Accompanying the story was a photograph of Burns's jubilant homecoming from the battle. The picture filled half of the front page of the issue. Two horses pull a small cart, carrying the war hero back to his home, a sturdy, if slightly run-down, two-story clapboard building visible in the background. Two men help Burns out of the cart, as several neighbors hover nearby, chatting excitedly. Children frolic in the street, while a woman dragging her own child by the hand runs toward the carriage waving a handkerchief in joyous welcome.

The caption reads, "Residence of John Burns, at Gettysburg, Pennsylvania—Photographed by Brady." It was "Mr. Brady, the photographer," *Harper's* explained, "to whose industry and energy we are indebted for many of the most reliable pictures of the war."

However, the "photograph" was not as reliable as *Harper's* made out—at least, not in the way that we think about photographic reliability today.

At the time the picture was published, photography was a burgeoning hobby and photojournalism was on its way to becoming a true profession. Mathew Brady, the photographer behind the *Harper's* cover image, had become one of the first celebrity photojournalists, putting on public exhibitions of his shocking Civil War battlefield images as early as 1862.

But newspaper printers couldn't yet technically combine photographs and text on a single news page. So in 1863, when *Harper's* and other newspapers and magazines claimed to "reproduce" photographs on their pages, what they meant was that a photograph had been used as the basis for an illustration. An artist would create a line drawing based on the original photograph, which would then be copied onto a block of wood. Skilled engravers would cut away the wood around the lines of the drawing, and the resulting woodcut could then be set in the printing press right alongside the movable type.

Along the way, the artists often took liberties with the photographs. The resulting illustrations were often more "inspired by a true story" than "unalloyed fact."

Brady's original photograph of the scene at John Burns's house was quite different from the joyous scene that ended up on the cover of *Harper's*. As Mia Fineman notes in *Faking It: Manipulated Photography Before Photoshop*, the woodblock illustration on the cover of *Harper's* "meticulously reproduces the architecture" of Burns's house, even including "the ramshackle wood structures around it." But where the cover of *Harper's* showed a spontaneous homecoming celebration, Brady's original photograph shows an empty, lifeless dirt street in front of the house. The only people visible in the photograph are Burns and his wife. Burns sits proudly in a chair on the house's porch while his wife stands next to him. His left foot is bandaged from a wound sustained in the battle, his crutches propped up behind him. His musket leans against the doorjamb, almost as tall as his wife.

Brady hadn't even been in Gettysburg when Burns returned from battle; he took the photograph several weeks after Burns's homecoming. And even if Brady had been there when the small community welcomed Burns home, and even if the welcome party had played out as dramatically as the *Harper's* artist later imagined, Brady's camera simply wouldn't have been able to capture the candid moment. The camera required a long exposure time and so wouldn't have been able to capture people in motion, as depicted on the magazine cover.

Taking these kinds of liberties with photographs was common practice in the newspapers and magazines of the day. Some justified it as merely compensating for the technical limitations of the camera. "We do not depend upon the accidental transmission of photographs, with their corpse-like literalness," wrote the publisher of one illustrated newsmagazine, "but upon our own special artists" to provide "living pictures of every incident of interest."

Indeed, readers expected such embellishment. Publishers happily played up the camera's perceived documentarian authority in recording reality. But at the same time, Fineman says, they felt the audience's "demand for lively, legible, visually engaging illustrations that conformed to existing pictorial and narrative expectations." This often meant representing a scene in melodramatic tableau, with people depicted in dramatic poses like actors hamming it up on the theater stage.

The first photograph printed in a newspaper without the involvement of an artist or engravers appeared in the *New York Daily Graphic* on December 2, 1873. The simple photograph showed Steinway Hall, an elegant New York concert hall on Fourteenth Street. An accompanying article trumpeted the technology that allowed photographs to be reproduced in this way. It called them "granulated photographs," referring to the halftone process of rendering black-and-white photographs as an array of tiny black dots, smaller and farther apart where the photograph is light, larger and closer together where it is dark. It was "a wonderful process," the paper enthused, and was quick to point out the realism of the photo. "We need not call attention to the faithfulness of the picture. The picture of Steinway Hall speaks for itself. All who have seen this building—and what New Yorker has not—will recall with delight the perfect rendering of all its well-known outlines."

By the 1890s, the printing of photographs had been refined and was in widespread use in many newspapers and magazines. Yet the relationship between photographs and reality remained tenuous. Wilson Lowrey, a journalism professor who specializes in emergent media, noted that, in the era when artists and engravers transformed dull photographs into vibrant tableaux, "the reference photo had no artistic integrity" to the art director, "just as it had no journalistic integrity to the editor. Why should halftone photos be any different?" The ability to reproduce photos directly did not immediately change the equation. Photographs were not seen as an inviolable snapshot of reality, but merely a jumping-off point—an unfinished canvas to be refined and perfected, or even completely overhauled.

Up until the mid-twentieth century, it was commonplace, in tabloids and broadsheets alike, to alter news
photographs—often substantially. Artists would use paint,
airbrushes, chemicals, scissors, and other tools to mani-
pulate the final product. People's facial expressions could
be changed, elements could be rearranged or removed,
photos were cropped, rotated, and given artistic borders
or backgrounds. By the time they appeared in print,
some photos had more in common with a painting
than the unaltered representation of reality that we now
expect a news photograph to convey.

Some publishers took greater liberties than others.
The *New York Graphic* of the 1920s earned the nickname
the *Pornographic* for its frequent use of fabricated images
to illustrate sensational stories. Its circulation swelled
during a bizarre scandal that gripped New York's tabloids
in 1925. A New York socialite who had married his maid
sought an annulment on the grounds that he hadn't
realized his spouse was biracial. During the trial an
attorney instructed the woman to strip so that the jury
could inspect the precise color of her nipples, the idea
being that this would establish both her race and whether
her husband would have been aware of it. Photographers
had been barred from the room, but the *Graphic* was
undeterred. Its artists simply put together an image of
the scene by compositing real headshots of some of the
people involved with photographs of actors standing in
for others. This kind of "composograph" became a
regular feature in the *Graphic*.

★

So when Photoshop and other digital image-manipulation tools came on the scene, they were merely replicating digitally what enterprising artists had been doing to photographs all along. Digital tools might make the fakery easier, and they certainly make photo trickery more accessible to amateur dabblers. But to imagine that they would cause an apocalyptic implosion of the very idea of photographic truth assumes that people always took photographic truth for granted, and it's just now being called into question.

As Mia Fineman documented, the public reception of photography has always been more complicated than that. "Does the camera lie?" Fineman asked. "People have answered this question differently at different times in photography's relatively brief history." As she trawled through the history of photo manipulation, Fineman discovered a cyclical ebb and flow of faith in photography's inherent realism. Faith in photographs fluctuated approximately in tandem with the actual credibility of news photographs.

Initially, Fineman explained, a kind of naive assumption among some practitioners and consumers of photography was that photographs were a pure, unmediated image of reality. William Henry Fox Talbot, an early photography pioneer, published the first commercial book of photography in 1844. He called it *The Pencil of Nature*, writing in the introduction that the images had been "impressed by Nature's hand" by "the mere action of Light upon sensitive paper." Photographs were seen as a kind of "natural magic," as images that created themselves, without the interpretation of an artist.

Yet within a couple of decades, skepticism had set in, Fineman says, as audiences became increasingly aware of just how much interpretation, manipulation, and outright fakery went into supposedly pure photographs.

To take one small example, if you look at a landscape photograph taken in the mid-nineteenth century, chances are good that a large part of it—the sky—is fake. Limitations of early photographic film made it almost impossible to capture both land and sky in a single, correctly exposed frame. The sky would usually come out as a blown-out white void. To produce a more aesthetically appealing final image, photographers employed several inventive solutions. Fluffy clouds could be painted directly onto the photographic negative, or the glass negative could be waved over a flame, producing dark deposits that appeared as wispy white clouds when the negative was developed. A little later, photographers figured out that two negatives could be combined, one exposed for the land and another exposed for the sky.

As Fineman notes, these faked clouds could be "at once truer and less true" than the unmanipulated photographs. The camera, for all its alleged objectivity, simply couldn't capture all the detail that would have been visible to the human eye. The faked clouds might, paradoxically, be closer to what the photographer actually saw when the image was captured. But aesthetic merit often trumped realism. Several artists made a habit of reusing a single dramatic cloudy sky to complement more than one landscape.

Some photographic trickery was less subtle. "Spirit photographers" of the 1860s claimed to be able to capture the translucent, spectral forms of deceased loved ones hovering behind the posed sitter. In 1869, one pioneer of the form, William Mumler, was arrested for fraud. The resulting court case received widespread media coverage, including the testimony of photographic experts who outlined the many tricks photographers could use to achieve the ghostly effects.

The judge eventually dismissed the case against Mumler, though not because he didn't think it was an obvious case of fraud. "I am morally convinced that there may be fraud and deception practiced by the prisoner," he said. He just didn't feel the prosecution had been able to prove, beyond a reasonable doubt, that Mumler had used darkroom trickery rather than capturing real spirits on film. As a writer for the *New York World* quipped, it is "difficult to prove a negative, even a photographic 'negative.'"

Yet the media didn't miss the implications of the case. "Who, henceforth, can trust the accuracy of a photograph?" asked a comically hyperbolic editorial in the *New York World*. "Heretofore, we have been led to believe that nature, the whole of nature, and nothing but nature, could be 'took'; but now whither shall we turn?" the writer swooned. "Photographs have been treasured in a belief that, like figures, they could not lie, but here is a revelation that they may be made to lie with a most deceiving exactness."

The complicated relationship of photographs to reality, Fineman says, was not lost on the public. For the next half a century or so, photography lost the sheen of "natural magic," as photographers pushed the limits of darkroom manipulation techniques, and audiences became increasingly familiar with all the ways photographs can mislead.

Trust in photographs was bolstered to an extent in the early- to mid-twentieth century, Fineman says, as photojournalism became a profession, and photojournalistic ethics and ideals were codified. That news photographs should be published unaltered became the rule rather than the exception. When *Life* magazine relaunched in 1936 with an emphasis on photojournalism, for example, "its policy against substantial retouching was something of a departure," noted Thomas Wheeler in *Phototruth or Photofiction?*, a book about the history and ethics of photojournalism. But the policy soon became the stated industry standard. Respectable newspapers and magazines began to favor printing unretouched photographs, just as the "yellow journalism" of the late nineteenth century gave way to more restrained, factual reporting over sensation and opinion.

Finally, Fineman says, skepticism reemerged in the seventies and eighties, as postmodernism questioned the idea of objective truth and digital manipulation brought renewed attention to the possibility of manipulating images.

"Our current crisis of faith in photography does not signal a break with a previously stable and monolithic belief in the photographic image as a reliable bearer of truth," Fineman wrote. "Just as digital manipulation has precedents in earlier photographic techniques, today's skepticism about the veracity of photographs is part of a dynamic history of belief that reaches back to the inception of the medium."

So viewers haven't always taken photographs at face value, and they never should have. Yet that didn't stop photography from becoming an essential element of

news. "Like journalistic writers and their readers, visual
journalists and their viewers share a set of assumptions
that provides the foundation for photography's long-
lived credibility," argued Thomas Wheeler. Wheeler
called the audience's assumption a "qualified expectation
of reality." What he meant is that we put our faith in
news organizations to the extent that they have earned
our trust though consistent adherence to ethical practices.
That trust is hard-won and easily lost.

Photos, in this respect, are a lot like quotes, Wheeler
argues. A nefarious reporter could easily make up a
quote to mislead readers. Even reliable reporting
usually involves manipulating quotes for publication.
"Edited for clarity and length" is a common disclaimer
at the top of interviews. Sometimes edits are explicitly
acknowledged in the text, such as through ellipses
where a thought has been abbreviated or sentences
strung together in a way that they weren't originally.
Sometimes the changes aren't signposted. In news
articles and television interviews, we know that the
sentence-or-two sound bite probably came from a
much longer interview. We know, when we stop to
think about it, that the journalist isn't necessarily telling
us everything that was said. Yet we expect the end
product to preserve the speaker's "fundamental
meaning," Wheeler says. This is the "qualified
expectation of reality."

We hold news images to the same standard. Despite
rumors to the contrary, we *know* the camera can lie. As
with any reporting, choices are made about what to
cover, how to cover it, what to put in the story, and
what to leave out. These choices are unavoidable.

Responsible news outlets handle the process with care and transparency; less responsible outlets, not so much. Just as a journalist who was discovered misrepresenting what an interview subject said would find his or her credibility diminished, so, too, would a responsible news organization found to have published misleading images.

That's why it was a big deal when *National Geographic* altered a photograph of the great pyramids at Giza for a 1982 cover image. The pyramids were merely moved slightly closer together to fit the vertical cover layout. Years later, *National Geographic* editor Bill Allen defended the alteration, arguing that it hardly misrepresented the reality of the scene; it was "the same effect as if the photographer had walked perhaps fifty yards to the left before taking the photograph." Yet the magazine had been founded on a reputation of photographic authenticity. Even a simple digital change of perspective called that reputation into question. "This reminds all of us just how fragile our credibility is," Allen said. "If you lose it, it's almost impossible to ever get it back. It's why we're such fanatics about disclosure now at *National Geographic*."

Put simply, photographer Pedro Meyer told *Wired* magazine back in 1995, "It isn't trustworthy simply because it's a picture. It is trustworthy if someone we trust made it."

★

So one reason that deepfakes might not lead to the end of all visual credibility is that audiences just aren't as gullible as the feverish concern about deepfakes makes out. We're used to seeing questionable, misleading, or outright fake images. So we take them with a grain of salt.

Another, somewhat darker reason is that if you want to mislead people, you don't need to go to the trouble of faking a photo or a video. Unmanipulated images can do the job just fine.

Maryanne Garry, an educational psychologist with a special interest in memory, has been behind a lot of the research. In one of Garry's studies, she and her colleagues had people play the role of a newspaper editor. They had to read a news article describing a hurricane causing damage on the coast of Mexico. The text of the article mentioned property damage, power outages, floods, and storms. Importantly, however, it made no mention of anyone being injured in the hurricane. Garry asked her volunteer editors to look out for typos in the article, and to decide where would be the best spot to place an accompanying image.

The crucial manipulation was in what the photo showed. One group of pretend editors were given a photo showing a fairly run-down street in the town before the hurricane hit. The second group was given a photo of the same street, from the same vantage point, but taken after the hurricane had passed through. The property damage was evident, but the photo showed no evidence of anyone being injured.

Two days later, Garry invited everyone back into the lab to test their memory of the news article they had read. The participants were good at recognizing claims that had been made in the article they read. But Garry also asked about some claims the article *hadn't* made. Had it reported a woman whose husband lay in the hospital seriously injured by flying debris in the office complex where he worked? Had the article reported that three fishing boats were missing and their crew presumed dead? Neither of these claims had appeared in the article.

A substantial difference emerged between the two groups who had seen the different photos. Just 9 percent of those who saw the "before" photo thought they had read about the injured husband and missing fishermen. Within the group who had seen the "after" photo, more than three times as many people—just under a third— falsely remembered reading those claims in the article. Again, both groups had read the exact same article, and neither had read or seen any evidence of injuries. But the photograph showing property damage led some people to falsely remember stories of injury and possible death.

So a real photograph accompanying a real news article can lead to false memories of what it reported. Another of Garry's studies demonstrated that real photos can help make people believe fake news.

For this study, she had people read a bunch of news headlines from the last three years. Some were true, such as "John Paul Sainthood Process Begins." But a couple were fake news. "Hussein Survives Assassination Attempt in Prison: Bush Denies US Involvement," claimed one. "Blair Under Fire for Botched Baghdad Rescue Attempt; Won't Step Down," the other reported, referring to former British prime minister Tony Blair.

Half of the time, the headlines people read were accompanied by news photographs. The photos deliberately didn't add anything to the stories. For example, the headline about John Paul's sainthood appeared with a

photo of the pope praying and an aerial shot of his funeral.
The fake news about Saddam Hussein appeared with two
photos of the famous toppling of his statue in Baghdad;
the false Blair headline appeared with one photo showing
Blair looking dejected alongside another photo showing
him speaking in Parliament. The photos provided no
evidence about whether each headline was true or false.
They were just photos for the sake of photos.

But that's not how people responded to them. Looking
just at the true headlines, when the headline was not
accompanied by a photo, only about a quarter of the
people said they remembered the event described in the
headline. (Some of the headlines were intentionally
obscure, so you can hardly blame the New Zealanders for
not being familiar with them.) But when the headlines
had been accompanied by photos, the proportion of
people who said they remembered the events rose to
almost half.

More troublingly, the same thing happened with the
fake news headlines. Without photos, only about 15
percent of people said they remembered Hussein's
assassination attempt, or Blair's blunder. With photos,
close to four in ten said they remembered the events,
which had never happened.

Remember, these weren't fake photos. They were just
barely relevant stock images of the people supposedly
involved in the news events. But, like the uninformative
photos of shoelaces and macadamia nuts, the news
photos "led people to immediately and confidently
remember false news events."

★

Not only do you not have to fake pictures of stuff—you might not need pictures at all. Other research shows that merely suggesting that a photo or a video exists might be enough to nudge at least some people toward remembering things that didn't happen.

On October 4, 1992, an El Al cargo plane lost both engines shortly after taking off from Amsterdam's Schiphol Airport. The crew tried to make the wide turn necessary to return to the airport, but the plane didn't make it. It crashed into an eleven-story apartment building in the suburb of Bijlmermeer. The four crew members and thirty-nine people in the building were killed. Within an hour of the crash, news cameras were on the scene, capturing firefighters battling the flames and rescuing people from the building while distraught onlookers searched for friends, family, and neighbors. The footage was played and replayed as the tragedy dominated the national news for days. However, there was no footage of the actual crash. "The most important part of the story in virtually everybody's mind," argued cognitive psychologist Hans Crombag, "must have been based on a mixture of hearsay and inference."

Crombag designed a study, together with colleagues Willem Wagenaar and Peter van Koppen, to test people's memory of the tragic crash. They simply asked people, "Did you see the television film of the moment the plane hit the apartment building?" More than half of the people Crombag asked said yes, they had seen the footage—footage which didn't actually exist.

Crombag was surprised by just how many people could be misled by the simple suggestion. Emboldened, he and his colleagues put together a second study asking

the same question about the nonexistent footage, this
time following it up with questions about specific details
of the video. They asked whether the plane had already
been on fire when it crashed into the building; about the
angle at which it hit; and about whether it disintegrated
or broke apart upon impact. This time, two-thirds of the
people the researchers asked said they remembered seeing
the footage. For each question about some detail of the
nonexistent footage, participants were offered the option
to say, "I can't remember." Yet only half of the people
chose that option; most confidently filled in details of the
footage that they couldn't possibly have seen.

Other researchers have run similar studies, asking
about, for example, nonexistent footage of the car crash
in which Princess Diana died, or about CCTV footage
of a nightclub bombing in Bali. Each time, a third or
more of people said they had seen the footage. Most
were happy to supply details, such as whom they'd been
with when they saw it, whether it was in black and
white or color, and what the image quality was like.

Again, this isn't unique to news images. Even our
memories for our personal experiences are susceptible
to manipulation, with or without faked photographs.
Kimberley Wade, who, back in 2002, had used
Photoshop to convince people they had ridden in a
hot-air balloon as a child, conducted a follow-up study
a few years later. She realized that she couldn't be sure
the faked pictures were responsible for people's false
memories in that earlier study. Without a control
condition in which people *didn't* see a photograph of
themselves riding in a balloon, it's impossible to say
whether *photos* convince people of fake experiences,

over and above simply having a psychologist suggest that it might be true.

So, for her follow-up study, Wade only created fake photos for half of her participants. The other half, she simply presented with a brief description of the time they had taken a hot-air balloon as a child, filling in some pertinent details to make it plausible, such as the person's age, whom they went with in the balloon, and where it had happened: "When you were between 4–6 years old, you and your dad went up in a hot-air balloon in Wanganui. You didn't go far off the ground because the ropes anchoring the balloon were still attached. It was around May/June; a colder season."

She found that the simple, forty-five word suggestion was even more effective than the photographs in getting people to remember the fictitious balloon ride. After a three-week-long interview process, like that she had used in her first study, Wade found that exactly half of the people shown fake photographs remembered the fake balloon ride—just as in her first study. But people shown no photograph, only the brief description, were even more likely to remember the balloon ride. Eight out of ten had some recollection.

Wade had a knack for coming up with catchy titles for her research. Remember, her first paper had been titled "A Picture Is Worth a Thousand Lies." She gave this second paper a title that seemed to respond directly to that first one: "Actually, a Picture Is Worth Less Than 45 Words."

★

"A photograph can be true in the way a sentence can be true," Thomas Wheeler wrote in his study of photojournalistic ethics. "Viewers will believe in its truth as long as they believe it corresponds in a meaningful way to reality."

Anyone can write about something that never happened, but we don't mindlessly believe everything we read. Likewise, almost anyone can fake up a reasonably convincing picture of something that didn't happen, but we know that seeing isn't always believing.

Soon it will be possible for anyone to fabricate videos just as easily. It's understandable why the idea of convincing facsimiles of famous people being made to say things they never said is so concerning. But, at this point, the fear outpaces the evidence of ill effects.

Generally we use new technologies to do what we've always done, just more and better. The tricks early photographers figured out to toy with their images were most often used not for political propaganda, but for fun and profit. As Mia Fineman documented, picture postcards showing—though darkroom trickery—comically oversize fruit loaded on the backs of flatbed trailers, or scantily clad women made to look as if they were riding on the back of butterflies, became enormously popular. Enterprising photographers could make it look as if you had been decapitated while holding your head in your arms, or as if you were shaking hands with your own reflection.

Deepfake technology will be put to the same uses. If the name *deepfake* sounds strangely erotic, perhaps that's because one of its first uses was to create porn videos with celebrities' faces swapped for those of the original actors. That certainly raises troubling issues of its own.

But the vast majority of viral deepfakes to date have been created for harmless shits and giggles. In one, for example, Steve Buscemi's face was pasted onto Jennifer Lawrence's body. ("I've never looked better," Buscemi joked on seeing the video.) In another, comedian Bill Hader's face transforms into that of Arnold Schwarzenegger as Hader slips into and out of a spot-on impersonation of the *Terminator* star. A bunch of deepfakes put Nicolas Cage's face on just about anyone else's body because, I guess, why not?

As David Perlmutter points out, overplaying the supposedly corrosive effects of fake images or video could have harmful consequences of its own. "Whatever the effects of images are, there is clearly a perception among the public, the press, and our leaders that images *are* powerful; this perception can be more influential than its less sensational reality." Proclaiming that truth is dead because deepfakes are upon us could provide a convenient explanation for governments and other authorities wishing to deny the veracity of documentary evidence of atrocities. When the Chinese government denied that ordinary citizens were killed in the 1989 Tiananmen Massacre, despite photographic evidence to the contrary, Perlmutter points out, it relied on the argument that news photographs in the age of digital imaging were inherently questionable. The hyperbolic accusations that videos are no longer evidence of anything could backfire.

The truth about how we respond to images, fake or otherwise, is complex. We can be manipulated by images, but we can also be manipulated without images. Perhaps even more important, nobody is better at manipulating you than you yourself. When it comes to figuring out what's true and what's not, what we see and what we're told is sometimes less important than what we make of it. The fear of deepfakes assumes that seeing is believing. But as we'll explore next, sometimes believing is seeing.

CHAPTER SEVEN

Post-Truth

At eight in the morning on April 20, 1831, William Cullen Bryant strode up Broadway looking for trouble.

He didn't have to look far. Across from City Hall, just a few blocks north of the office of the *Evening Post*, the paper Bryant edited, he spotted the man he was looking for: the editor of the rival *Commercial Advertiser*, William Leete Stone.

Over the clatter of passing horse-drawn carriages and the shouts of street vendors, Bryant called Stone's name. Stone turned around. As soon as he saw Bryant, Stone knew he was in for a fight. The pair had been trading insults on the pages of their respective newspapers for weeks. Evidently Bryant was looking to settle the score.

What Stone didn't know was that, as Bryant had put on his hat to leave the office, he had concealed beneath it a carefully coiled cowhide whip.

What Bryant didn't know was that the cane Stone carried concealed a blade within its bamboo shell.

The feud had started, Bryant wrote afterward, with "some harmless pleasantry." A few weeks earlier a dinner had been thrown in honor of the Federalist congressman Tristam Burges. The dinner had been attended by a number of the city's prominent Federalists, including Stone. When Stone's *Commercial Advertiser* published

Burges's stodgy after-dinner speech in full, Bryant, a staunch anti-Federalist, decided to poke a little fun at it. He published an article about the dinner brimming with highfalutin put-downs. "If there be any soundness in the critical doctrine of Napoléon, that there 'is but a step from the sublime to the ridiculous,'" Bryant wrote, for example, Burges's speech had come "very near to the sublime."

Bryant felt his snarky editorial had been a success. "The town did this paper the honour to be amused with the article," he wrote after the subsequent duel.

Stone, however, hadn't seen the humor. He responded in the pages of his *Commercial Advertiser* by printing a toast that had apparently been given at the dinner, disparaging Bryant's *Evening Post* along with another anti-Federalist paper: "The *Evening Post*, and the *Courier and Enquirer.*—Stupidity and Vulgarity."

In response, the *Evening Post* accused Stone himself of delivering the slanderous remark: "A correspondent informs us that the toast given at the Burgess [sic] dinner and published in the Commercial about ten days afterwards, respecting the Evening Post and the Courier and Enquirer, was given by Col Wm L STONE." The article reprinted the insult, so "that the public may see what kind of toasts this person is in the habit of giving on such occasions."

The next day, Stone sent a letter to Bryant denying the allegation: "This statement is utterly and in all respects untrue. May I therefore request the name of the correspondent who has palmed the falsehood upon you, or am I to understand that you adopt it as your own?" Stone gave Bryant until eleven o'clock to reply.

Bryant duly sent a copy of the letter he had received, but Stone was not placated. In his paper he ran an article calling the letter "a dirty anonymous scrawl, which seems to have been the only authority for the FALSEHOOD thus editorially endorsed by the Evening Post." Then Stone doubled down on the insult. The toast *had* been given at the dinner, he confirmed. "By whom it was given, or by whom written, we know not," he claimed. "But its truth and propriety were so manifest that it was drunk with universal applause."

The next day, the *Evening Post* ran a lengthy article directly accusing Stone of authoring the insulting toast: "The crowning proof on this subject" was "the denial of William L. Stone himself, whose character is such that his denial of a fact affords the strongest presumption of its truth."

Another editorial in the *Commercial Advertiser* put the final nail in the coffin. The editorial stated that Stone had "refuted the calumny of the Evening Post in regard to the authorship of a certain toast, the truth of which seems to have cut the conductors of that paper to the quick." The incident had left "the brand of a significant word spelt with four letters, which it would outrage ears polite to repeat, to blister upon the forehead of William C. Bryant, if a blister can be raised on brass."

Bryant was outraged, but torn over how to respond. Perhaps Stone was counting on Bryant's aversion to notoriety and violence to get away with the grievous public insult. "On the one hand," Bryant mused, "it occurred to me that no glory was to be gained from personal contests between editors—and least of all from one with the individual in question."

On the other hand, fuck that guy. "The most outrageous possible insult had been offered me, and if I submitted to it, it would probably be soon repeated." Honor demanded that Bryant inflict upon Stone "personal chastisement for a personal outrage."

So Bryant coiled his whip, slipped it under his hat, and went striding up Broadway looking for satisfaction. On encountering Stone, Bryant drew out his whip. Stone raised his cane. Bryant replaced his hat, and the editors advanced.

The fight was over almost as quickly as it began. In Stone's telling in the *Commercial Advertiser*, he was attacked from behind without warning, yet managed to heroically wrestle the whip from Bryant's hands before any damage was done.

Bryant's *Evening Post* told it differently. According to an account written by Bryant's editorial assistant William Leggett, who had been present for the scuffle, the pair came to blows simultaneously. Bryant brought the whip down on Stone's shoulders. Stone landed a blow of his cane on Bryant's arm. The cane's bamboo sheath shattered, revealing the blade beneath. Stone thrust the sword at Bryant. Bryant parried and landed a few more licks of the whip. Eventually, the sword was struck from Stone's hand, and three stout onlookers wrestled the whip from Bryant.

More than a hint of bias is in Leggett's account: "One gentleman at the first moment of the attack ran across the street, and seemed disposed to separate the parties. But on being informed of the nature of the affair both he and others who soon gathered to the spot declined interfering, notwithstanding the piteous and repeated cries of Stone, invoking the assistance of the by-standers."

The next day, Bryant wrote an embarrassed but defiant editorial explaining to readers what had happened: "It is with the greatest reluctance that I obtrude any thing relating to my personal concerns on the public. I feel that I owe an apology to society for having, in this instance, taken the law into my own hands." But, in his defense, he wrote, "The outrage was one for which the law affords no redress."

Besides, he suggested, the important thing was that public opinion was on his side. "I am happy to know that grave and good men, whose favorable opinion is an honor wherever it is bestowed, have shown a disposition, when acquainted with the circumstances, to make proper allowances for the difficult position in which I was placed."

★

The Bryant–Stone farrago was not unique. News in the early nineteenth century was a personal business. Political editorializing often descended into personal insults between editors, printed in the pages of their newspapers for their readers' enjoyment. More than once public tussles ensued.

Bryant's assistant William Leggett himself challenged James Watson Webb, of the *Courier and Enquirer*, on Wall Street one afternoon, proclaiming, "Colonel Webb, you are a coward and a scoundrel, and I spit upon you." Leggett then spit upon Webb, as promised, not once but twice; the ensuing fistfight had to be broken up by onlookers. Webb, for his part, referred in print to James Gordon Bennett, of the *New York Herald*, as a "beggar," and physically assaulted Bennett twice in the space of a few months.* Bennett, on another occasion, called Benjamin Day, founder of the *New York Sun*, "the garbage of society." That insult didn't lead to a fist fight; Day's *Sun* merely responded that Bennett's "only chance of dying an upright man will be that of hanging perpendicularly upon a rope." One Brooklyn paper suggested that Walt Whitman, during his stint as editor of the *Brooklyn Daily Eagle*, had kicked an important politician down a flight of stairs and out the door in retaliation for a personal insult. The *Daily Eagle*, after it fired Whitman, dismissed the allegation, though not out of fondness for Whitman: "Whoever knows him will laugh at the idea of *his kicking anybody*, much less a prominent politician. He is too indolent to kick a musketo [*sic*]."

And that was just the New York papers. Partly, in 1830s New York, the animosity among editors was a result of intense competition for readers among the swelling number of penny papers. But even earlier, the editor-reporters of the early United States infused their papers with their personalities and beliefs. Opinions weren't separate from the news, they were the news.

---

* Bennett, however, prevailed over Webb in the war of words. He blithely explained the outcome of the tussle: "My damage is a scratch, about three quarters of an inch in length, on the third finger of the left hand, which I received from the iron railing I was forced against, and three buttons torn from my vest, which any tailor will reinstate for a six-pence. His loss is a rent from top to bottom of a very beautiful black coat, which cost the ruffian $40, and a blow in the face, which may have knocked down his throat some of his infernal teeth for anything I know. Balance in my favor, $39.94."

Impartiality was out of fashion. *Partiality*—what we would now call bias—was to be expected.

"Professions of *impartiality* I shall make none," wrote William Cobbett in the inaugural issue of his *Porcupine's Gazette*, Philadelphia's newest newspaper in 1797. "They are always useless, and are besides perfect nonsense, when used by a news-monger." One who "does not exercise his own judgment, either in admitting or rejecting what is sent to him, is a poor passive tool, and not an editor."

"The printer, who under the specious name of impartiality jumbles both truth and falsehood into the same paper, is either doubtful of his own judgment or is governed by ulterior motives," another editor of the period suggested to his readers.

Papers that appeared insufficiently opinionated found themselves out of favor. Samuel Harrison Smith's *National Intelligencer* promised readers, "It will be his object to be impartial, and to exhibit as they exist, the varying opinions and actions of men." For his efforts, Smith's paper was contemptuously referred to as "Mr. Silky Milky Smith's National Smoothing Plane." According to an 1851 history of the turn-of-the-century news scene, the problem with Smith's *Intelligencer* wasn't the absence of partisan slant, but that it wasn't openly partisan enough. Smith "affected an almost prudish regard to decency and correctness of statement," the historian wrote. Toward his political rivals, however, "very little either of milkiness or silkiness was displayed. The long, formal, pedantic disquisitions in which the editor delighted to indulge, exhibited, indeed, a cold, clammy, political rancor, altogether more detestable and less easy to forgive than the passionate hate and vindictive malice" of other, more openly partisan, papers.

Newspaper editors of the day had several incentives to steer into partisan loyalties. The turn of the nineteenth century was a time of bitter party rivalry in the fledgling United States. Myriad threats to the fledgling nation were perceived from within and without. Being insufficiently partisan, or being loyal to the wrong party, was seen as unpatriotic at best, treasonous at worst.

Financial matters had to be considered, too. Advertising and subscription fees alone were rarely sufficient to sustain a newspaper. Government jobs and printing contracts helped. Personal advancement was also possible. Several editors of the day enjoyed the confidence of politicians they supported. Some papers were "virtual branches of the government," historian Eric Burns noted.

From those early days through the end of the nineteenth century, "the issue of the press's proper role in politics was never resolved," noted Hazel Dicken-Garcia, a professor of journalism who studied journalistic standards in the nineteenth century. "Articles late in the century reveal an inability to comprehend a nonpolitical press." Editors and journalists not infrequently took up political causes, ran for office, and, like Bryant and Stone, got into physical fights over political insults.

Rejecting a neutral reporting of the facts—indeed, *promising* readers bias—sounds odd to modern ears. We expect news to be factual, unbiased, nonpartisan. Current standards of objectivity coalesced in the early twentieth century, as journalism professionalized and developed codes of conduct that emphasized accuracy and neutrality. News providers are often accused of failing to live up to those ideals, but the general agreement is that those are the ideals to be aspired to.

Accordingly, mainstream news organizations generally do all they can to assure readers that they are providing just the facts.

"Give light and the people will find their own way," declares the motto of the Scripps newspaper chain, adopted in 1922.

The motto of the *New York Observer*, on its founding in 1987, was "Nothing sacred but the truth."

"No fear, no favor," declared Mississippi's *Aberdeen Examiner*.

USA Today promises to "deliver news, not noise."*

Even Fox News, widely regarded as suffused with political bias, described itself as "fair and balanced." When Fox dropped the slogan in 2017 the *New York Times* noted that it had long "caused conniptions among liberal critics of Fox News, who viewed it as an intentional needling of anyone who might question the network's view of the news." Fox replaced the slogan with "Most Watched, Most Trusted."

Yet there hasn't exactly been a steady shift from opinion-infused news to staid objectivity. Some of the earliest English-language newspapers, like their current-day descendants, bore mottoes promising nothing but the facts. London's *Mercurius Civicus*, which began publication in 1643, was subtitled *London Intelligencer, or, Truth impartially related from thence to the whole Kingdome, to prevent mis-information.*"

Even earlier, the author of an English newsbook printed in 1548 promised readers, "I shal never admit

---

* Not all news mottoes are so idealistic. The Itawamba County (MS) Times describes itself, endearingly, as "The Only Newspaper in the World That Cares Anything About Itawamba County."

for any affection towards countree or Kyn, to be so partial, as wil wittingly either bolster the falsehood or bery the truthe." (The newsbook went on to describe the Pope as a hideous monster, venomous snake, and the antichrist.)

Elizabeth Mallet, the publisher of the *Daily Courant*, founded in 1702, vowed that the editor would relate the news "fairly and Impartially." He would not "take upon him to give any Comments or Conjectures of his own, but will relate only Matter of Fact; supposing other People to have Sense enough to make Reflections for themselves." This, Mallet argued, would set the paper apart from "the Impertinences of ordinary News-Papers."

★

The tide of objectivity has advanced and receded at various times, in various places, for various reasons. Professions of impartiality aren't a recent innovation, though they never prevented outrageous claims from making it into print. When editors proudly declared their political partiality, they weren't dismissing the idea of truth—they did so in pursuit of truth. One of New York's penny-paper editors, Horace Greeley, captured the complicated relationship between fact and opinion as he reflected on the founding of his paper: "My leading idea was the establishment of a journal removed alike from servile partisanship on the one hand and from gagged, mincing neutrality on the other."

By some appearances, though, the tide may once again be on its way out. In 2016, Oxford Dictionaries declared *post-truth* the word of the year, defining it as "circumstances in which people respond more to feelings and beliefs than to facts." That November, the Poynter Institute noted that the idea that the world had entered a post-truth era had suddenly flourished. It was four months since the referendum that saw Britons vote by a narrow margin to leave the European Union, and a week before Americans went to the polls and narrowly elected Donald Trump president. In those four months, Poynter noted, more than fifty journalists or politicians had issued proclamations about the rise of post-truth politics.

The general thinking behind those allegations was that voters (at least, voters who vote differently from you) have become so blinded by partisanship that they simply reject facts that seem insufficiently amenable to their preferred conception of reality. Truth no longer matters. All that matters is what you believe.

But, to paraphrase Mark Twain commenting on his own alleged demise, rumors of the death of truth appear to be greatly exaggerated. People don't generally believe things they don't think are true. And, as we've seen, most people worry about bias in the news—about opinion masquerading as fact—just as much as they worry about outright fake news. Consumers don't want bias, they want truth. The difficulty is figuring out what's true. As the opinion-infused news of the nineteenth century illustrates, it has always been difficult to separate factual disputes from personal allegiances.

Even today, much as news makers might endeavor to keep fact and opinion apart, by, for example, having separate news and editorial sections, it remains a difficult task. Clark Hoyt, the *New York Times'* public editor from 2007 to 2010, wrote a thoughtful article on the sometimes subtle art of distinguishing fact from opinion.

Hoyt's article was motivated by a letter from a reader—a newspaper editor—lambasting him for not "explaining the difference between a news story and a column of opinion."

"If only it were that simple," Hoyt lamented. "The Times, like most newspapers, long ago ventured far from the safe shores of keeping opinions only on the opinion pages. The news pages are laced with columns, news analysis, criticism, reporter's notebooks, memos, journals and appraisals—all forms that depart from the straightforward presentation of facts and carry the risk of blurring the line between news and opinion."

In an effort to help readers navigate these choppy waters, Hoyt explained, the paper employs various signals when the news pages contain something other than straight news—yet, sometimes, he said, "the newspaper's efforts to define these forms seem strained." Uneven right-hand margins were one such signal, for example. The paper also distinguished between op-ed columns, which contain "opinion," and news columns, which have a "point of view."

"I couldn't figure out the difference between opinion and a point of view," Hoyt admitted, so he asked a colleague who wrote columns with a point of view about it.

"To be honest, I think it is distinction without a difference, and I don't really understand it," the colleague said.

Which is not to say it's necessarily a bad thing to have an element of opinion in news reporting. Suzanne Daley, then the *Times*' national editor, told Hoyt that reporters bring years of accumulated knowledge of their beats to their writing. Sticking merely to the facts would deprive readers of that wisdom, leaving them "with he-said, she-said, and you can't make head or tail of it." Interpreting facts is part of the job.

As usual, blame for the murky blending of fact and opinion doesn't reside solely with news producers. Uneven margins and linguistic distinctions without differences aside, the issue of telling fact from opinion is fundamentally psychological. Dramatic claims about people deserting the idea of truth en masse for a post-truth wasteland misconstrue the mundane challenge each of us faces every day of our lives: figuring out what to believe and what to doubt, what is opinion and what is simple fact.

★

To get to the bottom of how we manage this, we need to start deeper. How do we learn to tell the difference between reality and imagination, true and false, fact and fiction?

To answer that, consider another question: Do children believe in dancing carrots?

Sometimes psychological research is criticized for asking questions to which the answer seems obvious. Sometimes psychologists ask questions no one else would think to ask. "Do children believe in dancing carrots?" is, I think, somehow both.

Anyway, children do not typically believe in dancing carrots. We know this because psychologists have asked children whether they believe in dancing carrots, and the children denied it. "Most preschool-age children seem to be perfectly confident that dancing carrots do not exist in the real world," the researchers reported.

The finding is more noteworthy than it might first appear, however. Dancing carrots notwithstanding, children believe a lot of weird things. If you find yourself in a room with ten children, statistically speaking all but one will tell you that wishing is sometimes an effective way to get what you want. A couple will claim that wishing *always* works.

Probably six or seven members of your juvenile focus group will say they have an imaginary friend. These fictitious friends invariably share the power of invisibility. Some will be said to have additional powers, such as the ability to grant wishes. Most are reported to be magical humans, but some are said to be talking animals. Peak age for imaginary compadres is around five or six; most kids ditch their unreal amigos by age ten.

Even more common than claiming to have imaginary friends is believing in fantastical figures such as Santa, the Tooth Fairy, and the Easter Bunny, not to mention fairies, ghosts, monsters, witches, unicorns, mermaids, and so on.

If you're so inclined, you can even make something up and get kids to believe it. Around Halloween one year, developmental psychologist Jacqueline Woolley and colleagues told a bunch of preschoolers about the Candy Witch, a nice witch who eats candy for every meal. To satisfy the habit, she flies between children's houses on Halloween night and takes the candy children have collected while trick-or-treating and replaces it with a new toy.

Later, Woolley asked the kids whether they thought the Candy Witch was real or pretend, or if they were unsure. Around two-thirds of the children were convinced that the Candy Witch was real. Only a quarter were sure she was made up. The remaining few couldn't decide.

Children's apparent gullibility led some psychologists to see kids as innately magical thinkers, basically unable to distinguish reality from imagination. Jean Piaget, an influential early developmental psychologist, argued that children simply don't have the cognitive ability to tell the difference between their own thoughts and the outside world. If kids can imagine something, according to this view, they assume it's real. Skepticism, one psychologist suggested more recently, "is an adult characteristic acquired, if at all, with age."

This is all pretty flattering to adults. We start out dumb and credulous and gradually learn how to be smart and discerning. It also suggests that, if kids cared about what was going on in the world, they would be suckers for fake news. And it provides a ready-made explanation for why *other people* fall for fake news: they must be credulous rubes, like kids, not smart and skeptical, like us.

But if kids are so dumb, why don't they believe in dancing carrots?

Well, it turns out kids aren't as dumb as all that magical stuff makes it sound. Recent research, much of it by Jacqueline Woolley, the developmental psychologist behind the Candy Witch, reveals that children think a lot about what's real and what's not, making an effort to distinguish reality from magic and make-believe.

From as early as age three, they begin to realize the distinctions between pictures, toys, pretend, and reality. Even the magical stuff kids believe isn't without rules and internal logic. Woolley's research reveals that kids generally know that wishing isn't the same as normal thinking, that fantastical beings must have different qualities from real things, and that their imaginary friends aren't like their real friends.

Rather than believing anything and everything, sometimes kids can be *too* skeptical. It's asking a lot, after all, to expect kids to know that dinosaurs and knights are real but dragons and wizards aren't. Young kids often struggle with the distinctions, rejecting the reality of dinosaurs, for example, because "I've never seen one." In one study, three-year-olds commonly dismissed Michael Jordan as a fictitious being, presumably because they knew most of the things they saw on television were not real.

As they get a little older, children start making some pretty subtle distinctions. By age five or six, for example, most kids will understand that the difference between stage magic, such as the guy pulling a rabbit out of a top hat, and "real" magic. "Magicians can't make a house appear right at the instant—they have to make it by doing mirrors," an eight-year-old in one study explained, but "a fairy can make it appear just like that!"

And children make use of some surprisingly sophisticated strategies to evaluate evidence. You and I would probably agree that we should regard a claim as more or less dubious depending on its source. Turns out even preschoolers get that. They give more credence to adults who have provided correct information in the past, less to people who have given them bad information.

Children even realize that they should put more stock in claims that appear to have scientific validation. In one study, researchers made up something called a Surnit. By way of explanation, they told kids either that "dragons like to try to catch them" or that "scientists like to try to catch them." Kids were more likely to believe the latter.

Kids also use subtle conversational clues to figure out if they should trust a claim. From around age three or four, kids are more likely to believe counterintuitive claims when they're prefaced with a disclaimer such as "You're not going to believe it, but …" Around age nine, kids begin to realize that when adults discuss something that is definitely real, they don't usually say they "believe" in it; the assumption goes unstated. Only when talking about something with potential for disagreement do people tend to say they "believe" something to be true. Accordingly, kids put less faith in those kinds of statements. As a nine-year-old in one study explained, "You can tell they're not real because they said, 'I believe,' you know, like 'I believe in monsters.'"

That children often end up believing nonsense is less a testament to their innate credulity or lack of reasoning skills than to that someone is actively deceiving them: grown-ups.

Parents tell their kids to make a wish and blow out their birthday candles, even adding elaborate "rules," such as "Don't say it out loud or it won't work!" Parents help their kids leave cookies out for Santa, then make sure only a few crumbs are left in the morning. Kids believe in the Easter Bunny, ghosts, fairies, and unicorns because their parents and society give them the message that these things are real and should be believed.

I mentioned the Candy Witch before, as if kids were dumb for believing in the newly made-up creature. But Woolley and her colleagues didn't just stop kids on the street and ask if they believed in some candy-grubbing witch they'd never heard of before. The researchers put a lot of work into planting the mythology of the Candy Witch in the children's minds and making it seem credible. Kids in the study first heard about the Candy Witch from a seemingly trustworthy authority in a generally trusted setting—an adult visitor who was invited to their child-care center. The children's parents, another typically trustworthy source, were instructed to repeat the myth later at home.

Moreover, some kids in the study were treated to an apparent visit by the Candy Witch. Their parents were enlisted in the trickery, planting a piece of Halloween candy under the kid's pillow and switching it out for a toy while the unwitting child slept. Children who were visited by the Candy Witch were, understandably, more likely to believe in her than children who weren't. Slightly older children who received this kind of visit were more likely to subsequently believe in the Candy Witch than younger children because they were better able to construe it—entirely reasonably—as legitimate evidence for the existence of the Candy Witch. Sometimes the smarter you are, the easier you can be fooled.

So if you just make something up, such as carrots that can dance, kids are generally dubious. You could probably get your kids to believe in dancing carrots, if you wanted to, by telling them scientists have discovered a new species of undulating orange vegetable, having the kids make little tap shoes, and playing music by the fridge for the carrots in the crisper drawer to get down to. But it would probably say more about your parenting than your kid's inability to distinguish fantasy from reality.

*

So, for our first decade or so of life, we're by no means infallible when it comes to believing bullshit, but we're at least making a good honest effort to figure out what's true and what's not, using the best evidence available to us. Where we end up believing nonsense, it's often as much a product of active deception by the people we trust as of our limited cognitive abilities.

For all our sophisticated use of evidence in childhood, however, our underlying conception of knowledge is fairly simplistic. As educational psychologist Deanna Kuhn explained, children tend to be "absolutists," meaning that they think that reality is knowable, at least indirectly. Therefore, any claim must be either correct or incorrect. "If you and I disagree, one of us is right and one is wrong," absolutist thinking goes, Kuhn explains. "Resolving the matter is simply a matter of finding out which is which."

Then we reach adolescence, and we begin to realize that people don't just have to be either right or wrong. People have *opinions* about things. Even experts can disagree about what's true and what's not. Everything suddenly appears subjective. Everything is open to interpretation, all knowledge uncertain.

This is sometimes called relativism, in contrast to our earlier absolutism, and it makes the challenge of determining what's true infinitely more difficult. At this point in our intellectual development, Kuhn explains, many of us fall deep into "a poisoned well of doubt." After all, if knowledge consists not of facts but of opinions, and if opinions are basically chosen rather than ascertained from some absolute reality, then by what standard is any one opinion superior to any other, *man?*[*]

Hoisting oneself out of the deep well of doubt "is achieved at much greater effort than the quick and easy fall into its depths," Kuhn goes on. The key lies in reconciling the insights of both absolutism and relativism into a happy middle ground. Yes, all knowledge is uncertain; we can't usually crack reality open and peer directly into its depths to ascertain what's true. Some degree of judgment is required.

But neither is reality an entirely impenetrable black box, making all opinions equally valid. Usually we can measure opinions against reality by some kind of yardstick. "While everyone has a right to their opinion, some opinions are in fact more right than others, to the extent that they are better supported by argument and evidence," Kuhn explains. Kuhn calls this our "evaluativist" phase. Rather than being staunch absolutists or dismissing all knowledge as relative, we realize the necessity of evaluating claims on their merits.

Obviously this is easier said than done. Not everybody makes it out of the well. For those who do, evaluating

---

[*] I remember, embarrassingly, asking my high school chemistry teacher how we could possibly know that atoms and molecules and covalent bonds and all that stuff are real. I was not entirely persuaded by the answer that people had done extensive research and arrived at those conclusions based on the best available evidence. "That's just what *they* think," I thought, and my thought seemed just as valid as any other.

claims on their merits is rarely simple or straightforward. Just look at how rarely scientists can agree on seemingly straightforward questions, such as whether drinking a glass of wine a day is good or bad for you. The world is brimming with claims and evidence. The old cliché goes "Everyone is entitled to their own opinions, but not their own facts." But this implies that facts speak for themselves. They don't. As Michael Kinsley, a political journalist, has pointed out, there are plenty of facts; the trick is making them make sense.

This, it seems, is the cause of much of the trouble when it comes to the news, fake or otherwise. It's not that some people will simply believe any old rubbish. Even as children, we begin developing sophisticated strategies to figure out what's true and what's not. We want to be able to tell the difference between truth and fiction, fact and opinion, and we do our best. Rather, the difficult part is evaluating the myriad claims of fact and opinion, figuring out the appropriate yardsticks against which to measure them.

★

In 2018, the Pew Research Center (which calls itself "a nonpartisan fact tank") put the American public's ability to sort fact from opinion to the test. The findings, Pew reported, "reveal that even this basic task presents a challenge."

Pew presented more than five thousand people with some simple statements. Here they are. Think about how you would label each, either as a claim of fact (regardless of whether you think it is true or false) or as a statement of opinion (regardless of whether you agree or disagree with it).

1. Health care costs per person in the US are the highest in the developed world.
2. Democracy is the greatest form of government.
3. President Barack Obama was born in the United States.
4. Increasing the federal minimum wage to $15 an hour is essential for the health of the US economy.
5. Immigrants who are in the US illegally have some rights under the Constitution.
6. Abortion should be legal in most cases.
7. ISIS lost a significant portion of its territory in Iraq and Syria in 2017.
8. Immigrants who are in the US illegally are a very big problem for the country today.
9. Spending on Social Security, Medicare, and Medicaid make up the largest portion of the US federal budget.
10. Government is almost always wasteful and inefficient.

How do you think you did? If you'd like to check your answers, odd numbers are factual claims and evens are opinion. The key difference, the Pew researchers said, is that the factual claims are formulated such that they can be proved or disproved by objective evidence, while the opinion statements reflect some kind of belief or value. So, for example, there's a right answer as to whether the United States spends more on health care per person than any other country, but whether democracy is the greatest form of government depends on what you mean by *greatest*.

How did the American public do at parsing the facts from the opinions? Well, most people correctly labeled at least three of the five statements in each set. Which sounds pretty good—until you realize it's only slightly better than if everyone had just randomly guessed. "Far fewer Americans got all five correct," Pew reports. "Roughly a quarter got most or all wrong."

On the whole, people did a little better at labeling opinions than facts, though perhaps just because we are generally slightly more inclined to call something an opinion than a fact. A little over a third of people correctly labeled all five opinions, compared to a quarter who classified the five factual statements correctly.

Probing deeper, the survey asked people their own feelings about each statement. If someone called a statement factual, they were then asked if they thought it was accurate or inaccurate. If they called it an opinion, they were asked whether they agreed or disagreed with it. The findings revealed that people's own beliefs played a role in how they labeled the claims.

When someone called a statement factual, that person more often than not said they agreed with the statement. Typically, eight or nine out of ten people who said a statement was factual said they also thought it was accurate. People who called something a claim of fact and then said they thought it was inaccurate were in a small minority. Likewise, people who mistakenly labeled a factual statement as opinion tended to disagree with the statement.

So, for example most (just under eight out of ten) of the people who said "Immigrants who are in the US illegally have some rights under the Constitution" was a factual claim thought it was true. Most of the people (just over eight out of ten) who said it was an opinion thought it was a mistaken opinion.

As you might expect, then, calling claims fact or opinion was sometimes divided along political party lines. Democrats were more likely to call a claim factual when it was more amenable to the left. The same held for Republicans, though to a slightly lesser degree, when the appeal was to the right. Close to four out of ten Democrats said "Increasing the federal minimum wage to $15 an hour is essential for the health of the US economy" was factual, for example, versus just under two in ten Republicans. On the other hand, Republicans were more than twice as likely as Democrats to say "Immigrants who are in the US illegally are a very big problem for the country today" was factual.

Now, possibly this is just a linguistic misunderstanding. In everyday conversation, *fact* and *true* are often used interchangeably. But the researchers intended a more general meaning of *factual*, which would include mistaken claims of fact. So, "the Thames is the world's longest river" would be a factual claim, even though it is false, since it is open to refutation. "The Thames is the world's greatest river," on the other hand, would be opinion, since its not a claim that could be settled by reference to objective evidence.

But Amy Mitchell, the director of journalism research at the Pew Research Center, argued that the findings reflect more than a simple difference of interpretation of the meaning of *factual*. In a Q&A about the study, Mitchell pointed out that the question wording specifically asked people to label the claims regardless of whether they felt each was accurate or inaccurate. Moreover, the researchers tested out several variations on the language used in the question instructions, the wording of the response options, and the number of response options before opening the survey to the public, then incorporated feedback from those tested to figure out the best way to ask the questions.

Overall, the Pew research reveals just how tricky it can be to tell fact and opinion apart, even in the simplest of circumstances. The people who took the survey just had to sort through a handful of short, fairly unambiguous claims. In everyday life, we are bombarded by countless claims, some factual, some opinion, many a mix of fact and opinion.

It's not just that people sometimes mistake opinion for fact and vice versa. More revealing, people's mistakes are somewhat predictable. We see the world through the lens of our existing beliefs. When we think something is true, it looks more like a fact. When we think something isn't true, it looks like an opinion.

When it comes to the news, the Pew researchers point out, these findings raise caution: "News consumers today are confronted with a tangle of statements and assertions that run the gamut from purely factual to purely opinion. Being able to quickly tell where a news statement fits on that spectrum is key to being an informed reader or viewer."

The distorting lens of what we think is true or false, however, warps more than just how we interpret fact and opinion in the news. Our prior beliefs and group allegiances can affect our perception of anything we see.

As we saw in the previous chapter, sometimes seeing can be believing; but often believing is seeing.

Even a football game can become a testing ground for our ability to keep our opinions from clouding the facts.

★

"On a brisk Saturday afternoon, November 23, 1951, the Dartmouth football team played Princeton in Princeton's Palmer Stadium," a report in a 1954 issue of the *Journal of Abnormal and Social Psychology* began. It was the last game of the season for both teams, and Princeton had won all its games. Its star player, Dick Kazmaier, had just appeared on the cover of *Time* magazine and was being considered as an all-American in recognition of his outstanding performance. As he was a graduating senior, this would be his last college game.

The final score was 13–0 in Princeton's favor. But the game was far more noteworthy for how it was played than for its outcome. "A few minutes after the opening kick-off," the authors of the report note dryly, "it became apparent that the game was going to be a rough one." Unfortunately for Kazmaier, he would end this game in the second quarter with a broken nose and a concussion. A Dartmouth player had to be taken off the field with a broken leg. .

Exciting stuff, but its not immediately obvious why a football game would warrant a report in the *Journal of Abnormal Psychology*. What got the attention of the researchers, Albert Hastorf, a Dartmouth professor, and Princeton's Hadley Cantril, was not the game itself, but how fans—the students at each college—reacted to it

"This observer has never seen quite such a disgusting exhibition of so-called 'sport,'" a writer for Princeton's student newspaper, the *Daily Princetonian*, wrote. "Both teams were guilty but the blame must be laid primarily on Dartmouth's doorstep."

Over in the Dartmouth student newspaper's editorial office, however, things looked very different. A writer for the *Dartmouth* claimed that the game had "set the stage for the other type of dirty football. A type which may be termed as an unjustifiable accusation." Sure, Kazmaier got a broken nose, the writer admitted, but that kind of injury was hardly unusual. The real dirty play had come from Princeton. "The game was rough and did get a bit out of hand in the third quarter. Yet most of the roughing penalties were called against Princeton while Dartmouth received more of the illegal-use-of-the-hands variety."

So this is where the abnormal psychology came in. It seemed as if supporters of each side had witnessed a different game. "We took the opportunity presented by the occasion," Hastorf and Cantril wrote, "to make a 'real life' study of a perceptual problem."

A week after the game, they handed out questionnaires to both Dartmouth and Princeton students. Almost every Princeton student said the game had been "rough and dirty." Dartmouth students were not nearly as unanimous. Around four out of ten agreed the game had been rough and dirty, but another four out of ten saw it as "rough and fair." (Hastorf and Cantril hadn't thought to include the option on their survey; the 40 percent of students who saw the game that way went to the trouble of writing it in.) More than a tenth of Dartmouth students went so far as to say the game had been "clean and fair."

Moreover, close to 90 percent of the Princeton students said the Dartmouth team had started the rough play; the other tenth said both teams were equally culpable. Again, over at Dartmouth, students' interpretations were more mixed. A third conceded that Dartmouth had started the trouble, but half claimed both teams had been responsible.

In addition to the questionnaire, Hastorf and Cantril also showed a film of the game to groups of Dartmouth and Princeton students. As they watched the film, the researchers had them make note of any infraction of the rules they saw, and whether the infraction was "mild" or "flagrant." The students' allegiances even affected their basic perception of the video. Dartmouth students saw both teams make about the same number of infractions, though they saw far more flagrant infractions from Princeton than from Dartmouth. Princeton students saw the Dartmouth team make more than twice as many infractions, with far more of them flagrant than Princeton's.

For having been inspired by something as seemingly trivial as a college football game, Hastorf and Cantril's findings are deep, probing the very definition of reality. "In brief," they wrote, "the data here indicate that there is no such 'thing' as a 'game' existing 'out there' in its own right which people merely 'observe.'" Rather, "the 'game' actually was many different games and that each version of the events that transpired was just as 'real' to a particular person as other versions were to other people."

Though the study was published in the *Journal of Abnormal Psychology*, people seeing things differently is anything but abnormal. We each interpret the world through the lens of our experiences, beliefs, fears, and desires. "From this point of view," Hastorf and Cantril concluded, "it is inaccurate and misleading to say that different people have different 'attitudes' concerning the same 'thing.' For the 'thing' simply is not the same for different people whether the 'thing' is a football game, a presidential candidate, Communism, or spinach."

★

Hastorf and Cantril gave their research paper the catchy, enigmatic title "They Saw a Game." In 2012, Dan Kahan and a group of his fellow researchers updated the idea. Their paper was titled "They Saw a Protest."

Actually, there were two protests. One had taken place outside an abortion clinic, where protesters had gathered to oppose legal abortion. The other was outside a military recruiting office; the protesters were demonstrating against the military's then-existing ban on openly gay and lesbian people joining the armed forces.

Kahan holds professorships in both law and psychology at Yale Law School. His background in law led him to frame the study around a basic legal issue. Both protests, Kahan explained to participants in the study, had been shut down by police on the basis of an ordinance prohibiting "obstructing," "intimidating," and "threatening" persons seeking to use the facilities in question. In both cases, the protesters were suing the police on the basis that their freedom of speech had been curtailed. Kahan showed the two hundred or so people who signed up for the study a video of one of the protests and asked them to imagine they were a juror in a court case. The key question was whether the protesters had crossed the line from exercising free speech, which is protected under the US Constitution, to disorderly conduct, in which the police were right to intervene.

Being a psychologist, though, Kahan also designed the study with a trick up its sleeve. There was just one protest, not two. The two groups of people who took part in the study watched the same video of protesters gathered outside a building. One group was told the protest was against abortion, the other was told 'it was against discrimination.

For Kahan to get away with the ruse, the video had to be fairly ambiguous. He and his colleagues blurred the wording of the signs the demonstrators wielded, telling viewers that "the court had ordered the blurring to prevent jurors from being influenced by the messages they contained" because "the U.S. Constitution prohibits the police from breaking up a protest based on the messages the protestors are trying to communicate." A soundtrack of generic crowd noise—a "cacophony of shouts and chants"—was added so that nothing that anyone was actually saying could be made out. (The video was actually of members of the Westboro Baptist Church, an infamously intolerant sect that publicly condemns homosexuality.)

Crucially, the video didn't show much of anything happening, but it left room for interpretation. It was edited, the researchers explained, "to create grounds for opposing conclusions about the key facts." At no point did the film show physical contact between the protesters and bystanders, for instance, though a few passersby in the video seem to be approaching the building only to rethink and veer away from the protesters. The protesters' enthusiastic yelling and gesticulating, and their proximity to the entrance of the abortion clinic/recruiting center, gave reason to suspect that anyone wanting to enter the facility could have felt obstructed or intimidated. Yet, it could equally have been that people avoided entering because they were persuaded by the protesters' message, didn't want to listen to the protesters, or didn't want to be publicly condemned for their behavior.

The crafty editing was successful. Before running the real experiment, Kahan and colleagues showed the video to a group of a hundred lawyers and judges. They agreed that the protest looked plausible enough, and they were evenly split as to whether the protesters had crossed the line into obstruction and intimidation, and thus whether the police had cause for dispersing the protest.

The actual participants in the study were similarly divided, on the whole. Just under half of the people in each group agreed that the police were in the wrong for ordering the protesters to cease the demonstration. More revealing, people's support for the protesters or the police depended, in part, on what kind of protest they thought they were seeing and how it aligned with their political preferences. The majority of Democrats who saw the abortion clinic video said the police had been in the right to shut down the antiabortion protesters, while the majority of Republicans said the police were in the wrong. When people thought they were seeing a protest against military discrimination, however, the trend was reversed: most Republicans supported police intervention, and most Democrats opposed it.

It wasn't just that the mock jurors had a general feeling about who was in the right and who was in the wrong. They fundamentally perceived the video differently. For many of the Democrats watching the abortion protest and Republicans watching the military protest, they "saw" the protesters obstructing people seeking to enter the building, or at least a risk that the protesters might resort to violence if anyone tried to enter. Yet, from the other side of the aisle, people saw the protesters merely trying to persuade people not to go into the building, not to physically interfere with, intimidate, obstruct, or threaten anybody. Some viewers, watching a protest they disagreed with, even "saw" things that hadn't happened, such as protesters shoving and spitting at prospective facility users.

Kahan and colleagues called the phenomenon "cultural cognition," referring to the way that our beliefs and values can unconsciously influence how we perceive the world around us. "Who saw what," they concluded, depended "on the relationship between the demonstrators' causes and the subjects' own values.

"Our subjects all viewed the same video. But what they saw—earnest voicing of dissent intended only to persuade, or physical intimidation calculated to interfere with the freedom of others—depended on the congruence of the protestors' positions with the subjects' own cultural values."

★

All right, maybe we can all be biased in how we see the world. But probably the other side is *more* biased, right?

The psychologist Peter Ditto describes himself as interested in "hot cognition," meaning the kind of psychology where reason meets passion. There's hardly a better testing ground for the collision of reason and passion than contemporary politics.

Ditto and colleagues started out with a simple survey. They asked close to a thousand Americans how well they thought the term *biased* described the average Democrat and the average Republican. Democrats saw the average Republican as substantially more biased than the average Democrat, while Republicans said the average Democrat is more biased than the average Republican.

The trends for Democrats and Republicans were an almost perfect mirror image of each other. On the seven-point rating scale Ditto and colleagues used, people rated supporters of the opposing party, on average, between a five and a six. They didn't see their own party as completely immune from bias, just as substantially less biased than the other team; the average rating for people's own party members was a four.

As Ditto and colleagues note, the finding probably wouldn't come as a surprise to many people: "It is common in political discourse to hear politicians and pundits contrast the biased opinions of their political opponents with their own side's impartial view of the facts." Our political allies, we think, are generally pretty rational, well-informed, and reasonable. Our opponents, on the other hand, must be irrational "low-information voters," blinded by misinformation and partisan bias. Why else would they disagree with us?

But the survey got Ditto wondering about who, if anyone, is right. Does one political team have a monopoly on hypocrisy? Or is bias bipartisan? Or maybe we're all just seeing bias across the aisle where it doesn't exist.

To try to answer the question, Ditto and his colleagues went searching for all the empirical evidence they could find. Specifically, they gathered every study that had been published, and some that hadn't, looking at the extent to which liberals and conservatives evaluate identical information more favorably when it supports their own political beliefs.

The key feature of each study was that, like Kahan's protest study, it presented people with information that appears to support one or the other political side, but is otherwise identical. If people are more favorable when the information appears to support their side of the argument, less favorable when it appears to support the other side, they would be guilty of the kind of partisan bias that each party so often accuses the other side of. If one side routinely demonstrated the bias more than the other, Ditto reasoned, then the difference should shine through when the researchers analyzed the collective findings.

In addition to Kahan and his colleagues' protest study, Ditto and his fellow researchers found fifty other studies using a similar procedure. Some, like Kahan's, merely changed the label attached to some piece of information, making it appear to be from one political team or the other. One, for example, presented participants with identical welfare policies that were said either to be strongly supported by either the majority of congressional Democrats or the majority of congressional Republicans. When the policy was said to be favored by Democrats, self-described Democrats said it was a good policy, and Republicans said it was a bad policy. When the policy was said to be favored by Republicans, the pattern reversed.

Other studies, rather than manipulating the alleged source of information, varied its conclusions. Some, for instance, presented people with scientific evidence supposedly confirming or contesting the efficacy of some policy about, say, the death penalty or gun control measures. Again, when people liked the conclusions, they rated the "evidence" as more persuasive; when they didn't like the conclusions, they rated the evidence as weaker.

All told, the dozens of studies covered policies from farm subsidies, education, and abstinence to medical marijuana and even food irradiation. Others examined people's interpretation of events including protests, campaign tactics, and presidential gaffes.

After quantifying the strength of bias demonstrated by liberals and conservatives in each study, Ditto and colleagues concluded that the people in that initial study were half-right. The other side *is* biased. But what they failed to realize is that their own side is equally biased. There was no statistical difference between liberals and conservatives. Both were slightly, but consistently biased in favor of their own team. "We may simply recognize bias in others better than we see it in ourselves," Ditto and colleagues concluded.

The researchers took pains to point out the potential limitations of their analysis. Important asymmetries could exist between liberal and conservative psychology that their analysis simply couldn't pick up. Although the two sides were equally biased on the whole across a wide range of issues, conservatives' characteristic sensitivity to the risks of sweeping political changes, and, on the other hand, liberals' heightened sensitivity to inequality, could lead the groups to be more or less biased about specific issues. Likewise, the analysis doesn't account for ideological extremity, or more nuanced divisions than simple left–right, conservative–liberal dichotomy. Yet "the fact that neither side is immune to partisan bias may be the more important point than whether one side falls prey to it slightly more than the other."

Ditto and colleagues suggest that their findings shed light on the practical problem of partisan hostility and gridlock, and even, perhaps, receptivity to fake news. "It is increasingly clear in contemporary U.S. politics that liberals and conservatives often hold dramatically different factual beliefs about key political issues," they write. The partisan bias revealed by their review of the research likely contributes to the rise of "alternative facts" they argue, "by leading political partisans to readily accept 'facts' that support their side's positions rather than to carefully scrutinize them. These differences in factual belief can in turn contribute to political conflict and governmental dysfunction by making compromise and negotiation more difficult and fueling corrosive political stereotypes of the other side as deluded, hypo-critical, or just plain dumb."

Ditto also notes an unhappy implication of the findings. It's tempting to think that political disputes can be resolved by simply generating more and better facts. "Our data, however, present a potential obstacle for this proposed solution," Ditto and colleagues note. "Rather than being the final arbiter of truth—the impartial political referee that many people seem to crave"—scientific data is just as easily construed in light of your tribal allegiances as, say, a college football game. "People are less skeptical consumers of information that they want to believe than of information that they do not want to believe, and this pattern is as evident in the political realm as it is in other realms of life that evoke strong emotions, preferences and social allegiances."

The researchers summed up, "The prognosis for eradicating partisan bias with harder data and better education does not seem particularly rosy." Combating political prejudices won't be easy. "But a crucial first step is to recognize our collective vulnerability to perceiving the world in ways that validate our political affinities."

The title of their paper is a bittersweet nod toward reconciliation: "At Least Bias Is Bipartisan."

*

Everyone agrees that fake news is bad. The trouble is that it's harder to agree about which news, specifically, is fake. Facts don't speak for themselves; we're constantly tasked with evaluating the truth of the claims that bombard us from the news and elsewhere. The idea of a "post-truth" society suggests there was once a golden age when everyone could agree about what was true and what wasn't. But that was never the case. To some extent, we can't help being partial; our beliefs and allegiances not only influence how much stock we put in any given claim, but even whether we think of the claim as fact or opinion.

Though the ideas of post-truth and alternative facts have received renewed attention, the challenge isn't new. If anything, maybe we're better off now than in the days when newspaper editors openly flung allegations and insults at one another via their news pages, such as William Cullen Bryant and William Leete Stone. At least lately there haven't been any pubic whippings or fistfights between the editors of the country's most influential papers.

An ironic twist was revealed three decades after William Cullen Bryant's public tangle with Stone. In 1865, Stone's son wrote to Bryant, claiming that his father hadn't even written the insulting editorial that drove Bryant to go looking for Stone with a whip hidden beneath his hat.

Stone's son claimed it had been written by Stone's editorial assistant, Robert Sands, who was a close friend of Bryant's. A scholar who compiled a collection of Bryant's letters suggested it was not wholly unlikely that Sands "touched off the quarrel between the rival editors as a practical joke." Bryant himself noted that Sands possessed an "excessive and unrestrained exuberance" that, on at least one other occasion, had caused Bryant's newspaper embarrassment.

Bryant had spent the intervening years regretting his public tangle with Stone. Not long after the duel, he had written a short story, *Medfield*, about a loosely fictionalized version of himself. Medfield had been a hothead who frequently lost his temper. "If an insult was offered me," he admits, "I returned it with insults still more intolerable; I repaid scorn by bitterer scorn." Even his young daughter came to fear him before her untimely death, which was quickly followed by the death of Medfield's wife. On her deathbed, his wife made him promise to curtail his temper. Yet, insulted a short time later in a newspaper by a rival, he reverts to his old habits, rushing to his writing desk to pen a cutting reply. As he moves the pen, however, he feels the ghostly touch of his wife's hand restraining his own. Thereafter, whenever he embarks on some ill-tempered action, he feels the physical restraint of his promise to his dying wife.

Perhaps we'd all be better off if we had someone looking over our shoulder, pushing us to check our partiality and animosity. Yet our beliefs are often more than mere facts. They are personal. True impartiality is an unattainable ideal. And there's satisfaction, perhaps, in indulging partiality.

Bryant never again got into such vicious editorial debates. Yet *Medfield* hints that his restraint may have been more an effort of will than a change of heart. "I confess to you that with this perpetual restraint upon my actions, this sense of a presence which checks and chastises what is wrong, I am far from happy," Medfield confides. "I feel like a captive in chains, and my spirit yearns after its former freedom. My sole desire and hope is that, by a patient submission to the guidance appointed me, I may become fitted for a state where liberty and virtue are the same, and where in following the rules of duty we shall only pursue a natural and unerring inclination."

Bryant's reply to Stone's son hints at the lingering hostility he harbored about the public insult he had suffered some thirty years earlier. "The filial piety which induces you to exonerate your father from the share which I supposed he took in our quarrel does you honor," Bryant wrote to Stone Jr. "But I am exceedingly pained to learn that it is to be ascribed to *Sands*, from whom, considering the friendly and intimate footing on which we stood I could not have expected it.

"I must, however, accept your account of the matter which, although I hoped I had got rid of any rancor left on my mind by the affair, makes me think more kindly of your father."

CHAPTER EIGHT

Setting the Record Straight

Does the news sometimes get things wrong?

Is the pope Catholic?

Yes, and yes. As the *London Times* pointed out in 2015, the pope was indeed Catholic. The confirmation was necessary because a mistake in an article the day before had cast doubt on the theological credentials of former Pope John Paul II (née Karol Wojtyla). "Karol Wojtyla was referred to in Saturday's Credo column as 'the first non-Catholic pope for 450 years,'" the correction explained. "This should, of course, have read 'non-Italian.' We apologise for the error."

The news industry, built on churning out countless facts and opinions, has a lot of opportunities for mistakes. The simple typo is a regular occurrence. The very first issue of the first newspaper gave the publication date as "The 2. Of Decemember."

In another date-related misprint, the *New York Times* once dated an issue as 1075, rather than 1975. The next day, it issued a lighthearted correction: "In yesterday's issue, The New York Times did not report on riots in Milan and the subsequent murder of the lay religious reformer Erlembald. These events took place in 1075, the year given in the dateline under the nameplate on Page 1 in late editions. The Times regrets both incidents."

Britain's *Guardian* newspaper became so renowned for its prolific typographical gaffes that a satirical magazine dubbed it the *Grauniad*, implying that sooner or later it was bound to misspell its own name. The nickname stuck. This example, from the 1960s, dug out by the *Guardian*'s own style guide editor, is worth quoting in full:

> The Republican National Comittee decided in the spring that its chances of the White House in 1964 would be very slim indeed if it did not capture California, the second largest state, in 1962. Nobody less than its strongest possible vote-getter would do to defeat the incumbent Governor, Edmund (Pat) Brown. When it said this, Mr Nion was looking towards Washington, but the committee was liiking at Mr Nixon. He would have to oick the candidate, and if he oicked another man, eho lost, the party would be loth to nominate for the Preidency a national leader whose influence could not carry his own state in a state election. Yet, if Mr Noxon ran himself and won, he would practiclly forsweat the presidency; for, like allaspiring governors, he has been bocal and bitter about men who use the governor's mansion as a springboard int the White House.

Technology can help. There's no telling how many typos have been averted by spell-checking software. But the technology can occasionally introduce errors of its own. The *Rocky Mountain News* was forced to apologize for getting the name of a local business wrong: "Spellcheck changed the name of Leucadia National Corp. to La-De-Da National Corp. And we published it."

The *Liverpool Daily Post* likewise failed to notice an autocorrect error that inadvertently slandered an innocent organization. "The problem arose when the computer spell checker did not recognize the term 'WNO' (Welsh National Opera)," the erratum explained. "A slip of the finger caused it to be replaced with the word 'winos.'" The correction writer captured the precariousness of depending on technology to avoid error: "It just goes to show that it's hard to beat the good, old-fashioned dictionary."

Autocorrect isn't the only software that can introduce errors. "Because of an editing error involving a satirical text-swapping web browser extension, an earlier version of this article misquoted a passage from an article by the Times reporter Jim Tankersley," a 2018 *New York Times* article explained. "The sentence referred to America's narrowing trade deficit during 'the Great Recession,' not during 'the Time of Shedding and Cold Rocks.'" The correction ended with the sage advice "Pro tip: Disable your 'Millennials to Snake People' extension when copying and pasting."

An editor at *Wired* magazine made the same mistake. "Due to an oversight involving a haphazardly installed Chrome extension during the editing process, the name Donald Trump was erroneously replaced with the phrase 'Someone With Tiny Hands' when this story originally published." The extension's programmer "was tickled, to say the least," *Wired* reported later, that the app he'd cobbled together in about fifty minutes on a whim had led to such a high-profile gaffe. "Clearly," he reflected, "it got picked up and installed by just enough people that you got fucked by it."

Even copying and pasting can be fraught with peril. "Because of an editing error, an article on Monday about a theological battle being fought by Muslim imams and scholars in the West against the Islamic State misstated the Snapchat handle used by Suhaib Webb, one of the Muslim leaders speaking out," the *New York Times* noted in a correction to a May 2016 article. "It is imamsuhaibwebb, not Pimpin4Paradise786."

Misheard interviews are another common cause of corrections. "Because of a transcription error, an article yesterday about Senator Alfonse M. D'Amato's remarks about Judge Lance A. Ito misquoted the Senator at one point in some editions," the *New York Times* admitted, back in 1995. "In his conversation with the radio host Don Imus, he said: 'I mean, this is a disgrace. Judge Ito will be well known.' He did not say, 'Judge Ito with the wet nose.'"

The United Kingdom's *Daily Mail* issued a correction after misquoting the testimony of a man on trial for drunkenly stealing and crashing a speedboat. "Mr Smith said in court, 'I am terribly sorry. I have a dull life and I suddenly wanted to break away.' He did not say, as we reported erroneously, 'I have a dull wife and I suddenly wanted to break away.' We apologize to Mr Smith, and to Mrs Smith."

The *Wall Street Journal* offered this mea culpa after misquoting the Israeli prime minister: "An earlier version of this article incorrectly stated Benjamin Netanyahu said Moses brought water from Iraq. He said the water was brought from a rock."

Then there's the category of error that, in technical psychological jargon, we might call the brain fart: errors made by someone who had the correct information or could have checked, but let a mistake slide by regardless.

The non-Catholic pope seems to fit into this category. It might seem surprising that a whopper like that could slip by unnoticed, though a psychological quirk called—appropriately enough—the Moses effect makes it more understandable. People tend to fail to spot the error in a sentence like "How many animals of each kind did Moses take on the ark?" It wasn't Moses, it was Noah, who built an ark and welcomed aboard two of each animal, according to the Bible story. But the sentence makes enough sense—Moses was in the Bible, too—that, for many people, the error slips beneath the radar. The *non-* in *non-Catholic pope* might sneak by a generally eagle-eyed copy editor like Moses trespassing on Noah's ark.*

The Moses effect can't account for every mistake. Sometimes it's just hard to find the word you're looking for. "Amphibious pitcher makes debut," declared a headline in the *East Oregonian*, referring to a baseball player with the rare ability to pitch both lefty and righty. Obviously the word the headline writer had been looking for was *ambidextrous*, the paper admitted. It titled the correction "Big Frogging Mistake."

Somewhat more subtly, the *Guardian* made an unappetizing gaffe involving a suffix. "In our note on the Channel 4 program *The Sperminator*, page 20, G2, yesterday, we

---

* In the spirit of transparency, let me share a brain-fart of my own. A couple of chapters ago I mentioned Canada's Prime Minister Justin Trudeau. Well, in the first draft of the chapter I had written "Justin Theroux," mixing up the surnames of the Canadian leader and the studly American actor. Thankfully, my copy-editor spotted the mistake—as did my wife, much to her amusement.

referred to the 'sperm doner.' Someone who donates is a donor. A doner is a type of kebab."

Sometimes the wrong word can be a matter of life and death, at least figuratively speaking. In 2005, the *Los Angeles Times* ran a correction: "A Wednesday commentary on the nomination of John R. Bolton to be U.S. ambassador to the United Nations erroneously used the term 'the late Sen. Jesse Helms.' It should have said former Sen. Jesse Helms."

More than once, papers have earnestly reported the death of someone who was still alive. The classic of the genre is Mark Twain's (often misquoted) retort "The report of my death was an exaggeration." Rudyard Kipling also had a pithy response to a magazine that falsely reported his demise: "I've just read that I am dead. Don't forget to delete me from your list of subscribers."

Obituaries, even when the deceased really is dead, are a frequent source of errors. In an early example, the *Boston News Letter* was forced to issue a detailed correction on May 18, 1727. "It being the Design of this Paper to give as fresh & true account of things as may be ; we shall always desire & be ready to receive & publish corrections of the mistakes that we have already published," the paper proclaimed. Then it detailed how it had gotten almost every detail in a recent obituary of an English businessman wrong.

Whereas it was said, He died on *Saturday Morning in the 77 Year of his Age*; it shou'd be more exactly, *On the Evening before the Saturday, at 9 a. Clock, in the 79 Year of his Age*. And whereas it was said, *He was never ingag'd in a Law suit*; It shou'd be, *That he was but seldom ingag'd in the Law; especially considering how long & much* he traded, and with what variety of people. He was indeed a great Friend to the Poor ; But *the Report* of his charging his Children & Executors about them on his Death bed, was an intire mistake : and so was *That Report* concerning his Daughter *Church* at *Freetown*. Nor cou'd either of these be expected of him : For he had done abundantly, both for the Poor & that Daughter of his, in his Life Time.

"An obituary on Gore Vidal on Wednesday included several errors," the *New York Times* admitted more recently.

Mr. Vidal called William F. Buckley Jr. a crypto-Nazi, not a crypto-fascist, in a television appearance during the 1968 Democratic National Convention. While Mr. Vidal frequently joked that Vice President Al Gore was his cousin, genealogists have been unable to confirm that they were related. And according to Mr. Vidal's memoir *Palimpsest*, he and his longtime live-in companion, Howard Austen, had sex the night they met, but did not sleep together after they began living together. It is not the case that they never had sex.

Occasionally, corrections rise to the level of art. A paper once published the following convoluted correction:

The Ottawa Citizen and Southam News wish to apologize for our apology to Mark Steyn, published Oct. 22. In correcting the incorrect statements about Mr. Steyn published Oct. 15, we incorrectly published the incorrect correction. We accept and regret that our original regrets were unacceptable and we apologize to Mr. Steyn for any distress caused by our previous apology.

Craig Silverman, the author of *Regret the Error*, a book about corrections, explains that the bewildering erratum had been dictated by the disgruntled Mr. Steyn, himself a journalist, to make the paper look foolish.

★

These often-amusing, sometimes genuinely damaging mistakes make you wonder, Just how many news stories contain a mistake of some kind?

About half, apparently.

That was the answer Mitchell Charnley arrived at in the first study of newspaper accuracy, published in 1936. He titled his findings, modestly, "Preliminary Notes on a Study of Newspaper Accuracy." Yet Charnley's preliminary estimate appears to hold up surprisingly well.

Before becoming a professor at the University of Minnesota's newly founded school of journalism, Charnley had been a newspaper reporter and magazine editor. As such, he was keenly aware of both sides of the news accuracy debate. "As common as the layman's superficial generalization that 'the newspaper is always wrong' is the newspaper man's defense that the wonder is that so few errors get into print," Charnley wrote in his introduction to the study. "But, as far as I have been able to discover, neither has had reliable information on which to base his belief."

Given that people had been complaining about rampant mistakes and outright lies in newspapers since their inception roughly three centuries earlier, it's perhaps surprising that nobody before Charnley had thought to empirically examine the accuracy of the news. Previously, at least some news producers had paid lip service to the notion of truth and accuracy, but it was more a branding issue than a genuine ethical imperative. Only in the early twentieth century did a professional code of conduct began to coalesce. Journalism schools were flourishing around the United States—Charnley's department at the University of Minnesota had been established just over a decade earlier. The time had finally come to begin auditing news accuracy.

Charnley came up with a deviously simple approach to auditing the accuracy of news. He scoured local newspapers for relatively straightforward, factual reports— announcements, accident and police stories, drives and campaigns, business meetings, community celebrations, speeches and interviews, and the like—rather than opinion-based editorials, where accuracy would be harder to define. Crucially, the stories Charnley selected had to mention somebody who could be identified and contacted. This was how the accuracy of the stories would be determined—by asking the original source of the story if he or she thought it had gotten the story straight.

Charnley ended up with a sample of one thousand stories from three Minneapolis daily newspapers. He mailed copies of articles out to the people they reported on, along with a questionnaire about the story's accuracy and a return envelope. Just under six hundred of the questionnaires were returned.

In the final accounting, Charnley reported, "A few more than half of all the stories returned—319 of 591, or 54 per cent—were entirely accurate." Despite some variation among the three papers, they were all in the same ballpark: the best made an accuracy score of 57 percent; the worst, 52 percent.

If the former newsman was surprised to find that close to half of all the articles he'd mailed out were perceived to contain erroneous information, Charnley didn't let it show: "Only two conclusions seem justified by the data from this comparatively limited survey: That about half—perhaps more than half—of the simple factual news stories appearing in daily papers is completely free from error; and that errors occurring most frequently are those in meaning, in names and in titles." While cautious in his conclusions, Charnley was satisfied with the general approach. "This method of checking newspaper accuracy seems, however, basically sound," he wrote. "If a similar survey could be carried through on a wider scale, checking many more stories and selecting them from areas differing geographically, socially and economically, it seems altogether probable that a reliable body of data concerning newspaper dependability could be built up."

Since Charnley's pioneering study, other researchers have taken him up on the suggestion. These researchers have refined the methodology and broadened the scope of their investigations. The studies have looked at daily and weekly newspapers, both small and large circulation, local and national. Studies have examined not only news coverage, but also science stories, reports about social issues, and wire service coverage. In addition to scrutinizing newspapers, studies have examined the accuracy of television news (which seems to make fewer errors than newspapers) and newsmagazines (which seem to make fewer errors still). Charnley's estimate, that about half of newspaper stories contain some kind of mistake, has proven stubbornly consistent. Estimates of the proportion of stories that contain one or more inaccuracies have ranged between roughly 40 and 60 percent.

One researcher who has taken up Charnley's mantle is Scott Maier. Like Charnley before him, Maier, a journalism professor and former reporter, combined a professional understanding of how and why errors make it into the news with an academic interest in how media inaccuracy affects audiences.

The title of one of Maier's first investigations of news accuracy gives away the key finding: "Getting It Right? Not in 59 Percent of Stories." For that study, he used a procedure similar to Charnley's, sending surveys to a thousand people who had been mentioned in news stories in the *Raleigh (NC) News & Observer.* As the title suggested, the news sources reported errors in more than half of the local news stories they reviewed.

Maier was more pointed about his findings than Charnley had been: "The implications are sobering for anyone who cares about the media. If *The News & Observer*, a Pulitzer prizewinning newspaper rated by the *Columbia Journalism Review* as one of the nation's top 15 dailies, has such difficulty getting its facts straight, one can imagine what the results likely would be for news organizations less committed to quality journalism."

No need to imagine. A few years later, Maier published the results of a considerably more extensive study. This one encompassed close to five thousand stories, clipped from fourteen daily newspapers from across the United States. As in previous studies, Maier mailed the clippings to people mentioned in the stories with a questionnaire asking them to assess their accuracy.

The findings revealed the highest error rate of any study of newspaper accuracy since Charnley kicked off the research seven decades earlier. Of the thirty-two hundred sources who mailed surveys back to Maier, 61 percent disputed the accuracy of the story. Many of the disputed stories contained more than one error; the average was three. Again, some papers did better than others, and different categories of article were more or less error-prone. But even the best paper was found to have made mistakes in more than half of its news stories. The worst managed to avoid error in only a third of its feature news stories.

★

The research allows for a more nuanced dissection of media inaccuracy than simply labeling each story accurate or inaccurate. As Charnley had discovered in his preliminary study, many of the errors identified by news sources were simple slipups over facts, such as typos, misspelling someone's name, or getting details such as titles, ages, or addresses wrong.

Decades later, Scott Maier found that these kinds of simple factual goofs remained stubbornly persistent. Typos accounted for a tenth of all objective errors, only slightly lower than the rate reported by Charnley seventy years prior, despite the introduction of spell-checking software. At least, however, journalists seemed to have become better at spelling people's names correctly; only 3 percent of sources found their names misspelled in 2005, compared to more than a quarter in 1936.

But simple typos and mistaken facts were not the most pressing issue as far as sources were concerned. Charnley had found that "errors in meaning" were the most common single category of mistake that sources pointed out, accounting for a fifth of all the errors they reported. By this, Charnley meant that "the story errs in implication—in the impression it gives the reader, in emphasizing any point unduly or in failing to give any points due emphasis, in omitting information or details necessary to give the reader a fair understanding of its subject." More than a mere factual mistake, he pointed out, perceiving an error of meaning is "a commentary on the skill and understanding—or lack of them—of the news writers who handled the stories."

Maier found that sources perceived these kinds of subjective errors in half of all the news stories he mailed out. Close to a third of the sources said essential information was missing from the story. Almost a quarter complained that they had been misquoted or quoted out of context.

Maier also asked the sources to rate the severity of each type of error. "A cliché in journalism is that what really matters to news sources is that you get their names spelled right," he pointed out. But his data suggested otherwise. While the 3 percent of people who found their names misspelled were probably peeved, they rated the mistake as fairly inconsequential. People were significantly more concerned about misleading headlines, quotations, and numbers. "From the news sources' perspective, getting the facts straight clearly was not sufficient," Maier wrote. "Most bothersome were interpretive mistakes in which news sources believed the newspaper overplayed the story, left out vital information or made other 'errors of meaning.'"

As a former newsman, Charnley, back in 1936, had been quick to point out that these subjective errors are a little trickier to interpret than someone's simply pointing out that his or her name was spelled wrong. "To me it seems that the figure should not be taken at face value," Charnley wrote. People "might declare stories to be deficient in meaning merely because they did not present every fact, no matter how trivial." Journalists and the people they write about necessarily have different perspectives. What a source sees as a mistake, the journalist may deem a fair interpretation or omission. "The layman knows that the newspaper said he was going to spend the week-end with his cousin when he went only for Sunday," Charnley explained; "consequently 'the newspaper is always wrong,' even though his own name, his cousin's and other facts were accurate. The newspaper man, on the other hand, knows the appalling opportunities for error in the smallest story, and his own diligence and success in avoiding many of them."

A few newspapers have undertaken their own internal accuracy surveys. Their findings, where they have been made publicly available, have generally been much more favorable than surveys by academics. In one extensive review of papers' internal accuracy audits, most of the papers found errors in less than one in ten of their own stories—a sharp contrast with Charnley's and his ilk's estimate of one in two. Differences in methodology could account for part of the difference, as might the difference of opinion between sources and journalists. The true rate is probably somewhere between the estimates of the journalists and of the academics.

Whatever the true error rate, it seems fair to say that it is higher than either news makers or consumers would like. But it would hardly be reasonable to expect the news to be entirely error-free. "Reporters and editors make mistakes. Indeed, we are probably more likely than most to do so," wrote Craig Silverman in *Regret the Error*. "For just as bartenders break more glass because they handle more beer, so journalists who traffic in facts are bound to drop some along the way."

The *Montreal Gazette* offered up this type of justification after it printed the wrong lottery numbers one Saturday morning in 2006, causing a reader to momentarily believe he was a millionaire. After the man threatened to sue the paper, it published a frank explanation of the error: "The Gazette publishes about 100,000 words and numbers every day and we simply cannot guarantee all the information's accuracy. In the last 20 years we have published nine corrections of Loto [Loto-Québec] numbers. I wish I could say it was fewer, but then we have published lottery numbers on about 7,200 mornings in that time period."

So, mistakes happen. But, hey, maybe that's just the price of dealing in so many facts. As long as errors get corrected, no harm, no foul, right? Some particularly cynical media critics have even suggested that getting things wrong is good for business. Samuel Butler wrote, in a seventeenth-century satirical portrait of a news writer, that when the facts "do not prove sufficient, he is forced to add a Lye or two of his own making, which does him double Service; for it does not only supply his Occasions for the present, but furnishes him with Matter to fill up Gaps the next Letter with retracting what he wrote before."

If it really is profitable to publish bad information simply to have something to correct the next day, the media doesn't seem to be cashing in. Craig Silverman noted that, in 2005, the *Boston Globe* published close to sixty thousand stories and only just over one thousand corrections, implying that less than 2 percent of all stories contained any errors. In his own research, conducted around the same time, Scott Maier found a correction rate of 3 percent.

Things might be getting better. In 1982, the *New York Times* typically printed just one correction per day. By 2004, that had increased to an average of 9 corrections per day. In 2018, "We published more than 4,100 corrections on digital articles," the *Times* said. "We estimate that hundreds more ran on videos, podcasts and graphics features. Other corrections were published only in print. For perspective: The Times published more than 55,000 articles in 2018, and more than 50 million words." So that works out to around 7 or 8 percent of stories earning corrections—more than the *Boston Globe* in 2005, but still low compared to the proportion of mistakes that studies by Charnley, Maier, and others suggest might be lurking out there. Even allowing that the true rate of errors is lower than the 50 or 60 percent suggested by the large-scale studies, these correction rates still seem low.

"Errors in the press," Maier wrote, "are far more numerous than the 'corrections box' would indicate."

★

Well, any correction has to be a good thing, right? Even if only some fraction of mistakes get corrected, it's better than nothing. The important thing is that we set the record straight. If hearing some bogus claim can incline us to believe it, then being told the claim is bogus should persuade us to disbelieve it. At least in the case of mistakes that are noted and corrected, problem solved. Right?

Unfortunately, one of the earliest and most influential studies to test in a realistic format the efficacy of corrections raised a concerning possibility. Not only might corrections not do much good, the research suggested, they might do actual harm. The researchers coined a term for this: the *backfire effect*.

The study, conducted in 2005 and 2006 by Brendan Nyhan and Jason Reifler, used a fairly straightforward approach to see how well corrections nudge people's beliefs in the right direction. A few hundred people read realistic news stories containing some bogus claim. About half of them also saw a correction attached to the faulty information; the other half didn't.

One story, for example, concerned allegations that Iraq had been harboring weapons of mass destruction in the early 2000s. The correction pointed out, "The Central Intelligence Agency released a report that concludes that Saddam Hussein did not possess stockpiles of illicit weapons at the time of the U.S. invasion in March 2003, nor was any program to produce them under way at the time." A pretty definitive correction, you would think. After reading the article and the accompanying correction, however, some people, particularly conservatives, became *more* confident that Saddam Hussein had been hiding WMDs than people who hadn't read the correction. About a third of the conservatives who read the story without the correction agreed that Iraq had weapons of mass destruction before the US invasion. That almost doubled, to just under two-thirds, among conservatives who saw the correction. Agreement among liberals fell from around a fifth without correction to a tenth after correction.

Likewise, conservatives presented with evidence that President George W. Bush's tax cuts did not increase government revenues ended up more convinced about the benefits of Bush's tax plan than people who read the article without correction. On the other side of the aisle, liberals who read a story claiming that Bush had banned research on stem cells accompanied by a correction clarifying that no such ban existed believed the claim no more and no less than people who didn't read a correction. The correction didn't backfire, but it might as well not have been there at all.

So, that seems like bad news. Not only do corrections apparently fail to correct mistaken beliefs, but in some cases they might actually make misconceptions worse. Nyhan and Reifler's "backfire effect" was widely cited in think pieces on our alleged transition to a "post-truth" society. Craig Silverman, in 2011, called the effect an "entrenched human" failing, lamenting that it "makes it difficult for the press to effectively debunk misinformation. We present facts and evidence, and it often does nothing to change people's minds. In fact, it can make people dig in even more." A 2018 article in the *Guardian* asked, "Why are people today becoming so immune to facts?," citing the backfire effect. To be fair, it wasn't just the media. Other academics were just as enamored of the result: Nyhan and Reifler's paper became the most highly cited article in *Political Behavior*, the journal in which it was published.

The trouble is, the backfire effect might not be real. Or, at least, it might not reflect how most people react to corrections most of the time. When Full Fact, "The UK's Independent Factchecking Charity," fact-checked the backfire effect in 2019, they found that it "is in fact rare, not the norm."

Nyhan himself wrote an op-ed in the *New York Times* in 2016 titled "Fact-Checking Can Change Views? We Rate That as Mostly True."

"Sometimes people will change their minds about the facts," he conceded. "Despite all the hand-wringing, we do not seem to have entered a post-truth era."

The change of heart was the result, in part, of a follow-up study by a different pair of researchers, Ethan Porter and Thomas Wood. They hadn't set out to call the backfire effect into question. They just wanted their study to be bigger and better than Nyhan and Reifler's original because studies with relatively small samples can sometimes produce misleading results. "Originally, when Tom and I designed this study, we anticipated identifying backfire effects across the political and ideological spectrum," Porter told the Poynter Institute. "We thought we would see which issues would prompt liberals to backfire and which issues prompted conservatives to backfire."

But, as is often the case in scientific research, the data did not conform to their expectations. "As time went by and we conducted study after study, we found that no one was exhibiting backfire across any issue," Porter said.

Porter and Wood's research spanned a series of five studies, employing more than ten thousand participants, addressing fifty-two separate polarizing political issues. They used real instances of mistaken factual statements spoken by political leaders from both sides of the aisle. As with Nyhan and Reifler's study, half of the time the participant would be provided with a correction to the misstatement, consisting of neutral data from governmental sources. Half of the time the misinformation would go uncorrected.

For example, one of the statements was Hillary Clinton's assertion that the current "epidemic of gun violence knows no boundaries, knows no limits, of any kind." The correction randomly shown to half of the people who read the story clarified, "In fact, according to the FBI, the number of gun homicides has fallen since the mid 1990s, declining by about 50% between 1994 and 2013."

Another statement was Donald Trump's infamous slander of Mexican immigrants during his 2015 presidential campaign announcement: "When Mexico sends its people, they're not sending their best. They're sending people that have lots of problems, and they're bringing those problems to us. They're bringing drugs. They're bringing crime. They're rapists."

"In fact," the mildly worded but unequivocal corrective noted, "according to the Congressional Research Service, undocumented/illegal immigrants commit crimes at a lower rate than the general population."

Other statements came from the likes of Barack Obama, Bernie Sanders, Marco Rubio, Ted Cruz, and other prominent politicians from both sides of the aisle. The topics of their dubious assertions ranged from taxes and defense spending to teenage pregnancy and abortion. In no case did reading a correction lead people to believe more strongly in the claim. A few corrections didn't shift people's belief in a claim one way or the other, but in the vast majority of cases, the correction reduced people's endorsement of the mistaken claim, just as you'd hope. Conservatives were just as open to correction as liberals, in general—though moderates were generally the most responsive.

"We find that backfire is stubbornly difficult to induce, and is thus unlikely to be a characteristic of the public's relationship to factual information," Porter and Wood concluded. "Overwhelmingly, when presented with factual information that corrects politicians—even when the politician is an ally—the average subject accedes to the correction and distances himself from the inaccurate claim."

After Porter and Wood's surprising failure to replicate Nyhan and Reifler's backfire effect, the four researchers teamed up to conduct another study. In this one, the foursome tested corrections during the 2016 presidential election. In one study, they fact-checked then-candidate Donald Trump's convention acceptance speech after a few weeks. In a second experiment, they had people watch a live debate between Trump and Clinton and fact-checked some of Trump's claims immediately after the broadcast. Again, corrections seemed to do their job. "People express more factually accurate beliefs after exposure to fact-checks," the four researchers wrote, "even when fact-checks target their preferred candidate."

★

So, phew! Seems like corrections help after all. They're by no means a perfect cure for misinformation, but they're considerably better than nothing.

We shouldn't celebrate too quickly, though. Asking whether corrections change people's beliefs in some simple, easily measured way may be somewhat missing the point. It's not just that journalistic mistakes can lead to faulty beliefs about the facts. More important, the perception of error can undermine the media's credibility much more generally. Surveys over the years have found that around two-thirds of Americans think the media ignores or tries to hide its mistakes. "Errors can be forgiven, but confession is required," the American Society of News Editors (ASNE) said, in a report on the public perception of accuracy in the news. "Absent explanations, motives will be presumed."

I got some of those amusing corrections from the beginning of the chapter from the Poynter Institute's annual roundup of corrections, which, they say, is reliably one of their most popular articles of the year. You can see why. Aren't they fun? Non-Catholic pope! Amphibious pitcher! Lol!

In 2017, however, fake news came along to rain on the parade. "The internet ruins everything," Poynter quipped at the beginning of that year's collection of news errors, "even end-of-year listicles. What used to be a generally light-hearted column about the most outrageous corrections issued by media organizations over the past twelve months has to switch gears significantly this year."

Thanks to relentless accusations of mainstream news outlets trafficking in fake news, corrections had become a surprisingly contentious issue, Poynter said. "Media corrections are usually met with a mixture of guffaws and finger-wagging, even though fessing up to errors in public is the best way journalists can hold themselves accountable," another Poynter article earlier in the year had explained. "Something seems to have changed in recent months, however. Corrected articles are being heralded by critics of mainstream media as evidence that they, too, publish fake news."

As a case in point, the Poynter writer noted an unfortunate mistake printed in the *Bryan College-Station Eagle*. A front-page headline had suggested that President Donald Trump was considering replacing his vice president, Mike Pence. In reality, Trump wasn't contemplating ditching his VP; rather, as the article below the headline correctly explained, "President Donald Trump has asked U.S. Army superstar Lt. Gen. H. R. McMaster to serve as the new national security adviser, replacing Michael Flynn." Oops.

Kelly Brown, the editor of the *Eagle*, explained how the error made it into print: "A copy editor responsible for editing and designing eight pages of local and wire copy last night made the mistake. It was one of 25 headlines he wrote during his shift." In fact, the copy editor had written a headline about Vice President Pence before moving on to the main story, about McMaster and Flynn. "The back-up system—having another editor proof that work—failed," Brown admitted. "While we typically have another copy editor working the desk, we're currently shorthanded, which means fewer eyes making certain each sentence, every cutline, and all headlines are accurate."

Like Moses herding animals onto the ark, the mistake was simple enough to go unnoticed. "The Eagle's mistake was not a deliberate untruth or an alternative truth," Brown wrote. "It was an error made on deadline without enough back-up to catch the oversight. That falls on me."

Some readers who noticed the mistake, however, saw sinister intent.

One Facebook commenter wrote, "Fake news at its best. Sometimes I wonder why I continue to subscribe to your paper."

Another wrote, "Right, The Eagle is a typical fake news liberal site that posts propaganda and b.s. How pathetic you are to be so ignorant and unprofessional."

Yet another asked, "How could anyone miss a front page title like that?? Knowing you were against Trump. Just proves there is fake news out there." The comment ended with a sad-face emoji.

Another reader saw the mistake as evidence that "subconsciously, the copy editor must have wished that Pence was being replaced."

Someone else phoned the *Eagle*'s office, Brown said, "and accused us of being the 'alt-left liberal media pushing fake news' and bet that everyone in our newsroom was on Hillary Clinton's payroll."

"Journalism can't afford for corrections to be next victim of 'fake news' frenzy," the Poynter article urged;

"'Lol #fakenews' cannot become a standard, reflexive reaction to media corrections."

And while that's doubtlessly true, it's important to keep the issue in perspective, and not to give undue weight to a vocal minority of kneejerk cynics. Even amid the accusations of fake news, many of the comments on Brown's article explaining the error praised her and the paper for its openness in detailing the gaffe.

"Thanks for owning up to the mistakes," one commenter wrote. "Not sure how many other local publications would be able to take a mistake like this and explain what happened while also taking responsibility with such grace. Good stuff."

Other commenters scoffed at the idea that the mistake revealed any kind of hidden agenda. "Still trying to figure out how the wrong headline helps Hillary, or the left in general," one commenter wrote.

"Hahaha. A caller really said that the Eagle is an alt-left news source and everyone there is on Hillary's payroll? Holy crap. How delusional are people?" asked another.

More than one fellow news worker wrote to admit similar flubs. "Mistakes happen. Having made errors of my own on a copy desk, I immediately thought of the copy editors who missed it. That's the worst feeling in the world."

It's possible that at least some of the people crying "fake news" over the mistaken headline were joking, or piling on for the sheer enjoyment of being unpleasant to someone online. Some people will find something to complain about no matter what. Remember the

Wired writer whose browser extension exchanged the name "Donald Trump" with "Someone With Tiny Hands"? The writer reflected, "Predictably, our error wasn't viewed so kindly by Trump fans, who felt it revealed an unfair institutional bias against their candidate. I can understand that," the writer admitted, "though I could have done without their insinuations about my 'microphallus.'"

★

Nobody really expects reporting to be entirely error-free. "A newspaper with a zero level of factual error is a newspaper that is missing deadlines, taking too few risks or both," wrote Philip Meyer in *The Vanishing Newspaper: Saving Journalism in the Information Age*. "The public, despite the alarms raised in ASNE studies, does not expect newspapers to be perfect. Neither do most of the sources quoted in the paper. The problem is finding the right balance between speed and accuracy, between being comprehensive and being merely interesting."

So even though people complain about the news getting things wrong, and a correction is an admission of error, it is generally reassuring to see an attempt to set the record straight. In one ASNE survey, close to two-thirds of newspaper readers said they felt better about the quality of news coverage when they saw corrections. Only 8 percent said they felt worse. Unfortunately, surveys have found that a similar two-thirds of people think the media ignores or tries to hide its mistakes.

Even fastidiously correcting every mistake wouldn't be a perfect solution, however. Tolerance for error has limits. Whether corrections help or harm the perception of media credibility depends on what kind of mistakes were made, why they were made, and how they were subsequently handled.

A 2017 study by researchers in Sweden examined corrections to online news articles. The faster pace of news online increases the risk of errors, the researchers point out; with the 24-7 news cycle, "the lines between facts and information and interpretations and speculations are becoming increasingly blurred." However, the digital environment also means that errors can be corrected continuously, and that the process of erring and correcting errors could become more transparent.

To see how people felt about different kinds of errors and corrections, the researchers surveyed two thousand or so Swedes. Most claimed to be tolerant of small errors. The researchers gave the example of "a news item about a demonstration running riot, incorrectly describing the number of arrested people as 50, although it eventually turned out to be 49." Two-thirds of people agreed that kind of mistake wasn't a big deal, as long as the information was subsequently corrected.

The way in which it is corrected mattered, though. Most people in the survey—just under two-thirds— thought it was not okay to simply remove erroneous items without somehow informing readers. As long as small errors are inevitable, correcting them transparently, by acknowledging and explaining how the mistake was made, is preferable. Kelly Brown's explanation of the mistaken Pence headline is an admirable case study. It was a relatively trivial error, yet it got corrected as soon as it was noticed in an open, transparent way.

Not all mistakes are so easily forgivable, however. The consensus was that large errors are not okay, even if they get corrected. The Swedish researchers gave the example of "a news item about a demonstration running riot that incorrectly describes the police as using unprovoked violence although the disturbance really started with demonstrators throwing stones at the police and breaking shop windows." Unsurprisingly, nine out of ten people surveyed said that such a mistake going uncorrected would not be acceptable. Yet a substantial majority—three-quarters of people—thought an error like that wasn't okay, even if it was later corrected. The rush to report breaking news was not generally seen as a valid excuse; most of the Swedes surveyed disagreed that it was okay to publish erroneous information in the pursuit of reporting news quickly.

The conclusions of the study are a mix of good and bad news. "If news sites commit errors, the public is quick to forgive them should the errors be corrected and, most importantly, are small," the researchers wrote. Yet corrections are not a cure for every lapse of judgment. Hardly surprisingly, people do not like being fed inaccurate news. Journalists "might be forgiven for getting some of the details wrong, if they eventually get them right," the researchers advised, but "corrections cannot make up for bad journalism in the first place."

★

A wave of "fake news" media backlash may be cresting, but news audiences have always been concerned about mistakes. In the late nineties, the American Society of

Newspaper Editors undertook an extensive study of media credibility. The research included telephone interviews with a representative sample of three thousand Americans, in-person focus groups, and surveys of journalists and editors. The first lesson the research revealed, the report concluded, was that "the public and the press agree that there are too many factual errors and spelling or grammar mistakes in newspapers."

The report is an admirably brutal appraisal of the media's perceived shortcomings: "Even seemingly small errors feed public skepticism about a newspaper's credibility. Each misspelled word, bad apostrophe, garbled grammatical construction, weird cutline, and mislabeled map erodes public confidence in a newspaper's ability to get anything right. One focus group even laughed out loud when asked whether mistakes ever appeared in their paper."

Yet the credibility problem runs deeper even than that accounting suggests. When we think back to the research conducted by Mitchell Charnley, Scott Maier, and others, those simple typos and factual slipups are not the kind of mistakes that most rankle readers. The errors that news sources saw as most egregious were more subjective errors.

It's not that the facts are unimportant. Accuracy "is the foundation upon which everything else builds: context, interpretation, debate, and all of public communication. If the foundation is faulty, everything else is flawed," wrote Bill Kovach and Tom Rosenstiel, two veterans of the news industry, in *The Elements of Journalism*. But "a journalism built merely on accuracy fails to get us far enough," they insisted. It's important and admirable that news organizations issue corrections at all. But when stories do get corrected, it is usually to fix some mistaken fact. Perceived subjective errors, which present the greater threat to credibility, more often go unaddressed.

Reputable news organizations are not unaware of the issue. In an article about its own corrections policy, the *New York Times* noted parenthetically, "(Occasionally we publish an Editors' Note, generally to acknowledge a journalistic lapse other than a factual error: failure to include a response from a company criticized in an article, for example, or the omission of crucial information that might have altered readers' understanding of an issue.)"

It's laudable that the *Times* does this at all. But that it was mentioned as a parenthetical aside in an article focusing on the extensive resources the *Times* devotes to correcting "all its factual errors, large and small (even misspellings of names)," suggests that perhaps an important component is being neglected. Correcting flubbed facts is relatively easy. Providing appropriate context, nuance, and perspective for every story is a different matter.

Even owning up to every outright journalistic lapse would only scratch the surface. As we saw in the previous chapter, our fundamental conception of what is fact and what is opinion can be shaped by what we think is true to begin with. What one reader might see as a purely factual report, another might dismiss as hopelessly biased conjecture. This puts news producers in a delicate predicament. Omitting information that some readers might find relevant invites accusations of bias. On the other hand, bending over backward to incorporate every argument and counterargument invites accusations of bothsidesism, where fringe points of view are given the same weight as scientific consensus. There's no pleasing everybody.

Perhaps what would be pleasing to most is more openness and transparency, not only about mistakes that have been made, but about the entire news gathering and reporting industry—about the pressures and biases and uncertainty that necessarily pervade any attempt to document and explain the "great blooming, buzzing confusion," as the foundational psychologist William James put it, that is the world around us.

Again, this idea is far from new. The *Washington Post* political reporter and Pulitzer Prize winner David S. Broder went so far as to call failure to disclose such formative influences fraud: "The consumer fraud, if you will, begins right at the top, with the flagship of our business, the *New York Times*, and its famous slogan, 'All the News That's Fit to Print.'" In a speech Broder gave at the National Press Club in 1979, he said, "It is a great slogan, but it is also a fraud. Neither the *Times* nor the *Washington Post* nor any other newspaper—let alone the nightly network news shows—has space or time to deal with all the actions taken and the words uttered in the city of Washington with significance for some of its readers or viewers. And that says nothing of what is happening every day in the rest of the country and the world. All of us know as journalists that what we are mainly engaged in deciding is not what to put in but what to leave out."

The fix, Broder suggested, would be to change how the news organization portray their efforts to the reading public. "If we treated our audience with the respect its members deserve, and gave them an accurate understanding of the pressures of time and space under which we work, we could acknowledge the inherent limitations and imperfections in our work—instead of reacting defensively when they are pointed out. We could say plainly what we all know to be the case, that the process of selecting what the reader reads involves not just objective facts but subjective judgments, personal values and, yes, prejudices."

Returning to the *Times'* slogan, Broder suggested that rather than loftily claiming to contain all the news that's fit to print, "I would like to see us say—over and over, until the point has been made—that the newspaper that drops on your doorstep is a partial, hasty, incomplete, inevitably somewhat flawed and inaccurate rendering of some of the things we have heard about in the past 24 hours—distorted, despite our best efforts to eliminate gross bias, by the very process of compression that makes it possible for you to lift it from the doorstep and read it in about an hour… But it's the best we could do under the circumstances, and we will be back tomorrow with a corrected and updated version."

Consistent, proactive transparency could help reassure news audiences that the news is not only accurate, but, more fundamentally, credible. Examining data from an earlier ASNE survey, journalism researchers Cecilie Gaziano and Kristin McGrath found that newspaper and television news audiences' conception of news credibility was broad. Credibility was a product of the extent to which "newspapers and television news are fair, are unbiased, tell the whole story, are accurate, respect people's privacy, watch out after people's interests, are concerned about the community's well-being, separate fact and opinion, can be trusted, are concerned about the public interest, are factual, and have well-trained reporters." Merely patching up facts after they've been mishandled neglects much else of what makes the news appear credible more broadly.

"Perhaps the industry's quest for credibility should focus less on accuracy and more on 'authenticity'—how well each story provides balance, perspective and context," Scott Maier suggested.

Here we are venturing out of the relatively safe waters of what can be demonstrated in the clear-cut experiments that social scientists favor, into murkier depths. As the media scholar Thomas Hanitzsch put it, "The troubled nature of the relationship between news media performance and trust in journalism might well have to do with our quite limited knowledge about the nature of trust and what it essentially means to have trust in an institution." Yet sounding those depths may be the key to the news continuing to serve a valuable role in society, and maintaining the trust of the audiences on which it depends.

The stakes are high. "When the public distrusts what they read and see on the news," Maier wrote, "the media not only lose customers but, research suggests, community and democracy wither as the public becomes increasingly disengaged."

★

Which brings us back to where we started this book. "Fake news," meaning outright lies masquerading as news, is just

the highly visible tip of a much larger iceberg—one that
has been looming for a long time. News audiences are
understandably concerned about plainly fraudulent
information posing as news. But sensationalism, negativity,
bias, inaccurate facts, and misleading interpretations are
just as concerning, and far more pervasive. Focusing our
attention and ire on problems that evidence suggests aren't
as worrying as the breathless media coverage often implies—
echo chambers, deepfakes, information overload—distracts
from the deeper problems with how news is made and
consumed. Endless coverage of crime, scandal, disaster, and
other bad news invites accusations of sensationalism. The
relentless speed of news dictates the definition of
newsworthiness and introduces more opportunities for
error. The vast amount of news reported in the quest to
capture readers' fleeting attention is often framed to fit
existing story moulds, flattening reality by making every
story appear equally important—until the news cycle moves
on to the next one.

As we've seen, there's nothing new about this.
Audiences and critics have been complaining about
these problems for centuries. Yet the blame cannot be
placed entirely on the media. The news is business; it
only sells what people will buy. Despite our protestations,
we keep on reading, drawn to novelty, breaking news,
and blood on the sidewalks. We're quick to call bias on
news that we don't agree with, but more reluctant to
acknowledge bias in the news that we approve of. We're
slower still to realize how our own beliefs shape our
perception of the world to begin with. We may never be
able to agree about the facts if we can't even agree what's
fact and what's opinion.

Fake news is one small niche within the much broader news ecosystem. Deliberately putting out misinformation dressed up as news is emphatically not the same as reputable news outlets making mistakes. Yet every perceived misstep puts a dent in the credibility of the media. Facts are relatively easy to correct. The perception of a media that fails to acknowledge routine sensationalism, negativity, oversimplification and the wide penumbra of uncertainty that surrounds every seemingly incontestable fact is more difficult to fix.

That's the bad news.

The good news is that we don't have to navigate these waters blind. Long before *fake news*, *alternative facts*, and *post-truth* became buzzwords, researchers in the fields of psychology, journalism, communications, political science, economics, sociology, and beyond were probing our complicated relationship with the news. Moreover, history provides a too-often-overlooked guide to the successes and failures of the news industry, its problems and its promise.

Orson Welles didn't invent the idea of fake news, though his pioneering use of radio to shock and delight the people listening to his *War of the Worlds* adaptation certainly shone a light on how we consume news—and how we think other people consume news. The problem was less that so many people fell for Welles's fake news, more that so many people were ready to believe fake news had the potential to topple society. The unexamined question was why news—real or fake—could have that kind of power over us. Or, rather, why we think it has such power over everyone else.

There will always be fake news. Acknowledging the psychological foundations that have made news the way it is could be a step, perhaps, toward understanding not just fake news, but our relationship with news in general. So the next time some prankster—or propagandist or profiteer—uses fake news to try to persuade us that Martians are invading the Eastern Seaboard, that the pope has endorsed an unlikely American presidential candidate, or that any other untruth is news, we can be appropriately skeptical. And, perhaps, we'll have a little more faith in everyone else not to fall for it, too.

References

Chapter 1: Fake News

Page

14 **As Schwartz reports:** Schwartz, A. B. (2015). *Broadcast Hysteria: Orson Welles's War of the Worlds and the Art of Fake News.* New York, NY: Hill and Wang.

14 **just 2 percent of radio-owning households:** Divided reaction to Mars broadcast. (1938, Nov 15). *Broadcasting.* p. 28.

14 **something like 6 million listeners:** Cantril, H. (1966). *The Invasion from Mars: A Study in the Psychology of Panic.* New York, NY: Harper & Row. p. 56.

14 **a small fraction:** Ibid. p. 82. "The regular weekly survey of Hooper, Inc., a commercial research organization checking on the audiences of programs, estimated the ratio of listeners to Orson Welles and Charlie McCarthy as 3.6 to 34.7."

14 **"Most people who heard …":** Schwartz, A. B. (2015). *Broadcast Hysteria: Orson Welles's War of the Worlds and the Art of Fake News.* New York, NY: Hill and Wang. p. 7.

15 **"Of course, when the Martians…":** Ibid. p. 74.

15 **Those who fell for the prank:** Ibid. p. 82.

15 **"The infernal machines…":** Ibid. p. 87.

16 **twelve from people:** Ibid. p. 82.

16 **One listener sued CBS:** Emery, D. (2016, Oct 28). Did the 1938 radio broadcast of 'War of the Worlds' cause a nationwide panic? *Snopes.com.*

16 **a lot of telephone calls and telegrams:** Divided reaction to Mars broadcast. (1938, Nov 15). *Broadcasting.* p. 28.

16 **"Panicked scenes of flight…":** Schwartz, A. B. (2015). *Broadcast Hysteria: Orson Welles's War of the Worlds and the Art of Fake News.* New York, NY: Hill and Wang. p. 83.

16 **Web searches for the term:** See https://trends.google.com/trends/explore?date=all&geo=US&q=fake%20news

16 **"Pope Francis Shocks World…":** Apparently this was the top-performing fake news story in the run-up to the 2016

election: Silverman, C. (2016, Nov 16). This analysis shows how viral fake election news stories outperformed real news on Facebook. *BuzzfeedNews.com*.

16 **"word of the year"**: Hunt, J. (2017, Nov 2017). 'Fake news' named Collins Dictionary's official Word of the Year for 2017. *Independent.co.uk*.

17 **politicians around the world:** Erlanger, S. (2017, Dec 12). 'Fake news,' Trump's obsession, is now a cudgel for strongmen. *NYTimes.com*.

17 **used to refer to satirical news:** Etymology Corner – Collins Word of the Year 2017. (2017, Nov 2). *CollinsDictionary.com*.

17 **"false, often sensational, information..."**: https://www.collinsdictionary.com/us/dictionary/english/fake-news

17 **more than one hundred and fifty times:** Trump cries "fake news" and the world follows. (2018, Feb 5). *WashingtonPost.com*.

17 **"one of the greatest..."**: Quoted in Ibid.

17 **"a poorly-defined..."**: Disinformation and 'fake news': Interim Report: Government Response to the Committee's Fifth Report. (2018, Jul 29). *Publications.Parliament.uk*.

17 **called the term "tainted":** Sullivan, M. (2017, Jan 8). It's time to retire the tainted term 'fake news'. *WashingtonPost.com*.

18 **declared religion the original fake news:** Yuval Noah Harari extract: 'Humans are a post-truth species'. (2018, Aug 5). *TheGuardian.com*.

18 **"say they have lost trust..."**: Ingram, M. (2018, Sep 12). Most Americans say they have lost trust in the media. *CJR.org*.

19 **a Pew research poll:** Mitchell, A., Gottfried, J., Stocking, G., Walker, M., & Fedeli, S. (2019, Jun 5). 3. Americans think made-up news and videos create more confusion than other types of misinformation. *Journalism.org*.

19 **American, British, and Canadian surveys:** McCarthy, N. (2019, Jan 11). America's Most & Least Trusted Professions. *Forbes.com*.
Trust in Professions: Long-term trends. (2017, Nov 29). *Ipsos.com*.
Silverman, C. (2009). *Regret the Error*. New York, NY: Union Square Press.

19 **In 2017, the barometer declared:** 2017 Edelman Trust Barometer. (2017, Jan 21). *Edelman.com*.

19 **"the battle for truth."**: 2018 Edelman Trust Barometer: Global Report. (2018). *Edelman.com*.

20 **"trust at work."**: 2019 Edelman Trust Barometer: Global Report. (2019). *Edelman.com*.

20 **"By many accounts…":** Pavlik, J. V. (2001). News framing
    and new media: Digital tools to re-engage an alienated
    citizenry. In S. D. Reese, O. H. Gandy, & A. E. Grant (Eds.),
    *Framing Public Life: Perspectives on Media and Our
    Understanding of the Social World* (pp. 311–322). New York,
    NY: Lawrence Erlbaum Associates.

21 **"Note to Editors…":** Quoted in Schwartz, A. B. (2015).
    *Broadcast Hysteria: Orson Welles's War of the Worlds and the Art of
    Fake News.* New York, NY: Hill and Wang. p. 94.

21 **Reporters buttonholed Welles:** Maltin, L. (1988). Theatre of
    the Imagination. *MercuryThreatre.info.*

21 **"Mr. And Mrs. America… ":** Quoted in Brown, R. J. (1998).
    *Manipulating the Ether: The Power of Broadcast Radio in Thirties
    America.* Jefferson, NC: McFarland. p. 217.

21 **As Brad Schwartz points out:** Schwartz, A. B. (2015).
    *Broadcast Hysteria: Orson Welles's War of the Worlds and the Art of
    Fake News.* New York, NY: Hill and Wang. p. 94.

21 **front pages of newspapers:** These headlines are all from the
    October 31st, 1938 editions of the papers mentioned.

22 **foreign papers:** The end of the world: The 1938 War of the Worlds
    broadcast and press reaction. (2015, Aug 25). *Blog.BritishNewspaper
    Archive.co.uk.*

23 **An article in Joseph Goebbels's *Der Angriff*:** Quoted in
    U.S. to probe radio scare. (1938, Oct 31). *The Austin Statesman.*
    p. 1.

23 **"The newspapers are correct…":** Thompson, D. (1938, Nov
    2). Mr. Welles and mass delusion. *Daily Boston Globe.* p. 16.

23 **the *Boston Globe* simply reprinted…:** A look back / Mars
    attack panics radio listeners. (1971, May 23). *Boston Globe.* p. 47.

24 **"textbook example…":** Cruz, G. (2008, Oct 30). Orson
    Welles' War of the Worlds. *Time.com.*

24 **"H. G. Wells's *The War of the Worlds*…":** The Editorial Board.
    (2018, Aug 1). Mars close up. *NYTimes.com.*

24 **established in England in the early seventeenth century:**
    See, for example, Stephens, M. (2007). *A History of News.* New
    York, NY: Oxford University Press.

25 **"things true and false…":** Quoted in Muddiman, J. G. (1908).
    A History of English Journalism: To the Foundation of The Gazette.
    London: Longmans, Green, and Co. p. 34.

25 **These shamefull lies…:** Quoted in Sommerville, C. J. (1996).
    *The News Revolution in England: Cultural Dynamics of Daily
    Information.* New York, NY: Oxford University Press. p. 32.

25 **"I saw one once…":** Cleveland, J. (1613–1658). *The Character of a Diurnal-maker.* https://quod.lib.umich.edu/e/eebo/A33421.0 001.001/1:10?rgn=div1;view=fulltext

25 **"lies by the grosse.":** Cleveland, J. (1613–1658). *The Character of a Moderate Intelligencer.* https://quod.lib.umich.edu/e/eebo2/ A79952.0001.001?rgn=main;view=fulltext

25 **"Nothing can now be believed…":** Image 2 of Thomas Jefferson to John Norvell, June 11, 1807. *LOC.gov.*

26 **"The just rewarde…":** Quoted in Dutton, R. (1809). *The Harleian Miscellany, Or A Collection of Scarce, Curious, and Entertaining Pamphlets and Tracts, as Well in Manuscript as in Print, Found in the Late Earl of Oxford's Library: Interspersed with Historical, Political, and Critical Notes. Vol. III.* (1809). London. p. 228.

26 **"I have never published a falsehood.":** Quoted in Silverman, C. (2009). *Regret the Error.* New York, NY: Union Square Press. p. 42.

26 **"the froth and scum…":** Thoreau, H. D. (1906). *The Writings of Henry David Thoreau.* New York, NY: Houghton Mifflin. p. 460.

26 **"ribald slander":** Dickens, C. (1907). *The Works of Charles Dickens,* Vol 12. London: Chapman and Hall. p. 291..

26 **"Here's this morning's…":** Dickens, C. (1844). *The Life and Adventures of Martin Chuzzlewit.* London: Chapman and Hall. p. 193.

27 **"Our duty is…":** Quoted in Paine, A. B. (1912). *Mark Twain, a Biography.* New York, NY: Harper & Brothers. p. 228.

27 **20 percent of people:** The Relationship Among NGOs, Government, Media and Corporate Sector: Proprietary Research by Strategy One and Edelman PR Worldwide. (2001). *Edelman.com.*

27 **since 1983:** Trust in Professions: Long-term trends. (2017, Nov 29). *Ipsos.com.*

27 **a 1985 American survey:** McGrath, K., & Gaziano, C. (1986). Dimensions of media credibility: Highlights of the 1985 ASNE survey. *Newspaper Research Journal, 7(2),* 55–67.

27 **Another survey of American public opinion:** Smith, Tom W., Davern, Michael, Freese, Jeremy, and Morgan, Stephen, General Social Surveys, 1972-2018 [machine-readable data file] / Principal Investigator, Smith, Tom W.; Co-Principal Investigators, Michael Davern, Jeremy Freese, and Stephen Morgan; Sponsored by National Science Foundation. --NORC ed.-- Chicago: NORC, 2018: NORC at the University of Chicago [producer and distributor]. Data accessed from the GSS Data Explorer website at gssdataexplorer.norc.org.

28 **The moniker was based on a 1972 poll:** O'Connor, J. J. (1972, May 25). TV: Diverse ventures in news and public affairs. *New York Times.* p. 91. See also, Shafer, J. (2009, Jul 21). Why I didn't trust Walter Cronkite. *Slate.com.*

28 **"For reasons not entirely clear…":** Plissner, M. (1999). *The Control Room: How Television Calls the Shots in Presidential Elections.* New York, NY: The Free Press. p. 218.

28 **"one screaming mess…":** Pavlik, J. V. (2001). News framing and new media: Digital tools to re-engage an alienated citizenry. In S. D. Reese, O. H. Gandy, & A. E. Grant (Eds.), Framing Public Life: Perspectives on Media and Our Understanding of the Social World (pp. 311–322). New York, NY: Lawrence Erlbaum Associates.

28 **"No other profession…":** Colby, F. M. (1902). Attacking the newspapers. *The Bookman, Aug,* pp. 534–535.

29 **"As a staunch…":** Quoted in Schwartz, A. B. (2015). *Broadcast Hysteria: Orson Welles's War of the Worlds and the Art of Fake News.* New York, NY: Hill and Wang. p. 160.

29 **"Of course, with an elementary…":** Ibid. p. 83.

30 **"I suppose that by this time…":** Potter, L. A. (2003). "Jitterbugs" and "crack-pots": Letters to the FCC about the "War of the Worlds" broadcast. *Prologue Magazine, 35 (3). Archives.gov.*

30 **"molli coddled jitterbugs…":** Quoted in Schwartz, A. B. (2015). *Broadcast Hysteria: Orson Welles's War of the Worlds and the Art of Fake News.* New York, NY: Hill and Wang. p. 160.

30 **"Any normally intelligent man…":** The gullible radio public. (1938, Nov 10). *Chicago Daily Tribune.* p. 16.

30 **"Nothing whatever…":** Thompson, D. (1938, Nov 2). Mr. Welles and mass delusion. *Daily Boston Globe.* p. 16.

30 **"frothy craperoo":** Quoted in Schwartz, A. B. (2015). *Broadcast Hysteria: Orson Welles's War of the Worlds and the Art of Fake News.* New York, NY: Hill and Wang. p. 67.

31 **"moronic and inane.":** Quoted in Ibid. p. 67.

31 **"Perhaps this will be a lesson…":** Quoted in Ibid. p. 68.

31 **"Milwaukeeans are a canny lot…":** Quoted in Ibid. p. 101.

31 **The *Austin Statesman* reported:** US to probe radio scare. (1938, Oct 31). *The Austin Statesman.* p. 11.

32 **"Panic swept one apartment house…":** Quoted in 'War of the Worlds' broadcast causes chaos in 1938. (2015, Oct 29). *NYDailyNews.com.*

32 **"gripped impressionable Harlemites"**: Andrews, M. (1938, Oct 31). Monsters of Mars stampede radiotic America. *Washington Post.* p. 12.

32 **"the parlor churches..."**: Radio listeners in panic, taking war drama as fact. (1938, Oct 31). *New York Times.* p. 4.

32 **"Weeping and hysterical women..."**: Quoted in Radio play terrifies nation. (1938, Oct 31). *Daily Boston Globe.* p. 10.

32 **"Freshmen in a Mary Washington College..."**: Associated Press. (1938, Oct 31). Thousands flee, pray and weep as radio war play panics U.S. *The Baltimore Sun.* p. 2.

32 **"In girls' schools..."**: Andrews, M. (1938, Oct 31). Monsters of Mars stampede radiotic America. *Washington Post.* p. 12.

33 **"Rocket From Mars Misses Barnard."**: Ackerman, J. (1938, Nov 4). Rocket from Mars misses Barnard. *Barnard Bulletin.* pp. 1, 3.

33 **An article on Lifehacker.com**: Ocampo, J. (2019, Jul 25). How to stop your parents from sharing fake news online. *Lifehacker.com.*

33 **people "transformed"**: O'Neil, L. (2019, Apr 9). What I've learned from collecting stories of people whose loved ones were transformed by Fox News. *NYMag.com.*

34 **commercials**: Though the third-person effect seems to be weaker in the context of advertising than other types of communication, like news: Eisend, M. (2017). The third-person effect in advertising: A meta-analysis. *Journal of Advertising, 46(3)*, 377–394.

34 **political ads and debates**: Perloff, R. M. (1993). Third-person effect research 1983–1992: A review and synthesis. *International Journal of Public Opinion Research,* 5(2), 167–184.

34 **news stories**: Kim, H. (2016). The role of emotions and culture in the third-person effect process of news coverage of election poll results. *Communication Research, 43(1),* 109–130.
Lo, V., Wei, R., Lu, H.-Y., & Hou, H.-Y. (2015). Perceived issue importance, information processing, and third-person effect of news about the imported U.S. beef controversy. *International Journal of Public Opinion Research, 27(3),* 341–360.
Perloff, R. M. (1989). Ego-involvement and the third person effect of televised news coverage. *Communication Research, 16(2),* 236–262.

34 **works of fiction**: Perloff, R. M. (1993). Third-person effect research 1983–1992: A review and synthesis. *International Journal of Public Opinion Research, 5(2),* 167–184.

34 **conspiracy theories:** Douglas, K. M., & Sutton, R. M. (2008). The hidden impact of conspiracy theories: Perceived and actual influence of theories surrounding the death of Princess Diana. *Journal of Social Psychology, 148(2),* 210–221.

34 *more* **open to having our minds changed:** Golan, G. J., & Day, A. G. (2008). The first-person effect and its behavioral consequences: A new trend in the twenty-five year history of third-person effect research. *Mass Communication and Society, 11(4),* 539–556.

34 *third person effect:* Davison, W. P. (1983). The third-person effect in communication. *The Public Opinion Quarterly, 47(1),* 1–15.

35 **think of other people as less rational:** Cohen, G. L. (2003). Party over policy: The dominating impact of group influence on political beliefs. *Journal of Personality and Social Psychology, 85(5),* 808–822.

35 **the territory of fake news:** Jang, S. M., & Kim, J. K. (2018). Third person effects of fake news: Fake news regulation and media literacy interventions. *Computers in Human Behavior, 80,* 295–302.

35 **more vulnerable to the risks of social media:** Lev-On, A. (2017). The third-person effect on Facebook: The significance of perceived proficiency. *Telematics and Informatics, 34(4),* 252–260.

36 **The angrier we are:** Kim, H. (2016). The role of emotions and culture in the third-person effect process of news coverage of election poll results. *Communication Research, 43(1),* 109–130.

36 **and the more personally invested we feel:** Perloff, R. M. (1989). Ego-involvement and the third person effect of televised news coverage. *Communication Research, 16(2),* 236–262.

36 **researchers asked people in the area:** Johnson, M., Goidel, K., & Climek, M. (2014). The decline of daily newspapers and the third-person effect. *Social Science Quarterly, 95(5),* 1245–1258.

36 **More than half of the people in one survey:** Mitchell, A., Gottfried, J., Stocking, G., Walker, M., & Fedeli, S. (2019, Jun 5). 3. Americans think made-up news and videos create more confusion than other types of misinformation. *Journalism.org.*

36 **In a later reflection:** Davison, W. P. (1996). The third-person effect revisited. *International Journal of Public Opinion Research, 8(2),* 113–119.

37 **"A twist of the dial…":** Thompson, D. (1938, Nov 2). Mr. Welles and mass delusion. *Daily Boston Globe.* p. 16.

38 **picked it out on a map at random:** Schwartz, A. B. (2015). *Broadcast Hysteria: Orson Welles's War of the Worlds and the Art of Fake News.* New York, NY: Hill and Wang. p. 49.

39 **impression of President FDR's distinctive voice:** Ibid. pp. 78–79.

39 **"the most dramatic…":** Gabler, N. (1995). *Winchell: Gossip, Power and the Culture of Celebrity.* New York, NY: Vintage Books. p. 281.

39 **People calling newspaper switchboards:** E.g. Radio listeners in panic, taking war drama as fact. (1938, Oct 31). *New York Times.* p. 4.

39 **"For a long time… ":** Radio panic shows public jittery, Prof. Vaughan says. (1938, Nov 1). *Daily Boston Globe.* p. 5.

40 **"Monsters of Mars on a Meteor…":** Andrews, M. (1938, Oct 31). Monsters of Mars stampede radiotic America. *Washington Post.* p. 12.

40 **"a disease of the hand…":** Quoted in Schwartz, A. B. (2015). *Broadcast Hysteria: Orson Welles's War of the Worlds and the Art of Fake News.* New York, NY: Hill and Wang. p. 68.

41 **"By and large…":** The gullible radio public. (1938, Nov 10). *Chicago Daily Tribune.* p. 16.

41 **heard about the apparent invasion from friends:** Schwartz, A. B. (2015). *Broadcast Hysteria: Orson Welles's War of the Worlds and the Art of Fake News.* New York, NY: Hill and Wang. p. 68.

42 **"'My God,' roared one inquirer…":** Radio listeners in panic, taking war drama as fact. (1938, Oct 31). *New York Times.* p. 4.

42 **"Too bad really…":** Quoted in Schwartz, A. B. (2015). *Broadcast Hysteria: Orson Welles's War of the Worlds and the Art of Fake News.* New York, NY: Hill and Wang. p. 11.

Chapter 2: Bad News

Page

43 **The quick fade-in from black:** *ABC World News Tonight with David Muir.* Friday, May 17, 2019. Available online at https://archive.org/details/KGO_20190517_223000_ABC_World_News_Tonight_With_David_Muir/start/0/end/60

45 **I collected a year's worth of headline stories:** I gathered these from NexisUni. Because the database was missing the synopses of a few shows, I ended up with the chyrons and scripted comments from the introduction to each night's newscast for 340 broadcasts, spanning July 1, 2018 to July 4, 2019.

47 **A 1981 series of articles in the *Boston Globe*:** Thomas, J. (1981, Nov 10). What's going on in Boston TV?; Can Channel 7 close the gap? *Boston Globe.*

48 **"such tactics are those of desperation.":** Preparing for a Boston news war. (1982, Jul 19). *Broadcasting,* p. 63.

48   **"The 'if it bleeds, it leads' ethic…"**: Siegel, E. (1983, Nov
     30). 'Generic news' not funny. *Boston Globe*. p. 44.
48   **"A typical local news show begins with…"**: Cohen, R.
     (1986, Nov 16). No news is bad news. *Washington Post*. p. 9.
49   **"'If it bleeds, it leads' is Channel 5's unwritten policy…"**:
     Cartwright, G. (1984, Feb). Rating TV news: The good, the bad,
     and the merely pretty. *Texas Monthly*. p 104.
49   **"Grins, Gore and Videotape."**: Pooley, E. (1989, Oct 9).
     Grins, gore, and videotape. *New York*. p. 36.
50   **a 1990 *Newsweek* list of "buzzwords"**: Buzzwords. (1990,
     May 7). *Newsweek*. p. 8.
50   **the phrase showed up in the pages of the *New York Times***:
     Rosenthal, A. M. (1990, May 17). On my mind; Mayor, media,
     mongers. *New York Times*. p. 29.
51   **"Perhaps we should examine…"**: Rich, S. (1986, Jul 30).
     Revere's good side. *Boston Globe*. p. 14.
51   **"the old news adage."** Schulte, B. (2015, Aug 18). A great tip
     for improving your day: Start it by reading 'transformative' news,
     researchers find. *WashingtonPost.com*.
52   **"I hear new news every day…"**: Burton, R. (1621/1855).
     The Anatomy of Melancholy. Philadelphia, PA: J. W. Moore.
     p. 17.
53   **"The sixteenth century loved a murder…"**: Shaaber, M. A.
     (1929). *Some Forerunners of the Newspaper in England, 1476-1622*.
     Philadelphia, PA: University of Pennsylvania Press. p. 141.
53   **"the goriest single-crime story…"**: Frank, J. (1961). *The
     Beginnings of the English Newspaper: 1620-1660*. Cambridge, MA:
     Harvard University Press. p. 239.
54   **"abound in Police Intelligence…"**: Quoted in Stephens, M.
     (2007). *A History of News*. New York, NY: Oxford University
     Press. p. 185.
54   **"A Generation of Vipers"**: Starobin, P. (1995). A generation of
     vipers: Journalists and the new cynicism. *Columbia Journalism
     Review, 33*, p. 25.
55   **"It is nothing strange that men…"**: Quoted in Protess, D.
     (1991). *The Journalism of Outrage: Investigative Reporting in America*.
     New York, NY: Guilford Press. p. 30.
55   **"The sanctimony is…"**: Gopnik, A. (1994, Dec 12). Read all
     about it. *New Yorker*. pp. 86–87.
56   **President Theodore Roosevelt:** Retrieved from https://
     voicesofdemocracy.umd.edu/wp-content/uploads/2014/07/
     heyse-roosevelt-muckrake-ii1.pdf

56   **"The highest and primary obligation..."**: Retrieved from
     https://www.spj.org/pdf/spj-code-of-ethics.pdf
56   **Joseph Mitchell, a New York newspaper reporter, wrote:**
     Mitchell, J. (1938/2008). *Up in the Old Hotel.* New York, NY:
     Vintage. p. 137.
57   **"The public is interested..."**: Quoted in Taft, W. H.
     (1986/2016). *Encyclopedia of Twentieth Century Journalists.* New
     York, NY: Routledge. pp. 207–208.
57   **"they're thought to boost ratings..."**: Pooley, E. (1989, Oct
     9). Grins, gore, and videotape. *New York.* p. 42.
57   **In a 1985 survey:** Cited in Stone, G., Hartung, B., & Jensen, D.
     (1987). Local TV news and the good-bad dyad. *Journalism & Mass
     Communication Quarterly, 64,* 37–44.
57   **a Times Mirror poll:** Cited in Hume, E. (1995). *Tabloids, Talk
     Radio, and the Future of News: Technology's Impact on Journalism.*
     Washington, D.C.: The Annenberg Washington Program in
     Communications Policy Studies of Northwestern University.
58   **"People always say they want to hear..."**: Pooley, E. (1989,
     Oct 9). Grins, gore, and videotape. *New York.* pp. 42–43.
58   **"bad is stronger than good":** Baumeister, R. F., Bratslavsky,
     E., Finkenauer, C., & Vohs, K. D. (2001). Bad is stronger than
     good. *Review of General Psychology, 5(4),* 323–370.
58   **the opportunity to wear a sweater:** An example along
     these lines was used by Bruce Hood in Hood, B. (2009).
     Supersense: From superstition to religion-the brain science of belief.
     London: Hachette UK.
59   **his experiment with fruit juice and a cockroach:** Rozin, P.,
     Millman, L., & Nemeroff, C. (1986). Operation of the laws of
     sympathetic magic in disgust and other domains. *Journal of
     Personality and Social Psychology, 50(4),* 703–712.
61   **a later review paper:** Rozin, P., & Royzman, E. B. (2001).
     Negativity bias, negativity dominance, and contagion. *Personality
     & Social Psychology Review,* 5(4), 296–320.
61   **So in another study:** Rozin, P., Millman, L., & Nemeroff, C.
     (1986). Operation of the laws of sympathetic magic in disgust
     and other domains. *Journal of Personality and Social Psychology,
     50(4),* 703–712.; see also Rozin, P., Nemeroff, C., Wane, M., &
     Sherrod, A. (1989). Operation of the sympathetic magical law of
     contagion in interpersonal attitudes among Americans. *Bulletin of
     the Psychonomic Society, 27(4),* 367–370.
62   **In their review paper, Rozin and Royzman:** Rozin, P., &
     Royzman, E. B. (2001). Negativity bias, negativity dominance,

and contagion. *Personality & Social Psychology Review, 5(4)*, 296–320.

63 **how we view the people around us:** See Baumeister, R. F., Bratslavsky, E., Finkenauer, C., & Vohs, K. D. (2001). Bad is stronger than good. *Review of General Psychology, 5(4)*, 323–370.

63 **industrious, critical, warm, practical, and determined:** Asch, S. E. (1946). Forming impressions of personality. *Journal of Abnormal and Social Psychology, 41(3)*, 258.

64 **French college students:** Finkenauer, C., & Rime, B. (1998). Socially shared emotional experiences vs. emotional experiences kept secret: Differential characteristics and consequences. *Journal of Social and Clinical Psychology, 17(3)*, 295–318.

64 **American college students:** Klinger, E., Barta, S. G., & Maxeiner, M. E. (1981). Motivational correlates of thought content frequency and commitment. *Journal of Personality and Social Psychology, 39(6)*, 1222.

64 **looking either at pictures of death and violence:** Oosterwijk, S. (2017). Choosing the negative: A behavioral demonstration of morbid curiosity. *PLOS ONE, 12(7)*, e0178399.

65 **longer than pictures of good stuff:** Fiske, S. T. (1980). Attention and weight in person perception: The impact of negative and extreme behavior. *Journal of Personality and Social Psychology, 38(6)*, 889–906.

65 **Angry and threatening faces "pop out":** Pinkham, A. E., Griffin, M., Baron, R., Sasson, N. J., & Gur, R. C. (2010). The face in the crowd effect: Anger superiority when using real faces and multiple identities. *Emotion, 10(1)*, 141.

65 **We're quicker to respond:** Pratto, F., & John, O. P. (1992). Automatic vigilance: The attention-grabbing power of negative social information. *Journal of Personality and Social Psychology, 61(3)*, 380.

65 **We remember bad experiences:** See Baumeister, R. F., Bratslavsky, E., Finkenauer, C., & Vohs, K. D. (2001). Bad is stronger than good. *Review of General Psychology, 5(4)*, 323–370.

65 **we learn better when punished:** Ibid.

65 **Kimmo Eriksson and Julie Coultas:** Eriksson, K., & Coultas, J. C. (2014). Corpses, maggots, poodles and rats: Emotional selection operating in three phases of cultural transmission of urban legends. *Journal of Cognition & Culture, 14*, 1–26.

67 **Keely Bebbington and her colleagues:** Bebbington, K., MacLeod, C., Ellison, T. M., & Fay, N. (2017). The sky is falling:

Evidence of a negativity bias in the social transmission of
information. *Evolution and Human Behavior, 38(1),* 92–101.
69 **no novels about happy marriages:** Fiedler, L.A. (1966/1982).
Love and Death in the American Novel. New York, NY: Stein & Day.
69 **20 or 30 percent:** Meffert, M. F., Chung, S., Joiner, A. J., Waks,
L., & Garst, J. (2006). The effects of negativity and motivated
information processing during a political campaign. *Journal of
Communication, 56(1),* 27–51.
70 **accompanied by threatening graphics:** Sargent, S. L. (2007).
Image effects on selective exposure to computer-mediated news
stories. *Computers in Human Behavior, 23(1),* 705–726.
70 **remember the details of television news stories:**
Newhagen, J. E., & Reeves, B. (1992). The evening's bad news:
Effects of compelling negative television news images on
memory. *Journal of Communication, 42(2),* 25–41.
70 **People who say they're more interested:** Trussler, M., &
Soroka, S. (2014). Consumer Demand for Cynical and Negative
News Frames. *The International Journal of Press/Politics, 19(3),*
360–379.
70 **people who complain about too much negativity:** Ibid.
70 **Three German economists:** Arango-Kure, M., Garz, M., &
Rott, A. (2014). Bad News Sells: The Demand for News
Magazines and the Tone of Their Covers. *Journal of Media
Economics, 27(4),* 199–214.
70 **University of Michigan communications researchers:**
Soroka, & McAdams. (2015). News, politics, and negativity.
Political Communication, 32(1), 1–22.
71 **As far back as 1900, Delos Wilcox:** Wilcox, D. F. (1900). The
American Newspaper: A Study in Social Psychology. *The Annals
of the American Academy of Political and Social Science, 16(1),* 56–92.
72 **Yet when Morris Gilmore Caldwell:** Caldwell, M. G. (1932).
Sensational news in the modern metropolitan newspapers. *Journal
of Criminal Law and Criminology, 23(2),* 191–204.
73 **In 1987, three journalism professors:** Stone, G., Hartung, B.,
& Jensen, D. (1987). Local TV news and the good-bad dyad.
Journalism Quarterly, 64(1), 37–44.
74 **Paul Klite, a media critic:** Klite, P., Bardwell, R. A., &
Salzman, J. (1997). Local TV news: Getting away with murder.
Harvard International Journal of Press/Politics, 2(2), 102–112.
74 **computer scientist Julio Reis:** Reis, J., Benevenuto, F., Olmo,
P., Prates, R., Kwak, H., & An, J. (2015, Apr). Breaking the news:

First impressions matter on online news. In *Ninth International AAAI conference on web and social media.*

74 **"A word rarely mentioned…":** Klite, P. (1999, May 30). TV news and the culture of violence. *BizJournals.com.*

75 **"The very idea of news…":** Klite, P., Bardwell, R. A., & Salzman, J. (1997). Local TV news: Getting away with murder. *Harvard International Journal of Press/Politics, 2(2),* 102–112.

75 **"Scaring Us to Death…":** Kitman, M. (1984, Oct). Scaring us to death on the late-night news. *Washington Journalism Review,* 24–29.

76 **Any given news item:** Stephens, M. (2007). *A History of News.* New York, NY: Oxford University Press.

77 **"A group of Zulus…":** Stephens, M. (2007). *A History of News.* New York, NY: Oxford University Press. p. 24.

77 **most people watch the news not for the news, but for the weather:** Edmonds, R. (2019, Mar 26). Pew research finds that broadcast is the favorite source for local news and weather is the most valued topic. *Poynter.org.*

78 **"Why Good Is More Alike…":** Alves, H., Koch, A., & Unkelbach, C. (2017). Why good is more alike than bad: Processing implications. *Trends in Cognitive Sciences, 21(2),* 69–79.

78 **the Inuit people have more than a hundred different words for snow:** Steckley, J. (2007). *White Lies About the Inuit.* Toronto: University of Toronto Press.

79 **thirty-one adjectives describing pain:** Rozin, P., & Royzman, E. B. (2001). Negativity bias, negativity dominance, and contagion. *Personality & Social Psychology Review, 5(4),* 296–320.

79 **twice as many words for negative emotions:** Cited in Baumeister, R. F., Bratslavsky, E., Finkenauer, C., & Vohs, K. D. (2001). Bad is stronger than good. *Review of General Psychology, 5(4),* 323–370.

79 **"News time is deliberately shortsighted…":** Patterson, T. E. (1998). Time and news: The media's limitations as an instrument of democracy. *International Political Science Review, 19(1),* 55–67.

81 **"Half of marriages end in divorce…":** Sommerville, C. J. (1999). *How the News Makes Us Dumb.* Downers Grove, IL: InterVarsity Press. p. 101.

81 **"man bites dog.":** 'Dog Bites a Man' Is Not News.'Man Bites a Dog' Is News. (2013, Nov 22). *QuoteInvestigator.com.*

82 **"whether the subject is love…":** Stephens, M. (2007). *A History of News.* New York, NY: Oxford University Press. p. 119.

Chapter 3: Breaking News

Page

85   **On the morning of April 27, 1863:** Johnson, A. (1995). *The
      Tragic Wreck of the Anglo Saxon, April 27th, 1863.* Newfoundland:
      Harry Cruff Publications.

86   **the *Illustrated London News*:** Cape Race, Newfoundland. (1861,
      Aug 24). *Illustrated London News.* pp. 179, 193.

81   **"Yankee suggestion":** Quoted in Johnson, A. (1995). *The Tragic
      Wreck of the Anglo Saxon, April 27th, 1863.* Newfoundland: Harry
      Cruff Publications. p. 94.

88   **A small newsboat would head out from the Cape:**
      McGrath, P. T. (1904). Reporting the world's news before the
      Atlantic cable. *Telegraph Age, 24(22),* 574–576.

88   **The first cable:** Ibid.

89   **"an almost demonic...":** Johnson, A. (1995). *The Tragic Wreck
      of the Anglo Saxon, April 27th, 1863.* Newfoundland: Harry Cruff
      Publications. p. 22.

89   **"the steamers being under MAIL Contract..."** Retrieved
      from https://commons.wikimedia.org/wiki/File:Allan-Line-
      Fares-List-1890s.JPG

90   **"supposed the ship...":** Quoted in Johnson, A. (1995). *The
      Tragic Wreck of the Anglo Saxon, April 27th, 1863.* Newfoundland:
      Harry Cruff Publications. p. 27.

92   **"I looked to see...":** Quoted in Ibid. p. 46.

92   **There they found Captain John Murphy:** Ibid. p. 52.

92–93   **"Two hundred and thirty-seven lives were lost...":**
        General news. (1863, Apr 30). *New York Times.* p. 4.

93   **"The new tydings out of Italie...":** Reproduced in Frank, J.
      (1961). *The beginnings of the English newspaper: 1620-1660.*
      Cambridge, MA: Harvard University Press. p. 195.

93   **The *Acta Diurna*:** see Stephens, M. (2007). *A History of News.*
      New York, NY: Oxford University Press.

93   **Those writers never had to apologize:** Ibid. p. 141.

93   **"stale ballad-newes...":** Braithwaite, R. (1631/1859). *The
      Whimzies; Or a New Cast of Characters.* London: Thomas Richards.
      p. 19.

94   **"nauseate the Reader...":** Quoted in Sutherland, J.
      (1986/2004). *The Restoration Newspaper and its Development.*
      Cambridge: Cambridge University Press. p. 54.

94   **Those early papers were called corantos:** See Stephens, M.
      (2007). *A History of News.* New York, NY: Oxford University Press.

94   **"both the Reader and the Printer…":** Quoted in Shaaber,
     M. (1932). The History of the First English Newspaper. *Studies in
     Philology, 29(4),* 551–587.
94   **"I will directly proceed…":** Ibid.
95   **"if the Post…"; "The failure of all the mails…"; "No
     mail yesterday…":** Quoted in Stephens, M. (2007). *A History
     of News.* New York, NY: Oxford University Press. p. 211.
95   **"In every species of news…":** Quoted in Hudson, F. (1873).
     Journalism in the United States, from 1690–1872. New York, NY:
     Harper. p. 439.
95   **"skimming o'er the bright blue waters.":** The Fanny
     Elssler—Beating the Wall street loafers. (1840, May 18). *New York
     Herald.* p 4.
96   **"In one case…":** Anonymous. (1855). *Memoirs of James Gordon
     Bennett and His Times: By a Journalist.* New York, NY: Stringer &
     Townsend. p. 372.
96   **As Frank Mott notes:** Mott, F. (1962). *American Journalism: A
     History, 1690–1960.* New York, NY: Macmillan. p. 247.
96   **"One o'clock…":** Quoted in Ibid.
97   **twenty thousand miles:** Nonnenmacher, T. (n.d.). History of
     the U.S. Telegraph Industry. *EH.net.*
97   **Getting access to the telegraph wires was expensive:**
     Tucher, A. (1994). *Froth & Scum: Truth, Beauty, Goodness, and the
     Ax Murder in America's First Mass Medium.* Chapel Hill, NC:
     University of North Carolina Press. pp. 191–192.
97   **"The creation of the science…":** A telegraphic jubilee.
     (1958, Aug 9). *New York Times.* p. 4.
97   **"the paper which brings…":** Quoted in Hudson, F. (1873).
     Journalism in the United States, from 1690–1872. New York, NY:
     Harper. p. 548.
98   **unprecedented circulation figures:** Schiller, D. (1981).
     *Objectivity and the News: The Public and the Rise of Commercial
     Journalism.* Philadelphia, PA: University of Pennsylvania Press.
     p. 12.
98   **"a weekly cheat…":** Jonson, B. (1625). *The Staple of News.*
     http://hollowaypages.com/jonson1692news.htm
98   **"which performs constantly…":** Fielding, H. (1821).
     The Novels of Henry Fielding. London: Hurst, Robinson, and Co.
     p. 154.
98   **"the name and age of every dog…":** Summers, M. W.
     (2018). *The Press Gang: Newspapers and Politics, 1865-1878.*
     Chapel Hill, NC: University of North Carolina Press. p. 15.

98–99   **"Everyone now hurried to print:** Escott, T. H. S. (1911).
        Masters of English Journalism: A Study of Personal Forces.
        London: T. F. Unwin. p. 347.

99   **"The greatest felony in the news business…":** Bernstein, C.
        (1992, Jun 8). Idiot culture. *The New Republic.* pp. 22–28.

99   **reported that a third building had collapsed:** See Porter, R.
        (2007, Feb 27). Part of the conspiracy? *BBC.co.uk.*

99   **"We aim to be first with breaking news…":** Quoted in
        Lewis, J., & Cushion, S. (2009). The thirst to be first: An analysis
        of breaking news stories and their impact on the quality of
        24-hour news coverage in the UK. *Journalism Practice, 3(3),*
        304–318.

100   **"This is a developing story…":** Quoted in Mantzarlis, A.
        (2017, Feb 27). Journalism can't afford for corrections to be next
        victim of 'fake news' frenzy. *Poynter.org.*

100   **"When journalists or academics talk about…":** Lewis, J., &
        Cushion, S. (2009). The thirst to be first: An analysis of breaking
        news stories and their impact on the quality of 24-hour news
        coverage in the UK. *Journalism Practice, 3(3),* 304–318.

103   **"fetishism of the present.":** Manoff, R. K., & Schudson, M.
        (1986). *Reading the News: A Pantheon Guide to Popular Culture.*
        New York, NY: Pantheon Books. p. 81.

104   **"The past is a foreign country…":** Hartley, L. P. (1953). *The
        Go-Between.* London: Hamish Hamilton. p. 1.

104   **As philosophers have long argued:** See, for example, Gunn, J.
        (1929). The problem of time. *Philosophy, 4(14),* 180–191.

104   **"Psychological distance is a subjective experience…":**
        Trope, Y., & Liberman, N. (2010). Construal-level theory of
        psychological distance. *Psychological Review, 117(2),* 440–463.

105   **In one study, Liberman had people rate:** Liberman, N.,
        Sagristano, M. D., & Trope, Y. (2002). The effect of temporal
        distance on level of mental construal. *Journal of Experimental
        Social Psychology, 38,* 523–534.

106   **"We do not literally take…":** Trope, Y., & Liberman, N.
        (2010). Construal-level theory of psychological distance.
        Psychological Review, 117(2), 440–463.

106   **people use more abstract language:** Semin, G. R., &
        Smith, E. R. (1999). Revisiting the past and back to the future:
        Memory systems and the linguistic representation of social
        events. *Journal of Personality and Social Psychology, 76(6),*
        877–892.

107 **"reflects not only a literary convention…"**: Trope, Y., &
Liberman, N. (2010). Construal-level theory of psychological
distance. *Psychological Review, 117(2),* 440–463.

108 **psychological distance is subjective:** Ibid.

108 **the death of King William III:** Stephens, M. (2007). *A History
of News.* New York, NY: Oxford University Press. pp. 208–209.

109 **the Loch Ness monster:** Knowles, H. (2019, Sep 7). The Loch
Ness monster is still a mystery, but scientists have some new
evidence for a theory. *WashingtonPost.com.*

109 **"Loch Ness attracts people…":** Quoted in Ibid.

110 **to understand why people sigh:** Teigen, K. H. (2008). Is a sigh
"just a sigh"? Sighs as emotional signals and responses to a
difficult task. *Scandinavian Journal of Psychology, 49(1),* 49–57.

110 **"the sound of hope leaving the body.":** Teigen, K. H.
(2011, Nov 5). The sound of hope leaving the body.
PsykologTidsskriftet.no.

110 **Teigen was interested in the news:** Teigen, K. H. (1985).
Preference for news as a function of familiarity. *Scandinavian
Journal of Psychology, 26(1),* 348–356.
Teigen, K. H. (1987). Intrinsic interest and the novelty-familiarity
interaction. *Scandinavian Journal of Psychology, 28(3),* 199–210.

113 **The idea was pioneered by Pascal Boyer:** Boyer, Pascal.
(1994). *The Naturalness of Religious Ideas.* Los Angeles, CA:
University of California Press.

113 **a painting of the Virgin Mary:** Anderson, J. (2019, Sep 9).
Faithful see miracle in weeping icon of Mary with child Jesus at
Greek Orthodox church on Northwest Side. *ChicagoTribune.com.*

114 **Aiyana Willard and colleagues:** Willard, A. K., Henrich, J., &
Norenzayan, A. (2016). Memory and belief in the transmission of
counterintuitive content. *Human Nature, 27(3),* 221–243.

116 **began a 2011 report:** Upal, M. A. (2011). Why radicals win the
newsday: Ratcheting-up of cultural counterintuitiveness in
rumors and NRM doctrine. *Proceedings of the Annual Meeting of
the Cognitive Science Society, 33(33),* 1324–1329.

118 **The last battle of the War of 1812:** Howe, D. W. (2009). *What
Hath God Wrought: The Transformation of America, 1815-1848.*
Oxford: Oxford University Press.

118 **"a 'quick run'…":** The Loss of the *Anglo Saxon.* (1863, May
15). *Armagh Guardian.* From TheShipsList.com.

119 **An official enquiry:** The Loss of the *Anglo Saxon.* (1863, May
15). *Belfast Newsletter.* From TheShipsList.com.

119 **"There can be little doubt…":** Johnson, A. (1995). *The Tragic Wreck of the* Anglo Saxon, *April 27th, 1863.* Newfoundland: Harry Cruff Publications.

119 **"If the celebrated 'man bites dog'-paradigm…":** Teigen, K. H. (1985). Preference for news as a function of familiarity. *Scandinavian Journal of Psychology, 26(1),* 348–356.

Chapter 4: Too Much News

Page

121 **"struck by the epidemic.":** Strike still balks paper deliveries. (1945, Jul 2). *New York Times.* p. 8.

121 **13 million customers:** News strike ends under WLB terms. (1945, Jul 18). *New York Times.* p. 19.

122 **Berelson wasn't just *a* behavioral scientist:** Sills, D. L. (1981). Bernard Berelson: Behavioral scientist. *Journal of the History of the Behavioral Sciences, 17(3),* 305–311.

122 **Berelson dispatched research assistants:** Berelson, B. R. (1949). What missing the newspaper means. In P. F. Lazarsfeld & F. Stanton (Eds.), *Communications Research, 1948-1949* (pp. 111–129). New York, NY: Harper.

125 **coined the term *ambient news*:** Hargreaves, I., & Thomas, J. (2002). New news, old news: An ITC and BSC Research Publication. [via Web.Archive.org].

125 **"escaping the news is as difficult…":** Holton, A. E., & Chyi, H. I. (2012). News and the overloaded consumer: Factors influencing information overload among news consumers. *CyberPsychology, Behavior & Social Networking, 15(11),* 619–624.

125 **a 2018 Pew Research public opinion poll:** Gottfried, J., & Barthel, M. (2018, Jun 5). Almost seven-in-ten Americans have news fatigue, more among Republicans. *PewResearch.org.*

126 **researchers at the University of Texas:** Holton, A. E., & Chyi, H. I. (2012). News and the overloaded consumer: Factors influencing information overload among news consumers. *CyberPsychology, Behavior & Social Networking, 15(11),* 619–624.

126 **The Associated Press commissioned:** Associated Press. (2008, Jul 14). A new model for news: studying the deep structure of young-adult news consumption. *APO.org.*

126 **"3 Ways to Curb Your Addiction to News.":** Griffin, T. (2019, Sep 4). How to curb your addiction to news. *WikiHow.com.*

126 **"How I Ditched My Phone…"** Roose, K. (2019, Feb 23). Do not disturb: How I ditched my phone and unbroke my brain. *NYTimes.com.*

127 **Lack of Wi-Fi or phone reception:** See, for example, Worley, B. (2019, Aug 6). How and why you should go on a digital detox vacation. *GoodMorningAmerica.com.*

127 **Digital Wellness Escape:** https://www.mandarinoriental.com/ new-york/manhattan/luxury-spa/treatments-menu

128 **"A news-hungry public…":** Strike still balks paper deliveries. (1945, Jul 2). *New York Times.* p. 1.

128 **The figures climbed:** Sales of newspapers rise as strike goes on. (1945, Jul 13). *New York Times.* p. 22.

128 **"Despite the length of the strike…":** Paper deliverers ignore ultimatum; street sales rise. (1945, Jul 17). *New York Times.* p. 24.

128 **"Deliverers of afternoon papers…":** News strike ends under WLB terms. (1945, Jul 18). *New York Times.* p. 1.

129 **"probably no strike…":** The newspaper strike. (1945, Jul 12). *New York Herald Tribune.* p. 10.

129 **Berelson's interviews:** Berelson, B. R. (1949). What missing the newspaper means. In P. F. Lazarsfeld & F. Stanton (Eds.), *Communications Research, 1948-1949* (pp. 111–129). New York, NY: Harper.

131 **In October of 2009:** Hargittai, E., Neuman, W. R., & Curry, O. (2012). Taming the information tide: Perceptions of information overload in the American home. *The Information Society, 28(3),* 161–173.

132 **True enough, Pew found:** Gottfried, J., & Barthel, M. (2018, Jun 5). Almost seven-in-ten Americans have news fatigue, more among Republicans. *PewResearch.org.*

132 **But Pew has also asked people:** Horrigan, J. B. (2016, Dec 7). Information overload. *PewResearch.org.*

133 **The study by University of Texas journalism researchers:** Holton, A. E., & Chyi, H. I. (2012). News and the overloaded consumer: Factors influencing information overload among news consumers. *CyberPsychology, Behavior & Social Networking, 15(11),* 619–624.

133 **asked a few hundred Ohio residents:** Ji, Q., Ha, L., & Sypher, U. (2014). The role of news media use and demographic characteristics in the prediction of information overload. *International Journal of Communication, 8,* 699–714.

133 **Yet another study:** Schmitt, J. B., Debbelt, C. A., & Schneider, F. M. (2018). Too much information? Predictors of information

overload in the context of online news exposure. Information, *Communication & Society, 21(8),* 1151–1167.

134 **"In offering to the public *another newspaper...***": To the public. (1836, Mar 25). *Public Ledger.* p. 1.

135 **"The Magical Number Seven..."**: Miller, G. A. (1956). The magical number seven, plus or minus two: Some limits on our capacity for processing information. *Psychological Review, 63(2),* 81–97.

135 **"Fortunately," Miller later recalled:** Miller, G., A. (1989). George A. Miller. In L. Gardner (Ed.), *A History of Psychology in Autobiography VIII* (pp. 391–418). Stanford, CA: Stanford University Press.

136 **"I have been persecuted by an integer..."**: Miller, G. A. (1956). The magical number seven, plus or minus two: Some limits on our capacity for processing information. *Psychological Review, 63(2),* 81–97.

137 **"The idea of a magical number..."**: Miller, G., A. (1989). In L. Gardner (Ed.), *A History of Psychology in Autobiography VIII* (pp. 391–418). Stanford, CA: Stanford University Press.

137 **cited close to thirty thousand times:** Cowan, N. (2015). George Miller's magical number of immediate memory in retrospect: Observations on the faltering progression of science. *Psychological Review, 122(3),* 536–541.

138 **Nelson Cowan, a University of Missouri psychologist:** Ibid.

139 **Our capacity for information, Miller argued:** Miller, G. A. (1956). The magical number seven, plus or minus two: Some limits on our capacity for processing information. *Psychological Review, 63(2),* 81–97.

139 **MLBNHLNBANFL:** Lilienfeld, S. O., Lynn, S. J., & Namy, L. L. (2018). *Psychology: From Inquiry to Understanding.* New York, NY: Pearson.

140 **The procedure is quite simple:** Bransford, J. D., & Johnson, M. K. (1972). Contextual prerequisites for understanding: Some investigations of comprehension and recall. *Journal of Verbal Learning and Verbal Behavior, 11(6),* 717–726.

141 **media coverage of wildfires:** Not all fires are equal. (2018, Aug 10). *On the Media.* [transcript available at *WNYCStudios.org*].

142 **"We're not at war with fire..."**: Ibid.

142 **Pyne has written fifteen books:** Graham, A. (2015, Nov 22). How journalists fan the flames of wildfire in the West. *MJR.Jour. UMT.edu.*

143 **When the frame matches how we already think:** Shen, F. (2004). Effects of news frames and schemas on individuals' issue interpretations and attitudes. *Journalism & Mass Communication Quarterly, 81(2),* 400–416.

143 **"Can consumers be overloaded?":** Jacoby, J. (1984). Perspectives on Information Overload. *Journal of Consumer Research, 10(4),* 432–435.

144 **multiscreening:** Van Cauwenberge, A., Schaap, G., & van Roy, R. (2014). "TV no longer commands our full attention": Effects of second-screen viewing and task relevance on cognitive load and learning from news. *Computers in Human Behavior, 38,* 100–109.

145 **more time reading news articles:** Lagun, D., & Lalmas, M. (2016). Understanding user attention and engagement in online news reading. *Proceedings of the Ninth ACM International Conference on Web Search and Data Mining,* 113–122. ACM.

146 **when pilots have to make critical decisions quickly:** Devean, T., & Kewley, R. H. (2009). Overcoming Information Overload in the Cockpit. Retrieved from https://apps.dtic.mil/dtic/tr/fulltext/u2/a506356.pdf

147 **"visit the internet":** Rusbridger, A. (2018). *Breaking News: The Remaking of Journalism and Why It Matters Now.* New York, NY: Farrar, Straus and Giroux. p. 33.

147 **"the executive suite is awash...":** Jouzaitis, C. (1983, Feb 7). Execs buried by information overload. *Chicago Tribune.* p. D10.

147 **"Every executive I know...":** Grossman, J. (1987, Sep 27). The importance of being playful. *New York Times.* p. 28.

148 **"reduce the pressure...":** Quoted in Levine, N. (2017). The nature of the glut: Information overload in postwar America. *History of the Human Sciences, 30(1),* 32–49.

148 **Nick Levine points out:** Ibid.

148 **"Although there is no objective evidence...":** Bishop, J. E. (1979, Apr 16). Age of anxiety. *New York Times.* p. D14.

148 **"We have reason to fear...":** Quoted in Blair, A. (2003). Reading strategies for coping with information overload ca. 1550–1700. *Journal of the History of Ideas, 64(1),* 11–28.

149 **"Books, the multitude of...":** Rees, A. (1819). *The Cyclopaedia; Or, Universal Dictionary of Arts, Sciences and Literature Vol. IV.* London: Longman. p. 776.

149 **"information explosion":** Rosenberg, D. (2003). Early Modern information overload. *Journal of the History of Ideas, 64(1),* 1–9.

149 **something like sixty books:** Blair, A. (2003). Reading strategies for coping with information overload ca.1550–1700. *Journal of the History of Ideas, 64(1),* 11–28.

149 **Early medieval art:** Ibid.

150 **the range of creative solutions:** Ibid.

150 **Printers boasted of a "most complete":** Ibid.

151 **"nails for the convenience...":** Ibid.

151 **"Some books are to be tasted...":** Ibid.

152 **"So many summaries...":** Ibid.

152 **"Be careful...":** Ibid.

153 **"The first thing you hear in the morning...":** Quoted in DiGirolamo, V. (2019). *Crying the News: A History of America's Newsboys.* New York, NY: Oxford University Press. p. 31..

153 **a 2012 article in *The Atlantic*:** Jacobs, A. (2012, Jan 23). 'Commonplace books': The Tumblrs of an earlier era. *TheAtlantic.com.*

154 **"The news has the magical quality...":** Sommerville, C. J. (1999). *How the News Makes Us Dumb.* Downers Grove, IL: InterVarsity Press. p. 20.

154 **People who enjoy reading news:** York, C. (2013). Overloaded by the news: Effects of news exposure and enjoyment on reporting information overload. *Communication Research Reports, 30(4),* 282–292.

154 **we get more selective:** Holton, A. E., & Chyi, H. I. (2012). News and the overloaded consumer: Factors influencing information overload among news consumers. *CyberPsychology, Behavior & Social Networking, 15(11),* 619–624.

Chapter 5: Echo Chambers

Page

155 **"Every morning...":** Verne, J. (1965). In the twenty-ninth century. The day of an American journalist in 2889. In *Yesterday and Tomorrow*, pp. 107–124. London: Arco.
For an interesting discussion of the authorship of this short story, and how it changed somewhat across several versions, see Evans, A. B. (1995). The "New" Jules Verne. *Science Fiction Studies, 22(1),* 35–46.

156 **"This kind of newspaper...":** Negroponte, N. (1995). *Being Digital.* New York, NY: Knopf. p. 153.

157 **Cass Sunstein coined the term "echo chambers":** Sunstein, C. R. (2001). *Republic.com.* Princeton, NJ: Princeton University Press. p. 3.

158 **"More and more, your computer monitor..."**: Pariser, E. (2011). *The Filter Bubble: What the internet is hiding from you.* New York, NY: Penguin Press. p. 3.

158 **"Your filter bubble is destroying democracy"**: El-Bermawy, M. M. (2016, Nov 18). Your filter bubble is destroying democracy. *Wired.com*.

159 **"In the end..."**: Leetaru, K. (2019, Jul 20). The social media filter bubble's corrosive impact on democracy and the press. *Forbes.com*.

159 **"I think Twitter does contribute..."**: Murphy, M. (2018, Oct 15). Twitter creates filter bubbles, and 'we need to fix it,' says Jack Dorsey. *MarketWatch.com*.

159 **"I think we have created tools..."**: Murphy, M. D. (2017, Dec 11). Transcript of excerpt from Chamath Palihapitiya's Stanford Biz School talk. *Medium.com*.

161 **"Confirmed: Echo chambers exist on social media..."**: Emba, C. (2016, Jul 14). Confirmed: Echo chambers exist on social media. So what do we do about them? *WashingtonPost.com*.

161 **a single new study:** Quattrociocchi, W., Scala, A., & Sunstein, C. R. (2016, Jun 13). Echo chambers on Facebook. Available at SSRN: https://ssrn.com/abstract=2795110

161 **"There is much difference of opinion..."**: Aristotle, Nicomachean Ethics, 1155a. http://perseus.uchicago.edu/ perseus-cgi/citequery3.pl?dbname=GreekTexts

161 **"Similarity breeds connection..."'**: McPherson, M., Smith-Lovin, L., & Cook, J. M. (2001). Birds of a Feather: Homophily in Social Networks. *Annual Review of Sociology, 27(1),* 415–444.

162 **"is one of our best established social facts"**: Smith, J. A., McPherson, M., & Smith-Lovin, L. (2014). Social Distance in the United States: Sex, Race, Religion, Age, and Education Homophily among Confidants, 1985 to 2004. *American Sociological Review, 79(3),* 432–456.

162 **"a basic organizing principle"**: McPherson, M., Smith-Lovin, L., & Cook, J. M. (2001). Birds of a Feather: Homophily in Social Networks. *Annual Review of Sociology, 27(1),* 415–444.

162 **In 1922:** Almack, J. C. (1922). The influence of intelligence on the selection of associates. *School and Society, 16(410),* 529–530.

162 **The finding was recently replicated:** Boutwell, B. B., Meldrum, R. C., & Petkovsek, M. A. (2017). General intelligence in friendship selection: A study of preadolescent best friend dyads. *Intelligence, 64,* 30–35.

163 **The correlation between spouses' intelligence:** Plomin, R.,
& Deary, I. J. (2015). Genetics and intelligence differences: Five
special findings. *Molecular Psychiatry, 20(1),* 98–108.

163 **Donn Byrne:** Fisher, W. A., Fisher, J. D., Singh, R., & Baron, R.
A. (2015). Donn Byrne (1931–2014). *American Psychologist, 70(5),*
477–477.

163 **In his initial studies:** Byrne, D., & Nelson, D. (1965a).
Attraction as a linear function of proportion of positive
reinforcements. *Journal of Personality and Social Psychology, 1(6),*
659.
Byrne, D., & Nelson, D. (1965b). The effect of topic importance
and attitude similarity-dissimilarity on attraction in a
multistranger design. *Psychonomic Science, 3(1–12),* 449–450.

165 **a more ambitious project:** Byrne, D., Ervin, C. R., &
Lamberth, J. (1970). Continuity between the experimental study
of attraction and real-life computer dating. *Journal of Personality
and Social Psychology, 16(1),* 157–165.

165 **A 2017 article in the *New York Times*:** Rogers, K. (2017, Feb
10). Roommates wanted. Trump supporters need not apply.
NYTimes.com.

167 ***Voting: A Study of Opinion Formation ...*:** Berelson, B. R.,
Lazarsfeld, P. F., & McPhee, W. N. (1954). *Voting: A study of opinion
formation in a presidential campaign.* Chicago, IL: University of
Chicago Press.

168 **"Those who liked Ike...":** Retica, A. (2006, Dec 10).
Homophily. *NYTimes.com.*

168 **Likewise, a 1987 study:** Knoke, D. (1990). Networks of
political action: Toward theory construction. *Social forces, 68 (4),*
1041–1063.

168 **researchers examined real data from an online dating
website:** Huber, G. A., & Malhotra, N. (2017). Political
homophily in social relationships: Evidence from online dating
behavior. *The Journal of Politics, 79(1),* 269–283.

168 **shared affinity for smoking pot:** Kandel, D. B. (1978).
Homophily, selection, and socialization in adolescent friendships.
American Journal of Sociology, 84(2), 427–436.

169 **reviewed the research on the congeniality bias:** Hart, W.,
Albarracín, D., Eagly, A. H., Brechan, I., Lindberg, M. J., &
Merrill, L. (2009). Feeling Validated Versus Being Correct: A
Meta-Analysis of Selective Exposure to Information. *Psychological
Bulletin, 135(4),* 555–588.

169 **According to a document obtained by the website** *The Smoking Gun*: www.thesmokinggun.com/file/dick-cheneys-suite-demands

170 **In 1957, Danuta Ehrlich and colleagues:** Ehrlich, D., Guttman, I., Schönbach, P., & Mills, J. (1957). Postdecision exposure to relevant information. *Journal of Abnormal and Social Psychology, 54(1),* 98–102.

170 **J. Stacy Adams asked a hundred or so mothers:** Adams, J. S. (1962). Reduction of cognitive dissonance by seeking consonant information. *Journal of Abnormal and Social Psychology, 62(1),* 74.

171 **In the same study:** Berelson, B. R., Lazarsfeld, P. F., & McPhee, W. N. (1954). *Voting: A Study of Opinion Formation in a Presidential Campaign.* Chicago, IL: University of Chicago Press.

171 **people tend to read newspapers:** Lipset, S. M. (1953). Opinion formation in a crisis situation. *Public Opinion Quarterly, 17(1),* 20.

171 **In more recent experiments:** See Flaxman, S., Goel, S., & Rao, J. M. (2016). Filter bubbles, echo chambers, and online news consumption. *Public Opinion Quarterly, 80(S1),* 298–320.

172–173 **produced a report on echo chambers:** Guess, A., Nyhan, B., Lyons, B., & Reifler, J. (2018). Avoiding the echo chamber about echo chambers. *Knight Foundation White Paper.* Retrieved from https://kf-siteproduction. s3.amazonaws. com/media_elements/files/000/000/133/ original/Topos_KF_White-Paper_Nyhan_V1. pdf.

173 **Matthew Gentzkow and Jesse Shapiro:** Gentzkow, M., & Shapiro, J. M. (2011). Ideological Segregation Online and Offline. *Quarterly Journal of Economics, 126(4),* 1799–1839.

174 **studied the entire network of 2009 Twitter users:** Colleoni, E., Rozza, A., & Arvidsson, A. (2014). Echo chamber or public sphere? Predicting political orientation and measuring political homophily in Twitter using big data. *Journal of Communication, 64(2),* 317–332.

175 **More recently, Eytan Bakshy:** Bakshy, E., Messing, S., & Adamic, L. A. (2015). Exposure to ideologically diverse news and opinion on Facebook. *Science, 348(6239),* 1130–1132.

176 **researchers had fifteen hundred people install a browser plugin:** Krafft, T. D., Gamer, M., & Zweig, K. A. (2018). What did you see? Personalization, regionalization and the question of the filter bubble in Google's search engine. *arXiv preprint arXiv:1812.10943.*

176 **"Overall," concluded Axel Bruns:** Bruns, A. (2019). *Are Filter Bubbles Real?*. Medford, MA: Polity Press.

177 **William Hart and colleagues pointed out:** Hart, W., Albarracín, D., Eagly, A. H., Brechan, I., Lindberg, M. J., & Merrill, L. (2009). Feeling Validated Versus Being Correct: A Meta-Analysis of Selective Exposure to Information. *Psychological Bulletin, 135(4),* 555–588.

178 **In one, Garrett surveyed fifteen hundred Americans:** Garrett, R. K. (2009). Politically motivated reinforcement seeking: Reframing the selective exposure debate. *Journal of Communication, 59(4),* 676–699.

178 **"In another study, Garrett...":** Garrett, R. K., & Stroud, N. J. (2014). Partisan paths to exposure diversity: Differences in pro- and counterattitudinal news consumption. *Journal of Communication,* 64(4), 680–701.

181 **structural forces are at least as potent:** McPherson, J. M., & Smith-Lovin, L. (1987). Homophily in Voluntary Organizations: Status Distance and the Composition of Face-to-Face Groups. *American Sociological Review, 52(3),* 370.

181 **compared online news consumption:** Gentzkow, M., & Shapiro, J. M. (2011). Ideological Segregation Online and Offline. *Quarterly Journal of Economics, 126(4),* 1799–1839.

182 **the internet appears to be a better source:** Gentzkow, M., & Shapiro, J. M. (2011). Ideological Segregation Online and Offline. *Quarterly Journal of Economics, 126(4),* 1799–1839.

182 **According to another study, people who used social media:** Flaxman, S., Goel, S., & Rao, J. M. (2016). Filter bubbles, echo chambers, and online news consumption. *Public Opinion Quarterly, 80(S1),* 298–320.

182 **research conducted in Sweden:** Liang, C. Y., & Nordin, M. (2012). The internet, news consumption, and political attitudes. *B.E. Journal of Economic Analysis & Policy, 13(2),* 1071–1093.

182–183 **Gary King, Benjamin Schneer, and Ariel White:** King, G., Schneer, B., & White, A. (2017). How the news media activate public expression and influence national agendas. *Science, 358(6364),* 776–780.

184 **Another set of researchers had a dataset:** Flaxman, S., Goel, S., & Rao, J. M. (2016). Filter Bubbles, Echo Chambers, and Online News Consumption. *Public Opinion Quarterly, 80(S1),* 298–320.

184 **only about 10 percent of people's posts:** Colleoni, E., Rozza, A., & Arvidsson, A. (2014). Echo chamber or public

sphere? Predicting political orientation and measuring political homophily in Twitter using big data. *Journal of Communication, 64(2),* 317–332.

184 **people only clicked on 7 percent:** Bakshy, E., Messing, S., & Adamic, L. A. (2015). Exposure to ideologically diverse news and opinion on Facebook. *Science, 348(6239),* 1130–1132.

184–185 **one in every three hundred outbound clicks:** Flaxman, S., Goel, S., & Rao, J. M. (2016). Filter Bubbles, Echo Chambers, and Online News Consumption. *Public Opinion Quarterly, 80(S1),* 298–320.

185 **one in ten internet users:** Garrett, R. K. (2009). Politically motivated reinforcement seeking: Reframing the selective exposure debate. *Journal of Communication, 59(4),* 676–699.

185 **Andrew Guess found:** Guess, A. (2018). (Almost) everything in moderation: New evidence in Americans' online media diets. *Unpublished manuscript.* https://webspace.princeton.edu/users/aguess/Guess_OnlineMediaDiets.pdf

186 **"Polarized media consumption…":** Guess, A., Nyhan, B., Lyons, B., & Reifler, J. (2018). Avoiding the echo chamber about echo chambers. *Knight Foundation White Paper.* Retrieved from https://kf-siteproduction.s3.amazonaws.com/media_elements/files/000/000/133/original/Topos_KF_White-Paper_Nyhan_V1.pdf

186 **"we are paying far too much attention…":** Bruns, A. (2019). *Are Filter Bubbles Real?* Medford, MA: Polity Press.

186 **recent research by Levi Boxell:** Boxell, L., Gentzkow, M., & Shapiro, J. M. (2017). *Is the internet causing political polarization? Evidence from demographics* (No. w23258). National Bureau of Economic Research.

Chapter 6: Deepfakes

Page

189 **In 2019, some of the world's most powerful political leaders:** Seymour, M. (2019, Apr 12). Canny AI: Imagine world leaders singing. *FXGuide.com.*

191 **"AI brings people together…":** https://twitter.com/cannyai/status/1114101845880987648?lang=en

192 **"We're entering an era…":** Mack, D. (2018, Apr 17). This PSA about fake news from Barack Obama is not what it appears. *BuzzfeedNews.com.*

192 **showed House Speaker Nancy Pelosi:** Harwell, D. (2019, May 24). Faked Pelosi videos, slowed to make her appear drunk, spread across social media. *WashingtonPost.com.*

193 **"Call it a 'cheapfake'":** Donovan, J., & Paris, B. (2019, Jun 12). Beware the Cheapfakes. *Slate.com.*

193 **"We are deeply concerned…":** https://schiff.house.gov/ news/press-releases/schiff-murphy-and-curbelo-request-dni-assess-national-security-threats-of-deep-fakes

193 **"It's certainly clear…":** Taulli, T. (2019, Jun 15). Deepfake: What you need to know. *Forbes.com.*

193 **"Fake News Is About to Get Even Scarier…":** Bilton, N. (2017, Jan 26). Fake news is about to get even scarier than you ever dreamed. *VanityFair.com.*

193 **"Deep fakes are where truth goes to die.":** Schwartz, O. (2018, Nov 12). You thought fake news was bad? Deep fakes are where truth goes to die. *TheGuardian.com.*

193 **"Faster than you can say…":** Lasica, J. D. (1989, Jun). Photographs that lie: The ethical dilemma of digital retouching. *Washington Journalism Review,* 22-25.

194 **"Trademarks are not verbs":** https://www.adobe.com/legal/ permissions/trademarks.html

195 **"In the future…":** Grundberg, A. (1990, Aug 12). Ask it no questions: The camera can lie. *NYTimes.com.*

196 **opened his book with a joke:** Boorstin, D. J. (1992). *The image: A guide to pseudo-events in America.* New York, NY: Vintage.

196 **"The dry details of the telegraph…":** Picturephobia, the new epidemic. (1859, Apr 2). *Frank Leslie's Illustrated Newspaper.*

197 **"The public will have henceforth…":** Our address. (1842, May 14). *The Illustrated London News.*

197 **"What makes a news photo distinctive…":** Quoted in Wheeler, T. (2002). *Phototruth Or Photofiction?: Ethics and Media Imagery in the Digital Age.* Mahwah, NJ: Routledge. p. 5.

197 **"News pictures have a special ability…":** Perlmutter, D. D. (1998). *Photojournalism and foreign policy: Icons of outrage in international crises.* Westport, CT: Praeger.

197 **"I saw you with my own eyes…":** Mankiewicz, H. J. (Producer), & McCarey, L. (Director). (1933). *Duck soup* [Motion Picture]. United States: Paramount Pictures.

198 **the little plastic or metal tube things:** Cave, J. (2016, Jun 22). Behold, the aglet: That thing on the end of your shoelace. *HuffPost.com.*

199 **He apparently made $2.5 million:** Invine, A. (1902). Incomes
of successful inventors. *Scientific American, 86, 201*. The writer
doesn't mention whether he's talking in 1790 dollars or equivalent
1902 dollars. Either way, it comes out to more than $70 million in
2020 dollars, according to https://www.officialdata.org/1790-
dollars-in-2020?amount=2500000&future_pct=0.03

199 **When cognitive psychologist Eryn Newman:** Newman, E.
J., Garry, M., Bernstein, D. M., Kantner, J., & Lindsay, D. S. (2012).
Nonprobative photographs (or words) inflate truthiness.
Psychonomic Bulletin & Review, 19(5), 969–974.

200 **In a later study, Newman:** Fenn, E., Newman, E. J., Pezdek,
K., & Garry, M. (2013). The effect of nonprobative photographs
on truthiness persists over time. *Acta Psychologica, 144(1),*
207–211.

200 **Newman cites a real court case:** Newman, E., & Feigenson,
N. (2013). The truthiness of visual evidence. *Jury Expert, 25,* 1–4.

201 **"I'm going to go with yes...":** Newman, E. J., Garry, M.,
Unkelbach, C., Bernstein, D. M., Lindsay, D. S., & Nash, R. A.
(2015). Truthiness and falsiness of trivia claims depend on
judgmental contexts. *Journal of Experimental Psychology: Learning,
Memory, and Cognition, 41(5),* 1337.

202 **In one of the largest studies of its kind:** Frenda, S. J., Knowles,
E. D., Saletan, W., & Loftus, E. F. (2013). False memories of
fabricated political events. *Journal of Experimental Social Psychology,
49(2),* 280–286.

203 **"A Picture Is Worth a Thousand Lies.":** Wade, K. A., Garry,
M., Don Read, J., & Lindsay, D. S. (2002). A picture is worth a
thousand lies: Using false photographs to create false childhood
memories. *Psychonomic Bulletin & Review, 9(3),* 597–603.

208 **"old man JOHN BURNS...":** Reminiscences of Gettysburg.
(1863, Aug 22). *Harper's Weekly.* pp. 529, 534.

210 **As Mia Fineman notes:** Fineman, M. (2012). *Faking It:
Manipulated Photography before Photoshop.* New York, NY:
Metropolitan Museum of Art.

211 **"We do not depend upon...":** Picturephobia, the new
epidemic. (1859, Apr 2). *Frank Leslie's Illustrated Newspaper.*

211 **"demand for lively, legible...":** Fineman, M. (2012). *Faking It:
Manipulated Photography before Photoshop.* New York, NY:
Metropolitan Museum of Art.

212 **appeared in the *New York Daily Graphic*:** Steinway Hall [From
a photograph by Pach]. (1873, Dec 2). *New York Daily Graphic.*

212 **"the reference photo had no artistic integrity..."**: Lowrey, W. (1998, August). *Altered plates: Photo manipulation and the search for news value in the early and late twentieth century*. Paper presented to the Visual Communication Division, AEJMC National Convention , Baltimore, MD. https://list.msu.edu/cgi-bin/wa?A 2=ind9810d&L=AEJMC&P=7372

213 **Its artists simply put together an image:** See Fineman, M. (2012). *Faking It: Manipulated Photography before Photoshop.* New York, NY: Metropolitan Museum of Art. p. 144.

214 **"Does the camera lie?":** Ibid. p. 18.

214 **"impressed by Nature's hand..."**: Talbot, H. F. (1844). *The Pencil of Nature*. London: Longman, Brown, Green and Longmans.

215 **"at once truer and less true":** Fineman, M. (2012). *Faking It: Manipulated Photography before Photoshop.* New York, NY: Metropolitan Museum of Art. p. 15.

216 **"I am morally convinced..."**: Quoted in Kaplan, L. (2008). *The Strange Case of William Mumler, Spirit Photographer.* Minneapolis, MN: University of Minnesota Press. p. 206.

216 **"difficult to prove a negative..."**: Ibid. p. 206.

216 **"Who, henceforth, can trust the accuracy of a photograph?":** Ibid. p. 207.

217 **"its policy against substantial retouching..."**: Wheeler, T. (2002). *Phototruth Or Photofiction?: Ethics and Media Imagery in the Digital Age.* Mahwah, NJ: Routledge. p. 22.

217 **"Our current crisis of faith..."**: Fineman, M. (2012). *Faking It: Manipulated Photography before Photoshop.* New York: Metropolitan Museum of Art. p. 19.

218 **"Like journalistic writers..."**: Wheeler, T. (2002). *Phototruth Or Photofiction? : Ethics and Media Imagery in the Digital Age.* Mahwah, NJ: Routledge. p. 131.

218 **"qualified expectation of reality":** Ibid. p. 127.

219 **"the same effect as if..."**: Ibid. pp. 44–45.

219 **"It isn't trustworthy simply because it's a picture...":** Rosenberg, S. (1995, Dec 1). You can't believe your eyes. *Wired. com.*

220 **In one of Garry's studies:** Garry, M., Strange, D., Bernstein, D. M., & Kinzett, T. (2007). Photographs can distort memory for the news. *Applied Cognitive Psychology, 21(8),* 995–1004.

221 **Another of Garry's studies:** Strange, D., Garry, M., Bernstein, D. M., & Lindsay, D. S. (2011). Photographs cause false memories for the news. *Acta Psychologica, 136(1),* 90–94.

223 **"The most important part of the story…"**: Crombag, H. F.
M., Wagenaar, W. A., & van Koppen, P. J. (1996). Crashing
Memories and the Problem of "Source Monitoring." *Applied
Cognitive Psychology, 10(2),* 95–104.
224 **Other researchers have run similar studies:** Ost, J., Vrij, A.,
Costall, A., & Bull, R. (2002). Crashing memories and reality
monitoring: Distinguishing between perceptions, imaginations
and 'false memories.' *Applied Cognitive Psychology, 16(2),* 125–134.
Wilson, K., & French, C. C. (2006). The relationship between
susceptibility to false memories, dissociativity, and paranormal
belief and experience. *Personality and Individual Differences, 41(8),*
1493–1502.
225 **So, for her follow-up study:** Garry, M., & Wade, K. A. (2005).
Actually, a picture is worth less than 45 words: Narratives
produce more false memories than photographs do. *Psychonomic
Bulletin & Review, 12(2),* 359–366.
226 **"A photograph can be true…"**: Wheeler, T. (2002). *Phototruth
Or Photofiction?: Ethics and Media Imagery in the Digital Age.*
Mahwah, NJ: Routledge. p. 5.
227 **Steve Buscemi's face was pasted onto Jennifer Lawrence's
body:** Locker, M. (2019, Feb 7). Here's Steve Buscemi's reaction
to that haunting fake Jennifer Lawrence mashup video. *Time.com.*
227 **In another, comedian Bill Hader's face:** Collins, B. (2019,
Jun 12). This viral Schwarzenegger deepfake isn't just
entertaining. It's a warning. *NBCNews.com.*
227 **A bunch of deepfakes put Nicolas Cage's face:** Purdom, C.
(2018, Jan 29). Deep learning technology is now being used to
put Nic Cage in every movie. *AVClub.com.*
227 **"Whatever the effects of images are…"**: Perlmutter, D. D.
(1998). *Photojournalism and Foreign Policy: Icons of Outrage In
International Crises.* Westport, CT: Praeger. p. xvi.

Chapter 7: Post-Truth

Page
229 **At eight in the morning:** Muller, G. H. (2008). *William Cullen
Bryant: Author of America.* Albany, NY: SUNY Press. p. 93.
229 **"some harmless pleasantry."**: Bryant, W. C., & Leggett, W. M.
(1831, Apr 21). Evening post. *New York Evening Post.* p. 2.
230 **"The town did this paper"**: Ibid.

230 **"The *Evening Post*, and the *Courier and Enquirer*…"**: Quoted in Evening post. (1831, Apr 11). *New York Evening Post*. p. 2.

230 **"A correspondent informs us…"**: Ibid.

230 **"This statement is utterly and in all respects untrue…"**: Quoted in Bryant, W. C., & Leggett, W. M. (1831, Apr 21). Evening post. *New York Evening Post*. p. 2.

231 **"a dirty anonymous scrawl…"**: Ibid.

231 **"The crowning proof…"**: Evening post. (1831, Apr 11). *New York Evening Post*. p. 2.

231 **"refuted the calumny…"**: Quoted in Bryant, W. C., & Leggett, W. M. (1831, Apr 21). Evening post. *New York Evening Post*. p. 2.

231 **"On the one hand…"**: Ibid.

232 **In Stone's telling:** Ibid.

232 **According to an account written by Bryant's editorial assistant:** Ibid.

233 **"It is with the greatest reluctance…"**: Ibid.

233 **"Colonel Webb, you are a coward…"**: Burrows, E. G., & Wallace, M. (1998). *Gotham: A History of New York City to 1898*. New York, NY: Oxford University Press. p. 572.

233 **Webb, for his part:** Hale, W. H. (1950). *Horace Greeley: Voice of the People*. New York, NY: Harper & Brothers. p. 21.

234 **"My damage is a scratch…"**: Anonymous. (1855). *Memoirs of James Gordon Bennett and His Times: By a Journalist*. New York, NY: Stringer & Townsend. p. 214.

234 **"the garbage of society."**: Quoted in Goodman, M. (2008). *The Sun and the Moon*. New York, NY: Basic Books. p. 89..

234 **"only chance of dying…"**: Ibid.

234 **One Brooklyn paper suggested that Walt Whitman:** Loving, J. (2000). *Walt Whitman: The Song of Himself*. Los Angeles, CA: University of California Press. p. 146.

234 **"Whoever knows him…"**: Ibid.

235 **"Professions of *impartiality*…"**: Quoted in Dicken-Garcia, H. (1989). *Journalistic Standards in Nineteenth-Century America*. Madison, WI: University of Wisconsin Press. p. 99.

235 **"The printer, who under…"**: Quoted in Stewart, D. H. (1969). *The Opposition Press of the Federalist Period*. Albany, NY: SUNY Press. p. 29.

235 **"It will be his object…"**: National intelligencer. (1800, Oct 31). *The National Intelligencer and Washington Advertiser*. p. 1.

235 **Smith "affected an almost prudish…"**: Hildreth, R. (1851). *The History of the United States of America Vol. 5*. New York, NY: Harper & Brothers. pp. 421–422.

236 **"virtual branches of the government":** Quoted in Crossen, C. (2006, Oct 30). In Early Newspapers, Only 'Mr. Silky Milky' Would Be Impartial. *WSJ.com*.

236 **"the issue of the press's proper role…":** Dicken-Garcia, H. (1989). *Journalistic Standards in Nineteenth-Century America.* Madison, WI: University of Wisconsin Press. p. 32.

237 **"Give light and the people…":** https://scripps.com/company/about-scripps/

237 **"Nothing sacred but the truth.":** Snyder, G. (2009, Apr 22). With Peter Kaplan's Exit, a New York Media Era Closes. *Gawker.* https://gawker.com/5223565/with-peter-kaplans-exit-a-new-york-media-era-closes

237 **"No fear, no favor,":** Mitchell, J. (2017, Feb 22). Slogans state a newspaper's truth in changing times. *USAToday.com*.

237 **"deliver news, not noise.":** Ibid.

237 **"fair and balanced.":** Grynbaum, M. M. (2017, Jun 14). Fox News Drops 'Fair and Balanced' Motto. *NYTimes.com*

237 **"The Only Newspaper…":** Mitchell, J. (2017, Feb 22). Slogans state a newspaper's truth in changing times. *USAToday. com*.

237 **London's *Mercurius Civicus*:** Muddiman, J. G. (1908). *A History of English Journalism: To the Foundation of The Gazette.* London: Longmans, Green, and Co. p. 45.

237 **"I shal never admit…":** Quoted in Stephens, M. (2007). *A history of news.* New York, NY: Oxford University Press. p. 244.

238 **Elizabeth Mallet, the publisher of the *Daily Courant*:** Dicken-Garcia, H. (1989). *Journalistic Standards in Nineteenth-Century America.* Madison, WI: University of Wisconsin Press. p. 11.

238 **"My leading idea…":** Greeley, H. (1868). Recollections of a busy life. New York, NY: J. B. Ford and Company. p. 137.

238–239 **Oxford Dictionaries declared post-truth:** 'Post-truth' declared word of the year by Oxford Dictionaries. (2016, Nov 16). *BBC.com*.

239 **the Poynter Institute noted:** Mantzarlis, A. (2016, Nov 2). Fact-checking doesn't 'backfire,' new study suggests. *Poynter.org*.

239 **to paraphrase Mark Twain:** This is actually something of a misquote, but we'll spend more time thinking about reporting errors in Chapter 8. See Petsko, E. (2018, Nov 2). Reports of Mark Twain's Quote About His Own Death Are Greatly Exaggerated. *MentalFloss.com*.

239 **Hoyt's article:** Hoyt, C. (2008, Apr 13). The blur between analysis and opinion. *NYTimes.com*.

242 **"Most preschool-age children..."**: Woolley, J. D., &
Ghossainy, M. E. (2013). Revisiting the fantasy–reality distinction:
Children as naïve skeptics. *Child Development, 84(5),* 1496–1510.

242 **wishing is sometimes an effective way:** Woolley, J. D., Phelps,
K. E., Davis, D. L., & Mandell, D. J. (1999). Where theories of
mind meet magic: The development of children's beliefs about
wishing. *Child Development, 70(3),* 571.

242 **imaginary friend:** Taylor, M. (1999). Imaginary Companions and
the Children Who Create Them. Oxford: Oxford University Press.

242 **believing in fantastical figures:** Sharon, T., & Woolley, J. D.
(2004). Do monsters dream? Young children's understanding of
the fantasy/reality distinction. *British Journal of Developmental
Psychology, 22(2),* 293–310.

242 **Jacqueline Woolley and colleagues:** Boerger, E. A., Tullos, A.,
& Woolley, J. D. (2009). Return of the Candy Witch: Individual
differences in acceptance and stability of belief in a novel
fantastical being. *British Journal of Developmental Psychology, 27(4),*
953–970. Woolley, J. D., Boerger, E. A., & Markman, A. B. (2004).
A visit from the Candy Witch: Factors influencing young
children's belief in a novel fantastical being. *Developmental Science,
7(4),* 456–468.

243 **Jean Piaget:** Piaget, J. (1929). *The Child's Conception of the World.*
London: Routledge. http://archive.org/details/
childsconception01piag

243 **"is an adult characteristic..."**: Vyse, S. A. (1997). *Believing in
Magic: The Psychology of Superstition.* Oxford: Oxford University
Press. p. 155.

244 **Woolley's research:** Woolley, J. D., & Ghossainy, M. E. (2013).
Revisiting the fantasy–reality distinction: Children as naïve
skeptics. *Child Development, 84(5),* 1496–1510.

244 **"I've never seen one."**: Woolley, J. D., & Van Reet, J. (2006).
Effects of context on judgments concerning the reality status of
novel entities. *Child Development, 77(6),* 1778–1793.

244 **dismissed Michael Jordan as a fictitious being:** Woolley, J.
D., & Van Reet, J. (2006). Effects of context on judgments
concerning the reality status of novel entities. *Child Development,
77(6),* 1778–1793.

244 **"Magicians can't make a house appear..."**: Phelps, K. E., &
Woolley, J. D. (1994). The form and function of young children's
magical beliefs. *Developmental Psychology, 30(3),* 385–394.

244 **They give more credence:** Jaswal, V. K., & Neely, L. A. (2006).
Adults Don't Always Know Best: Preschoolers Use Past

Reliability Over Age When Learning New Words. *Psychological Science, 17(9)*, 757–758.

245 **researchers made up something called a Surnit:** Woolley, J. D., & Van Reet, J. (2006). Effects of context on judgments concerning the reality status of novel entities. *Child Development, 77(6)*, 1778–1793.

245 **"You're not going to believe…":** Jaswal, V. K. (2004). Don't believe everything you hear: Preschoolers' sensitivity to speaker intent in category induction. *Child Development, 75(6)*, 1871–1885.

245 **"You can tell they're not real…":** Woolley, J. D., Ma, L., & Lopez-Mobilia, G. (2011). Development of the use of conversational cues to assess reality status. *Journal of Cognition and Development, 12(4)*, 537–555.

247 **As educational psychologist Deanna Kuhn explained:** Kuhn, D., & Dean, D. (2004). Metacognition: A bridge between cognitive psychology and educational practice. *Theory into Practice, 43(4)*, 268–273.

249 **As Michael Kinsley, a political journalist, has pointed out:** Hirschorn, M. (2018, Nov 4). How MSNBC created a cable-news addiction epidemic. *VanityFair.com*.

249 **In 2018, the Pew Research Center:** Mitchell, A., Gottfried, J., Barthel, M., & Sumida, N. (2018, Jun 18). Can Americans tell factual from opinion statements in the news? *Journalism.org*.

252 **In a Q&A about the study:** DeSilver, D. (2018, Jun 18). Q&A: Telling the difference between factual and opinion statements in the news. *PewResearch.org*.

254 **"On a brisk Saturday afternoon…":** Hastorf, A. H., & Cantril, H. (1954). They saw a game; a case study. *Journal of Abnormal and Social Psychology, 49(1)*, 129.

255 **"This observer has never seen…":** Quoted in Ibid.

255 **"set the stage…":** Quoted in Ibid.

257 **"They Saw a Protest.":** Kahan, D. M., Hoffman, D. A., Braman, D., & Evans, D. (2012). They saw a protest: Cognitive illiberalism and the speech–conduct distinction. *Stanford Law Review, 64*, 851.

261 **Peter Ditto describes himself:** https://faculty.sites.uci.edu/phditto/

261 **Ditto and colleagues started out:** Ditto, P. H., Liu, B. S., Clark, C. J., Wojcik, S. P., Chen, E. E., Grady, R. H., … Zinger, J. F. (2019). At least bias is bipartisan: A meta-analytic comparison of partisan bias in liberals and conservatives. *Perspectives on Psychological Science, 14(2)*, 273–291.

261 **"touched off the quarrel…"**: Voss, T. G. (1975). *The Letters of William Cullen Bryant, 1809–1836.* New York, NY: Fordham University Press. p. 302.

Chapter 8: Setting the Record Straight

Page
269 **"Karol Wojtyla was referred to…"**: Corrections and clarifications: August 11, 2015. (2015, Aug 10). *TheTimes.co.uk.*
269 **"The 2. Of Decemember."**: Quoted in Silverman, C. (2009). *Regret the Error.* New York, NY: Union Square Press. p. 15.
269 **"In yesterday's issue…"**: Quoted in Kuntz, T. (2001, Nov 14). 150th Anniversary: 1851-2001; The Facts That Got Away. *NYTimes. com.*
270 **The Republican National Committee…**: Quoted in Marsh, D. (2009, Aug 23). Mind your language. *TheGuardian.com.*
270 **"Spellcheck changed the name…"**: Temple, J. (2006, Jan 14). Once in print, there are no mulligans. *RockyMountainNews.com.* [via Web.Archive.org].
271 **"The problem arose…"**: Quoted in Silverman, C. (2009). *Regret the Error.* New York, NY: Union Square Press. p. 105.
271 **"Because of an editing error involving a satirical …"**: Qiu, L. (2018, Mar 6). President Trump's Exaggerated and Misleading Claims on Trade. *NYTimes.com.*
271 **"Due to an oversight…"**: Tanz, J. (2016, Mar 9). Never mind Trump. The internet wants to watch what's behind him. *Wired.com.*
271 **"Clearly," he reflected:** Tanz, J. (2016, Mar 9). So, about that 'tiny hands' Trump Chrome extension…. *Wired.com.*
271 **"Because of an editing error, an article on Monday…"**: Goodstein, L. (2016, May 8). Muslim Leaders Wage Theological Battle, Stoking ISIS' Anger. *NYTimes.com.*
272 **"Because of a transcription error…"**: Corrections. (1995, Apr 7). *New York Times.* p. 2.
272 **"Mr Smith said in court…"**: Quoted in Silverman, C. (2009). *Regret the Error.* New York, NY: Union Square Press. p. 107.
272 **"An earlier version of this article…"**: Puko, T. (2018, Mar 27). Sheldon Adelson Facilitated EPA Connection for Israeli Firm. *WSJ.com.*
273 **the Moses effect:** Park, H., & Reder, L. M. (2004). Moses illusion. In R. F. Pohl (Ed.). *Cognitive Illusions.* Psychology Press. pp. 275–292.

273 **"Amphibious pitcher…"**: See Big Frogging Mistake. (2015, Jun 9). *EastOregonian.com.*

273 **"In our note on the Channel 4 program…"**: Corrections and clarifications. (2005, Aug 30). *TheGuardian.com.*

274 **"A Wednesday commentary…"**: Heilbrunn, J. (2005, Mar 9). U.N. May Need Bolton's Bitter Medicine. *LATimes.com.*

274 **"The report of my death…"**: Petsko, E. (2018, Nov 2). Reports of Mark Twain's Quote About His Own Death Are Greatly Exaggerated. *MentalFloss.com.*

274 **"I've just read that I am dead…"**: Quoted in Silverman, C. (2009). *Regret the Error.* New York, NY: Union Square Press. p. 171.

274 **"It being the Design of this Paper…"**: Correction. (1727, May 18). *Boston News-Letter.*

275 **"An obituary on Gore Vidal…"**: McGrath, C. (2012, Aug 1). Gore Vidal dies at 86; Prolific, elegant, acerbic writer. *NYTimes.com.*

275 **The Ottawa Citizen and Southam News:** Quoted in Silverman, C. (2010, May 14). Correction as weapon: Self-inflicted wounds. *CJR.org.*

276 **That was the answer Mitchell Charnley arrived at:** Charnley, M.V. (1936). Preliminary notes on a study of newspaper accuracy. *Journalism Bulletin, 13(4),* 394–401.

278 **science stories, reports about social issues, and wire service coverage:** See Maier, S. R. (2005). Accuracy matters: A cross-market assessment of newspaper error and credibility. *Journalism & Mass Communication Quarterly, 82(3),* 533–551.

278 **the accuracy of television news:** Hanson, G., & Wearden, S.T. (2004). Measuring newscast accuracy: Applying a newspaper model to television. *Journalism & Mass Communication Quarterly, 81(3),* 546–558.

279 **and newsmagazines:** Burriss, L. L. (1985). Accuracy of news magazines as perceived by news sources. *Journalism Quarterly, 62(4),* 824–827.

279 **"Getting It Right?…"**: Maier, S. (2002). Getting it right? Not in 59 percent of stories. *Newspaper Research Journal, 23(1),* 10–24.

279 **A few years later, Maier published:** Maier, S. R. (2005). Accuracy matters: A cross-market assessment of newspaper error and credibility. *Journalism & Mass Communication Quarterly, 82(3),* 533–551.

282 **internal accuracy surveys:** See Silverman, C. (2009). *Regret the Error.* New York, NY: Union Square Press.

283 **"Reporters and editors make mistakes…"**: Ibid. p. xxv.

283 **"The Gazette publishes…"**: Quoted in Ibid. p. 122.

284 **"do not prove sufficient…"**: Butler, S. (1908). *Characters and Passages From Notebooks* (A. R. Waller, Ed.). Cambridge: Cambridge University Press. p. 86.

284 **the *Boston Globe* published close to sixty thousand:** Silverman, C. (2009). *Regret the Error.* New York, NY: Union Square Press. p. 76.

284 **Maier found a correction rate:** Maier, S. R. (2009, Sep 16). Confessing Errors in a Digital Age. *NiemanReports.org.*

284 **In 1982, the *New York Times* typically printed:** Maier, S. R. (2007). Setting the record straight. *Journalism Practice, 1(1),* 33–43.

284 **"We published more than 4,100…"**: Moore, L. (2019, Jan 3). The news in 2018 was memorable. So were these corrections. *NYTimes.com.*

285 **"Errors in the press…"**: Maier, S. R. (2009). Confessing Errors in a Digital Age. *NiemanReports.org.*

285 **the *backfire effect*:** Nyhan, B. (2010). When corrections fail: The persistence of political misperceptions. *Political Behavior, 32(2),* 303–330.

286 **Craig Silverman, in 2011, called the effect:** Silverman, C. (2011, Jun 17). The backfire effect. *CJR.org.*

287 **"Why are people today becoming so immune to facts?":** Tillmans, W. (2018, Feb 28). Wolfgang Tillmans: my two-year investigation into the post-truth era. *TheGuardian.com.*

287 **became the most highly cited:** Wood, T., & Porter, E. (2019). The elusive backfire effect: Mass attitudes' steadfast factual adherence. *Political Behavior, 41(1),* 135–163.

287 **"is in fact rare…"**: Sippitt, A. (2019, Mar 20). Does the "backfire effect" exist—and does it matter for factcheckers?. *FullFact.org.*

287 **"Sometimes people will change…"**: Nyhan, B. (2016, Nov 5). Fact-Checking Can Change Views? We Rate That as Mostly True. *NYTimes.com.*

287 **a follow-up study:** Wood, T., & Porter, E. (2019). The elusive backfire effect: Mass attitudes' steadfast factual adherence. *Political Behavior, 41(1),* 135–163.

287 **"Originally, when Tom and I…"**: Mantzarlis, A. (2016, Nov 2). Fact-checking doesn't 'backfire,' new study suggests. *Poynter.org.*

289 **the four researchers teamed up:** Nyhan, B., Porter, E., Reifler, J., & Wood, T. J. (2019). Taking fact-checks literally but not seriously? The effects of journalistic fact-checking on factual beliefs and candidate favorability. *Political Behavior.*

290 **around two-thirds of Americans:** Silverman, C. (2009). *Regret the Error.* New York, NY: Union Square Press.

290 **"Errors can be forgiven…":** Credibility initiatives show promise, but must be long-term. (2000, Apr 11). *ASNE.org.* [via Web.Archive. org].

290 **"The internet ruins everything…":** Mantzarlis, A. (2017, Dec 18). Not fake news, just plain wrong: Top media corrections of 2017. *Poynter.org.*

291 **"Media corrections are usually…":** Mantzarlis, A. (2017, Feb 27). Journalism can't afford for corrections to be next victim of 'fake news' frenzy. *Poynter.org.*

291 **"A copy editor responsible…":** Brown, K. (2017, Feb 21). Apologies to Eagle readers—and to Pence. *TheEagle.com.*

292 **"Fake news at its best…":** Quoted in Mantzarlis, A. (2017, Feb 27). Journalism can't afford for corrections to be next victim of 'fake news' frenzy. *Poynter.org.*

292 **"Right, The Eagle is…":** Quoted in Ibid.

292 **"How could anyone…":** Quoted in Ibid.

292 **"subconsciously, the copy editor…":** Quoted in Ibid.

292 **"and accused us of being…":** Brown, K. (2017, Feb 21). Apologies to Eagle readers—and to Pence. *TheEagle.com.*

292 **"Journalism can't afford…":** Mantzarlis, A. (2017, Feb 27). Journalism can't afford for corrections to be next victim of 'fake news' frenzy. *Poynter.org.*

293 **"Thanks for owning up…":** https://www.facebook.com/ bcseagle/posts/10154978336286904

293 **"Still trying to figure out…":** Ibid.

293 **"Hahaha. A caller really said…":** Ibid.

293 **"Mistakes happen…":** Ibid.

294 **"Predictably, our error…":** Tanz, J. (2016, Mar 9). So, about that 'tiny hands' Trump Chrome extension…. *Wired.com.*

294 **"A newspaper with a zero level…":** Meyer, P. (2009). *The Vanishing Newspaper [2nd Ed]: Saving Journalism in the Information Age.* Columbia, MO. University of Missouri Press. p. 87.

294 **In one ASNE survey:** Urban, C. D. (1999). *Examining our credibility: Perspectives of the public and the press.* American Society of Newspaper Editors.

294 **two-thirds of people think the media ignores…:** Silverman, C. (2009). Regret the Error. New York, NY: Union Square Press. p. 237.

295 **A 2017 study by researchers in Sweden:** Karlsson, M., Clerwall, C., & Nord, L. (2017). Do not stand corrected:

Transparency and users' attitudes to inaccurate news and corrections in online journalism. *Journalism & Mass Communication Quarterly, 94(1),* 148–167.

297 **"the public and the press agree..."**: Urban, C. D. (1999). *Examining our credibility: Perspectives of the public and the press.* American Society of Newspaper Editors.

297 **"is the foundation..."**: Kovach, B., & Rosenstiel, T. (2001). *The Elements of Journalism: What Newspeople Should Know and the Public Should Expect.* New York, NY: Three Rivers Press. p. 43.

298 **"(Occasionally we publish...)"**: Jacquette, R. (2018, Jun 7). We stand corrected: How the times handles errors. *NYTimes.com.*

299 **"great blooming, buzzing..."**: James, W. (1890). *The Principles of Psychology.* New York, NY: Holt. p. 488.

299 **"The consumer fraud..."**: Broder, D. S. (1987). *Behind the Front Page: A Candid Look At How The News Is Made.* New York, NY: Simon & Schuster. p. 14.

300 **Cecilie Gaziano and Kristin McGrath:** Gaziano, C., & McGrath, K. (1986). Measuring the concept of credibility. *Journalism Quarterly, 63(3),* 451–462.

301 **"Perhaps the industry's quest..."**: Maier, S. (2002). Getting it right? Not in 59 percent of stories. *Newspaper Research Journal, 23(1),* 10–24.

301 **"The troubled nature..."**: Hanitzsch, T. (2013). Journalism, participative media and trust in a comparative context. In C. Peters & M. J. Broersma (Eds.), *Rethinking Journalism: Trust and Participation in a Transformed News Landscape* (pp. 200–209). London: Routledge.

301 **"When the public distrusts..."**: Maier, S. R. (2005). Accuracy matters: A cross-market assessment of newspaper error and credibility. *Journalism & Mass Communication Quarterly, 82(3),* 533–551.

Acknowledgments

For the second time Jim Martin, commissioning editor at Bloomsbury Sigma, dropped into my life and persuaded me to write a book. The first time we met in person, over Thai food in London, it led to *Suspicious Minds: Why We Believe Conspiracy Theories*. The second time we met in person, in the shadow of the Empire State Building, he took my scattered thoughts and gave me the outline for this book. Thanks again, Jim. And thanks to everyone else at Bloomsbury and beyond who worked to make this book a reality, particularly my editor Anna MacDiarmid, copy editor Steve Boldt, my agents Kristina Moore, Jessica Friedman, and Alex Christie, and to the New York Public Library for once again providing an inspiring place to think and write.

Thanks are due to my family and friends, especially to my wife Lindsay for being my unofficial editor, copy editor, and cheerleader, and to my parents, not only for their services as unofficial research assistants, but for a lifetime of love and support. It's hard to grasp all your parents have done for you until you have a child of your own. Speaking of which: to my son, who was born as I was finishing up the first draft of this book, thanks for being a patient and encouraging test-audience. I hope your first words aren't "fake news."

Index